ELEMENTARY PRINCIPAL'S SURVIVAL GUIDE:
Practical Techniques and Materials for Day-to-Day School Administration and Supervision

MARCIA KALB KNOLL, Ed.D.

Prentice-Hall, Inc.
Englewood Cliffs, New Jersey

Prentice-Hall International, Inc., *London*
Prentice-Hall of Australia, Pty. Ltd., *Sydney*
Prentice-Hall Canada, Inc., *Toronto*
Prentice-Hall of India Private Ltd., *New Delhi*
Prentice-Hall of Japan, Inc., *Tokyo*
Prentice-Hall of Southeast Asia Pte. Ltd., *Singapore*
Whitehall Books, Ltd., *Wellington, New Zealand*
Editora Prentice-Hall do Brasil Ltda., *Rio de Janeiro*

© 1984 by

PRENTICE-HALL, INC.

Englewood Cliffs, N.J.

10 9 8 7

Special thanks to Sydell Kane for her help in
providing the concepts for the illustrations.

Library of Congress Cataloging in Publication Data

Knoll, Marcia Kalb
  Elementary principal's survival guide.

  Includes index.
  1. Elementary school administration. 2. Elementary
school principals. I. Title.
LB2822.5.K57 1984   372.12   84-4825
ISBN 0-13-259564-8

Printed in the United States of America

HOW THIS BOOK WILL GUIDE YOU TO A SUCCESSFUL SCHOOL YEAR

At times, do you find yourself in the role of father, mother, secretary, custodian, guidance counselor, sister, brother, teacher, speaker, babysitter, supervisor, typist, lunch worker, traffic director, author, translator, recorder, messenger, planner, film projectionist, troubleshooter, fund collector, hall monitor, observer, host or hostess, administrator, nurse, disciplinarian, listener, and organizer? Then you must be a school principal, and this book is for you.

Here are specific and detailed ideas, strategies, and techniques for successfully administrating and supervising an elementary school in such diversified areas as:

- instructional staff performance
- pupil performance
- curriculum
- program development
- kindergarten registration
- teacher absence
- discipline
- staff deployment
- budgets
- instructional materials
- plant operation
- details
- parents

Over 70 sample forms are presented that will save you countless hours of preparation and help ensure efficient, effective performance of your varied tasks. The forms are designed to be easily adapted to any school, so in most cases, only names or titles need to be changed.

Included, for example, are samples of commendation cards, incident reports, observation reviews, and reports to parents. These, along with practical and detailed suggestions, help you to:

- use your time more efficiently
- identify needs and plan to effectively meet them
- avoid usually unavoidable problems and headaches
- boost staff morale
- be a more effective supervisor
- be a more efficient administrator

Because this book is intended to be a daily guide, it may become a handy reference to be used by topic as the need arises, or it may be read in its entirety. Either way, you will want to keep it close at hand.

Marcia Kalb Knoll

CONTENTS

1

HOW TO MAXIMIZE INSTRUCTIONAL STAFF PERFORMANCE

Staff development can be accomplished through several types of observations, since only one type will not serve all your purposes. The various types of observations in this chapter will enable you, the elementary principal, to best use your time to:

- monitor improvement in teaching
- spot potential trouble that may be avoided
- note the teacher's daily delivery of material that is vital to improving instruction

OBSERVE LESSON CONTENT

At times, you may want to see and evaluate how a particular teacher presents a subject. But a content observation evaluates more than the content area; it judges the general "art" of teaching: the questioning techniques, the motivation, the scope and sequence of the lesson and its pace, the medial and final summary, the review, reinforcement, and the follow-up.

In a content observation, you will also consider the students' interaction during the lesson, and to whom comments are directed. Students generally tend to speak to the teacher, but it's better if the students direct their answers to each other, rather than the teacher.

OBSERVE THE LEARNING ENVIRONMENT

In the environment observation, instead of evaluating the "art of teaching" in a specific content area, you evaluate the structure and climate of the learning environment—the classroom. The aim is to see what students do and how they perform when not directly involved with the teacher.

This type of evaluation becomes more important as teachers instruct small groups and individual students. Self-directed materials such as learning kits, skill books, activity cards and computer-assisted instruction have directed the teacher's attention away from the whole class as a group and toward smaller groups of students with similar needs. As a result, students have become more self-directed.

The items listed in Figure 1-1 make up an optimal setting for teachers and students. Experts in the field agree on the items that are essential for self-directed student learning.* The items, listed in behavioral terms, describe the teacher's and students' visible actions in the classroom.

ENVIRONMENT OBSERVATION

Teacher _____ Class _____ Date _____ Time _____

DIAGNOSING LEARNING EVENTS/EVALUATING DIAGNOSTIC INFORMATION

Teacher

Gathers information by:
_____ observing
_____ questioning
_____ testing
_____ correcting work
_____ checking work
_____ moving about

Students

Respond in:
_____ writing
_____ orally
_____ seek help
_____ get help
_____ give help
_____ self-check work
_____ peer-check work
_____ keep records

Outcomes

_____ lists of student needs
_____ students grouped by need
_____ students evaluated

Students know:
_____ where and how to get help

Teacher records:
_____ student progress
_____ test results
_____ cumulative folders of work for each student

TEACHING—GUIDING AND EXTENDING LEARNING

Teacher

_____ Instructs individuals
_____ Instructs small groups
_____ Instructs whole class
_____ Plans for group instruction visible

Students

_____ Plan for themselves morning/day/week

Work:
_____ individually
_____ with a peer
_____ in a small group
_____ individually with the teacher
_____ in a group with the teacher

Outcomes

Prescriptions:
_____ for individuals
_____ for group
_____ in reading
_____ in mathematics
_____ in writing
_____ are recorded
_____ are updated

Prescriptions include:
_____ contracts
_____ texts
_____ skill books
_____ activities/games
_____ kits
_____ rexographs

Figure 1–1

---

*Marcia Knoll. "Achievement, Attitudes, and Attendance of Third Grade Urban Classes Categorized by Degree of Deformalization and Socio-Economic Setting." Unpublished Doctoral Dissertation, St. John's University, 1977, pp. 258–273.

OPPORTUNITIES FOR LEARNING

Teacher	Students	Outcomes
Manages:	Interact with resources	Resources are provided
_____ student activity	_____ select	_____ for varied ability
_____ student behavior	_____ use	_____ in diversity
_____ noise level	_____ care for	for varied learning styles
Teacher rating = _____	_____ replace	_____ oral _____ visual
(1 = low to 5 = high)	_____ share	_____ tactile
Student Frequency = _____	Work:	_____ in profusion
A = All of the students	_____ on planned studies	(at least four items)
M = Most of the students	_____ with varied materials	_____ with organization
S = Some of the students	_____ on different levels	_____ neatly
F = Few of the students	_____ in different areas	Room demonstrates:
N = None of the students	_____ speak freely & softly	_____ space effectively used
	_____ move freely & orderly	_____ specified learning areas
		_____ materials readily available
		_____ student work displayed
		_____ neatness/order
_____	_____	
Teacher's signature	Principal's signature	

Figure 1–1 (continued)

The items in the learning environment fall into three groups: teacher, students and outcomes. The items describe what the teacher and students may be doing during the observation, along with the results of previous actions you have not observed but whose effects you can see. For example, you may not see the teacher prepare a box of individual folders for each student, but you can see the box of folders on the table.

Teacher and student activities and their outcome in the classroom fall into three categories:

- *Diagnosing Learning Events/Evaluating Diagnostic Information:* The items in this category address the diagnosis of learning need and the actions of both the teacher and the students and the outcomes that are involved in evaluating students' progress.

- *Teaching—Guiding and Extending Learning:* These items address the manner in which the students, the teacher, and the outcomes work toward meaningful instructional activities for the students.

- *Opportunities for Learning:* These items address how the classroom provides for maximum learning opportunities. Consider whether an effective management system is in place, and if there is a diversity of resources for meeting the needs of all the students.

Before using the Learning Environment Observation form (Figure 1-1), become familiar with its items and categories. Then introduce the form to the faculty, explaining its purpose and how it will be used. Tell the teachers that they will not be notified of the date and time of the observation, since it is intended to reflect what usually occurs in class. If the class's activity is inappropriate when you arrive for the observation, leave the room and return at another time.

Only visible actions and outcomes are noted in observations. What is not visible is not recorded. Everything in the classroom should be included in the observation, including student notebooks, writing on the chalkboard, signs posted, and learning centers. The teacher's actions may be rated for quality on a scale of 1 (low) to 5 (high). The frequency of students' actions may be rated using A (All students), M (Most), S (Some), F (Few), and N (None).

In all cases, a post-observation conference should be held with the teacher as soon as possible. At that time, the items observed, the ratings given, and other details can be discussed. Give the teacher specific suggestions for improvement and record these on a separate conference form.

HOW TEACHERS CAN EVALUATE THEMSELVES

Most professional teachers are interested in self-improvement, even though they are usually proud of their teaching. The teacher can use the Environment Observation form (Figure 1-1) to evaluate themselves in the classroom. It is not necessary for the teacher to show you the results of this self-evaluation. It is more important that each teacher honestly compares his or her classroom conditions to the specific items listed on the form in deciding if their classroom is operating efficiently and effectively. A second method for teachers to use in evaluating themselves is for two teachers to observe each other's environment. In this case, each teacher visits the other's class using the Learning Environment Observation form. The two teachers then meet to discuss what each observed about the other.

USE VIDEOTAPES FOR OBSERVATIONS

If you can use a video camera to film a teacher as he or she conducts a lesson, it can be very revealing. This type of self-observation examines the "art of teaching" and includes all aspects of a formal observation. The videotaped observation focuses especially on teacher and student behavior during the lesson. A videotaped observation is less threatening if the supervisor is not present, and only the technician operating the equipment is in class with the teacher and students. The teacher might want to view the videotape without the supervisor to check the quality of the lesson. This type of self-evaluation is extremely effective.

CONDUCT AN INFORMAL OBSERVATION

Informal observations are part of your daily routine as principal. It includes walking into the classroom, unannounced, to observe what is happening. This type of informal visit, if consistently practiced, becomes an expected and welcomed part of the teacher's day. Many teachers will show you something of which they are very proud, or tell you about a problem. However, the informal visit is primarily a way for you to see what actually goes on in the classroom.

For example, you may have noticed several students who could have profited from the use of counting frames, which were not available in the classroom. You can then tell the teacher that this equipment should be ordered for the class. Or, if you saw a superior lesson being taught, you can then write to the teacher and praise the lesson.

DO AN EIGHT-STEP OBSERVATION

The preceding paragraphs describe several types of observation techniques, but exactly how do you go about initiating, conducting, and finalizing the observation? Here are the eight steps to follow.

Step 1: How to Plan the Pre-Observation Conference

Give the teacher who is to be observed a copy of the form in Figure 1-2, notifying him or her of the date of the pre-observation conference and requesting the teacher to prepare for the conference by thinking through what the observed lesson will be about and how it will be conducted.

The Pre-Observation Conference form first requires the teacher to identify the lesson's subject area. Next, the teacher is asked if the lesson is to include the whole class or only a group of students. If you are concerned with the teacher's ability to get and hold the attention of all the students, ask to see a full class lesson. On the other hand, if you are concerned with the teacher's ability to provide meaningful activities for the rest of the class during a group lesson, you may request to see this type of lesson. The form then asks the teacher to record both the topic and the specific aim of the lesson.

The next item requests that the teacher outline the lesson's procedures and materials. The teacher is then asked to select a particular teaching technique to focus upon during the observation. It is helpful if the teacher identifies a problem area or weakness. Following the observation, you can then make suggestions. Finally, the teacher is informed of other non-curriculum matters that will be observed during the lesson. -

Step 2: How to Conduct the Pre-Observation Conference

The teacher brings the prepared form to this scheduled conference so that you both can discuss the lesson to be observed. Your aim, at this conference, is to assist the teacher in strengthening the lesson as much as possible. Give the teacher specific suggestions in planning all areas of the lesson. For example, you might offer suggestions on improving the lesson's motivation, or using a different sequence of activities to make the lesson more effective.

The pre-observation conference ends with the mutual selection of a time and date for the observation. You and the teacher each keep a copy of the pre-observation form.

Step 3: How to Use Guidelines in Your Observation

Make every effort to be prompt for the scheduled observation. When you enter the classroom, greet the teacher and then find a place to sit where you will have a good view of the students and the teacher during the lesson. During the observation, take notes about the lesson. These include what was good as well as what could be improved. Short phrases and simple sentences will help you keep a running notation of what is happening. You may also wish to head two columns, one with a plus and the other with a minus. Note commendable items in the plus column, and items needing improvement in the minus column. Whenever possible, quote several questions the teacher asked, along with student responses for future analysis. Be sure to take note of the lesson sequence as it moves from motivation to

PRE-OBSERVATION CONFERENCE

_____
Date

_____
Observation Date

Dear _____,

    Please meet with me on _____, _____ at _____ for a pre-observation conference. Please prepare the form below and bring it with you.

1. Subject area of the observation: _____

2. Instructional mode (Class / Group)

3. Topic of the lesson (e.g., Subtraction):

4. Specific aim (e.g., to learn to subtract with exchange in tens place):

5. The procedures of the lesson:

6. The materials to be used:

7. An area of teaching techniques to focus upon for the observation:

    questioning techniques   teacher delivery
    use of instructional aids   lesson pace
    motivational techniques   lesson sequence
    arrow of recitation   student involvement

8. Additional non-curriculum matters to be observed:

    use of bulletin boards   behavioral code of the class
    material selection and placement   housekeeping procedures
    management system in the classroom student self-direction

_____
Teacher's Signature

_____
Principal's Signature

Figure 1-2

summary. Also note the manner in which the teacher uses related materials, as well as the students' general behavior and their attention to the teacher. If a task is given to the students, circulate among them to examine their progress and make notes of what you see.

Step 4: How to Analyze the Observation

As soon as possible after the observation, review your notes. Organize them into categories so that you can comment in the written review. From the following list of comprehensive categories, select the ones that suit your observation:

1. Preparation of the class/group for instruction
2. Motivation of the lesson
3. Scope of the lesson
4. Sequence of the lesson
5. Provision for the lesson's summary
6. Review and reinforcement aspects of the lesson
7. Pupil participation
8. Development of language skills
9. Arrow of recitation
10. Teacher's use of questions
11. Use of instructional aids
12. Use of bulletin boards, material placement, management system, behavioral code, housekeeping procedures

Your written review should contain both a positive and negative comment. The following are positive and negative sample comments.

Categories for Comments	Comment Type	Sample Comments
1. Preparation of the class/group for the lesson	positive	The students were instructed to clear their desks and face the chalkboard.
		The group to be instructed was called to the round table.
		The other students, not in the instructional group, were instructed about the specific tasks to be completed.
	negative	Students' desks were filled with unrelated materials that were distracting.
		The students not in the instructional group were unsure of which tasks they should complete.

Categories for Comments	Comment Type	Sample Comments
		The students not in the instructional group did not understand how to complete the tasks given them.
2. Motivation of the lesson	positive	The lesson was motivated using an experience that was well within the understanding of the students.
	negative	The lesson was not meaningful to the students.
3. Scope of the lesson	positive	The lesson included the introduction of two new concepts for which the group demonstrated a readiness.
	negative	The lesson did not relate to any previous material learned.
4. Sequence of the lesson	positive	The lesson was developmental, beginning with a review of the facts of five, and moving to the division of a two-place dividend by a five as the divisor, then continuing to the new concept of a three-place dividend.
	negative	The sequence of the lesson could have been improved by first allowing the students to see, tell, and touch the materials before continuing a generalization.
5. Provision for summary	positive	The teacher provided for a medial summary of the review material before proceeding to the new concept.
	negative	The teacher did not provide a summary, or give the students an opportunity to express what they had learned.
6. Review and reinforcement aspects of the lesson	positive	The teacher gave the group/class an example to complete independently before proceeding to the next level of understanding.
	negative	The teacher did not provide for review or reinforcement of the concepts taught.

Categories for Comments	Comment Type	Sample Comments
7. Pupil participation in the lesson	positive	All students were involved in the lesson. The teacher called on volunteers and nonvolunteers.
	negative	The teacher did most of the talking, allowing little opportunity for the students to express their ideas.
8. Development of language skills	positive	The students were encouraged to explain and clarify their answers.
	negative	The teacher accepted student answers that were stated in phrases or single words.
9. Arrow of recitation	positive	The students spoke to each other, rather than direct their comments only to the teacher.
	negative	The students did not listen to the responses of their peers.
10. Teacher's use of questions	positive	The teacher used a multitude of "why and how" questions.
	negative	The teacher asked mostly "yes or no" questions.
11. Use of instructional aids	positive	The teacher made an appropriate game to be used as a review.
	negative	The teacher used no visual or tactile instructional materials.
12. Non-curriculum matters: Use of bulletin boards	positive	The bulletin boards in the classroom attractively display students' work.
	negative	The bulletin boards contain out-of-date work.
Material placement	positive	The classroom is appropriately filled with materials to be used by students in the learning process.
	negative	The materials in the classroom appear abused, as if they are used without care or respect.
Management system	positive	Procedures for leaving the room, sharpening pencils, and getting materials are well established and followed by the students.

Categories for Comments	Comment Type	Sample Comments
	negative	There is a lack of order and regular procedures are not used.
Behavioral code	positive	The students not in the instructional group were meaningfully involved in other activities.
	negative	The students were generally disruptive and easily distracted from the lesson.
Housekeeping procedures	positive	The classroom's neatness and order are conducive to learning.
	negative	Books and other learning materials were on the floor.

Step 5: How to Complete a Written Evaluation

After the observation has been analyzed, complete the write-up. Use a short, clear format to clarify what actually happened during the lesson and the factors that should be discussed during the post-observation conference. The form in Figure 1-3 groups your various types of comments about the lesson.

Lesson Summary. The lesson summary should briefly state the lesson's subject area, instructional mode, topic, and specific aim. Three or four sentences should then outline the lesson's scope and sequence. This summary helps remind you and the teacher of the lesson's details.

Commendable Items. Positive items should be listed in this category. If you were favorably impressed by the lesson, the list of favorable items may be long. If, on the other hand, the lesson was beneath your expectations, the list of favorable items may be very short. In any case, it is important to make some favorable remarks about *every* lesson. Morale is hurt and staff development is hampered if you give a teacher the impression that everything about the lesson was unacceptable.

Suggestions for Improvement. Negative items should be listed in this category. As with commendable items, the length of the list will depend upon your positive or negative reactions to the lesson.

Two ideas are important in writing this category. First, monitor the number of negative items that are listed. The purpose of the observation and write-up is to help the teacher improve. The post-observation conference should produce a mutually-agreed-upon plan to help the teacher. Therefore, limit the negative statements to a few prime targets for the teacher to develop. Save other negative comments for a later date, when you can point to a new direction for the teacher to improve.

Second, accompany each negative statement with a suggestion of how to improve the item. In general, glean these suggestions from the positive statements previously made.

Lesson Focus. The focus area the teacher selected during the pre-observation conference should be commented upon in this category. Your comments may be positive or negative,

OBSERVATION REVIEW

Teacher:

Class:

Date:

LESSON SUMMARY

COMMENDABLE ITEMS

1.
2.
3.
4.
5.

SUGGESTIONS FOR IMPROVEMENT

1.
2.
3.
4.
5.

LESSON FOCUS

LEARNING ENVIRONMENT

Sincerely,

_____

Principal

I have read and received a copy of this observation review.

_____

Teacher's signature

Figure 1-3

depending upon the observation and, if a comment is of a negative nature, give specific suggestions for the area's improvement. Do not comment about this category in any other categories in the write-up. For example, if the teacher selected questioning techniques as the area of focus, make no remarks about questioning under commendable items or suggestions for improvement. Save those comments for this section only.

Learning Environment. Items in this category are included under non-curriculum matters, with the exception of behavior. As with all other categories, negative comments should be accompanied by specific suggestions.

One original and one copy of the Observation Review should be prepared, and you and the teacher should sign both copies at the post-observation conference. The teacher retains the original, and you place the copy in an individual teacher file. The statement above the teacher's signature indicates that the teacher has read the observation and has received a copy. This could be an important factor if the teacher later objects to the observation write-up and begins legal action for its removal.

Figures 1-4 and 1-5 show two sample Observation Reviews.

OBSERVATION REVIEW

Teacher: Thomas Rogers

Class: Fourth-Room 203

Date: April 11, 1983

LESSON SUMMARY

The stated aim of this class math lesson was "to read the Farenheit thermometer" and "to predict the kind of clothing one should wear depending upon the weather." The lesson was motivated by the teacher's statement about not knowing what to wear in the morning. Through multi-questions during the lesson, the teacher referred to mercury rises and falls in a thermometer as it expands and contracts; the other term Celcius; the relationship of temperature to clothing worn; the concept of 0°; finding degrees on the thermometer that were listed as numerals, as slashes, and between the slashes; the freezing and boiling points of water; and a workbook page that practices subtraction and addition using rise and fall of daily temperature. Review and reinforcement were planned with another workbook page and the class construction of an 8 a.m. temperature chart.

COMMENDABLE ITEMS

1. You used one piece of representative material.
2. You used the chalkboard.
3. Many students were called upon during the lesson, both volunteers and non-volunteers.
4. Good student behavior was maintained during the lesson.

SUGGESTIONS FOR IMPROVEMENT

1. Your questioning strategies need drastic improvement.

a. You ask double or triple questions such as "What will happen as the days go on into spring?" "What will happen to the outdoor temperature?" "What will it feel like outside?" You do not stop for a student response and, as a result, confuse the students.

b. You ask elliptical questions such as "Mother cooks water to make it …?"

c. You ask yes/no questions such as "Would there be ice on the ground?"

d. You ask multiple choice questions such as "At 104° would you be very hot, comfortable, or chilled?"

e. You ask questions that require a one-word answer, such as "In a metric scale, what is temperature called?"

Only once during the entire lesson did you ask why. The lesson was devoid of thought questions that required a complete sentence for response.

2. The one representative material used to teach gradations of degree on a thermometer was insufficient and ineffective. It was too small to be easily seen by all of the children, let alone be used for calculations of degrees. It would have been far more effective to have prepared transparencies of several different thermometers with different degree intervals illustrating one degree, two degrees, and five degrees. You then could have taught reading gradations of degrees on a thermometer.

LESSON FOCUS (Student Involvement)

The students participated but were not involved in this teacher-dominated lesson. You did not give opportunities for their contributions, either verbally or through active participation.

LEARNING ENVIRONMENT

The classroom is divided into learning stations equipped with some of the appropriate materials present in the room. Many of the appropriate materials are placed on the windowsill or the back ledge. The bulletin boards contain examples of students' work, most of which is dated January. The papers are shabby. Both the teacher's desk and the top of the file cabinet are in a state of chaos. The room has a disorganized appearance that is not conducive to learning. We will plan together for ways to improve.

Sincerely,

_____

Principal

I have read and received a copy of this observation.

_____

Teacher's Signature

Figure 1-4

OBSERVATION REVIEW

Teacher: Sally Jones

Class: Kindergarten-Room 3

Date: March 2, 1983

LESSON SUMMARY

The stated aim of the lesson was "to introduce the letter S." The lesson was motivated by an S story well within the students' experience involving cooking a supper of spaghetti on a stove, requiring the stirring of the food, and later cleaning up with soap and a sponge. The introduction of a mystery box containing the new letter, to be opened later, heightened the excitement. The students guessed the letter successfully and continued to complete three pages in their S book. Provision for review and reinforcement was distributed in several appropriate homework sheets.

COMMENDABLE ITEMS

1. The teacher provided appropriate activities for those students not in the reading group.
2. The teacher began the lesson with "follow the teacher" hand and arm exercises.
3. The teacher's motivational techniques were well within the students' experience and were interesting to them.
4. The teacher used oral, visual and tactile experiences in the lesson to provide for all learning styles.
5. The teacher insisted and got appropriate responses from the children in whole sentences.
6. The students appropriately responded to the teacher's request to raise their hands before responding.
7. The teacher used positive directional statements rather than call attention to negative behavior.
8. The teacher circulated and supervised each student during the lesson.
9. The teacher used appropriate motivational materials that included the actual item as well as large demonstration samples.
10. The teacher encouraged peer assistance.
11. The teacher gave clear and specific instructions throughout the lesson and for the homework.

SUGGESTIONS FOR IMPROVEMENT

1. Although this was an excellent lesson, it was extremely long, lasting over 45 minutes. You would have focused more specifically on your stated aim by not including the writing of both capital and small S.

2. Having this focus only (recognition of S in oral, visual and tactile forms) would have given the time for additional experiences. For example, the flannel board mentioned in your pre-conference plans but not used in the lesson, a bag of objects that included S and non S objects to be identified by sound and name, a review of letter names previously studied, opportunities for verbalization by students of S stories based on the objects they selected from the bag.

3. Although you circulated among the students, you did not notice the errors in their work.

LESSON FOCUS (Lesson Pace)

The pace of the lesson was good as you moved with good tempo from one activity to another.

LEARNING ENVIRONMENT

The room was neat and well organized with books and some activities and materials appropriately placed. The bulletin boards were attractive and contained students' work. Recordkeeping for completion of students' homework was visible.

Sincerely,

_____
Principal

I have read and receeived a copy of this observation.

_____
Teacher's Signature

Figure 1-5

Step 6: How to Conduct the Post-Observation Conference

As soon as the observation review is completed, a note should be sent to the teacher inviting him or her to a post-observation conference. Do not allow more than a few days to pass between the observation and the post-observation conference, because the teacher will naturally be anxious to hear your reaction to the observation. Also consider that the longer you wait between the actual observation and the post-observation conference, the more difficult it will be to remember the details.

Notes should be taken during the conference. These can be completed by using the form in Figure 1-6.

POST-OBSERVATION CONFERENCE

Teacher:

Class:

Date:

Observation date:

ITEMS DISCUSSED:

SUGGESTIONS:

Figure 1-6

The post-observation conference begins with your asking the teacher for a reaction to the lesson. The teacher's statements concerning what was good or bad about the lesson or any explanation for actions during the lesson should be recorded under "Items Discussed."

Following the teacher's discussion of his or her impressions of the lesson, the observation write-up should be read by the teacher. Spend some time commenting on the commendable items. It is necessary to discuss with the teacher the important aspects of the lesson. A notation under "Items Discussed" should indicate the commendable items you talked about.

Next, discuss suggestions for improvement. Fully explain and talk over with the teacher the active items that need improvement, including the specific suggestions stated in the write up. The teacher's comments about these items should be recorded under suggestions. As you discuss each of these items, develop a plan for improvement with the teacher.

The post-observation conference ends with both you and the teacher understanding how and what will be improved. The teacher signs both copies of the observation review and the post-observation conference form. Both originals are given to the teacher, and the copies are stapled to the pre-observation form in the teacher's folder.

At times, the teacher may object to portions or statements in the observation write-up. You must then consider modifying the review. In general, your objective is to improve the teacher's performance. If the objectionable comments will prevent a good working relationship between you, it is better to change them. Try to get the teacher's agreement to the joint action plan before the post-observation conference ends.

Step 7: How to Develop a Joint Action Plan

The observation's purpose is to identify areas of the teacher's performance that need improving. As mentioned in the observation review, it is not a good idea to design action plans for more than two items. Select what you think is the most important item, or else choose one the teacher feels is most important to his or her classroom performance. Then develop a specific action plan, including:

- specific details of what the teacher wants to accomplish
- a list of the teacher's responsibilities, as well as your own
- a realistic amount of time to complete these goals
- a way to evaluate the teacher's actions

The specific plan will depend on the item to be improved. For example, if the item involves the classroom's appearance and the placement of materials, you might wait and make a second informal observation to observe the change. If the item to be improved involves the teacher's questioning techniques, you might schedule a second observation to check only questioning skills. You should then devote the pre-observation conference to helping the teacher develop appropriate questions to be asked during the observation. Make it clear to the teacher how and when you will help him or her improve.

Most of all, be fair, honest and supportive. Few teachers improve if you project hostile feelings or attitudes. Keep in mind that your only objective is to help the teacher to improve. The teacher will appreciate any positive actions you take toward this end.

Step 8: How to Put the Plan into Action

Once you develop the plan, you must lend all the support pledged. This may include conducting a second pre-observation conference to help the teacher plan the sequence of the lesson, identify a type of motivational experience, or write the questions he or she will use in the second observation. You may need to go into the classroom and help the teacher arrange materials more meaningfully, or show the teacher how to better organize the room so that it is neat, attractive and functional.

Once the plan is put into action, give the teacher some breathing space before having a follow-up evaluation. Avoid waiting too long, but be sure there is enough time between implementing the plan and evaluating its results, so the teacher has a chance to see an actual change in behavior, attitude, or skill. Then, be sure that the evaluation is fair and supports the teacher's efforts. The results may be less than you expected, but if a sincere effort was made by the teacher, praise those efforts, and make suggestions for further improvement.

ACCOMPLISH ONGOING MONITORING

How to Gather Data from Teacher Plans

You can consider teacher plans a blueprint for instructional excellence. Without them it is very difficult for a teacher to be effective. Specific plans include:

- working on specific graded goals for each content area
- providing review and reinforcement of new skills
- giving remedial work to students who have a skill weakness
- developing critical thinking skills in all content areas
- working on a wide range of state mandated areas

You should regularly schedule a review of teacher plans. It is unrealistic to try to review the plans of your entire staff each week, unless your staff is small. It is far more effective to review the plans of two or three grades in depth, rather than superficially review them all. Each Monday you could collect the plans of a few grades using a three-week cycle. For example, begin with the kindergarten, and grades one and two on the first Monday, grades three and four the next Monday, and so on. Teachers of music, gym, art, remedial reading, learning disabilities, etc., should be included with specific grades. When the plans of any grouping of grades are reviewed, look at the whole three-week span, but randomly pick any one of the three weeks to check in detail.

Use a copy of Figure 1-7 as a guide when reviewing teacher plans. This memo will help you zero in on all the specifics that should be a part of the lesson plans. You can also use it to notify teachers of your comments related to any of their plans. If you fill out the memo with a carbon or make a photostat, you will have a copy you can refer to the next time plans are collected, or if you need to remember a question you asked the teacher to answer within a few days.

How to Strengthen Teacher Planning

You can strengthen a teacher's plans by helping them understand what they should include in their planning for the week. The form shown in Figure 1-7 is the initial way to inform the teacher that his or her planning is lacking in the specified area(s). Next, you follow up the memo. If a meeting is necessary, request it on the memo, then meet the teacher and discuss what is lacking in the plans. If the memo indicated a specific problem, you should request that teacher's plans again in the next week's review cycle.

```
┌─────────────────────────────────────────────────────────────────┐
│                            MEMO                                   │
│                                                                   │
│  To: _____                             │
│                                                                   │
│  Fr: Sidney Smith, Principal                                      │
│                                                                   │
│  Re: Your plans, as indicated below                               │
│                                                                   │
│  ITEMS MISSING:                     SPECIFICS OMITTED:            │
│                                                                   │
│  _____ content area (    )          _____ remediation lesson in   │
│                                     _____                     │
│                                                                   │
│  _____ related written content      _____ enrichment lesson in    │
│                                     _____                     │
│                                                                   │
│  _____ plans for _____      _____ materials to be used    │
│                                     _____ pages to be covered     │
│                                     _____ objectives of the lesson│
│                                     _____ lesson for class or group│
│                                                                   │
│  COMMENTS:                          ADDITIONAL COMMENTS:          │
│                                                                   │
│  _____ plans are insufficient                                     │
│  _____ plans are not clear                                        │
│  _____ plan form is not effective                                 │
│  _____ please see me on _____                                 │
│  _____ plans are outstanding                                      │
│  _____ plans are late                                             │
└─────────────────────────────────────────────────────────────────┘
```

Figure 1-7

How to Improve the Teacher Plan Format

To shorten and improve a teacher's plans have them each incorporate the items from the following checklist.

1. The teacher should include all content areas:
   a. reading, including new skills, review, and reinforcement needs
   b. mathematics, including new skills, review, and reinforcement needs
   c. language arts, including writing skills, structural skills, and spelling strategies
   d. handwriting, including new and diagnosed needs
   e. social studies, including the topic of study and the method to use
   f. science, including the aim, materials, and process
   g. library skills, including the weekly skill lesson to be conducted
   h. other areas, such as current events, art, and television viewing
2. The teacher should state for each content area the:
   a. instructional mode (class, group, individual)

    b. specific aim to be accomplished

    c. materials to be used specifying pages

    d. conferences planned with students

Remember that the specific items on the checklist will vary, depending on your requirements for each teacher.

How to Broaden Teacher-Plan Effectiveness

Many teachers become frustrated when individual students are excused from the classroom for special group activities such as sports practice. It is often difficult to find a specific time to instruct the whole class or groups of students without excluding at least one student. When this problem occurs, help the teacher complete a form similar to the one shown in Figure 1-8, showing possible time blocks that won't be interrupted. This simple schedule helps the teacher to determine when all of the students and some groups are available for instruction.

POSSIBLE INSTRUCTIONAL TIME

TIME	O/A*	MON	TUES	WED	THURS	FRI
9-9:30	O	Juan(R1, M2) Mary(R2, M1)	NONE	Juan(R1, M2) Mary(R2, M1)	NONE	Juan(R1, M2) Mary(R2, M1)
	A	Read Gp 3 Math Gp 3	ALL	Read Gp 3 Math Gp 3	ALL	Read Gp 3 Math Gp 3
9:30-10	O	Tom(R3, M1)	Tom(R3, M1)	Tom(R3, M1)	Tom(R3, M1)	Tom(R3, M1)
	A	Read Gp 1,2 Math Gp 2,3	Read Gp 1,2 Math Gp 2,3	Read Gp 1,2 Math Gp 2,3	Read Gp 1,2 Math Gp 2,3	Read Gp 1,2 Math Gp 2,3
10-10:30	O	NONE	NONE	NONE	NONE	NONE
	A	Read Gp 1,2,3 Math Gp 1,2,3	GYM	Read Gp 1,2,3 Math Gp 1,2,3	GYM	Read Gp 1,2,3 Math Gp 1,2,3
10:30-11	O	NONE	NONE	NONE	NONE	NONE
	A	MUSIC	Read Gp 1,2,3 Math Gp 1,2,3	ART	Read Gp 1,2,3 Math Gp 1,2,3	CLASS
11-11:30	O	Marie(R1, M1)	Marie(R1, M1)	Marie(R1, M1)	Marie(R1, M1)	Marie(R1, M1)
	A	Read Gp 2,3 Math Gp 2,3	Read Gp 2,3 Math Gp 2,3	Read Gp 2,3 Math Gp 2,3	Read Gp 2,3 Math Gp 2,3	Read Gp 2,3 Math Gp 2,3
11:30-12	O	NONE	NONE	NONE	NONE	NONE
	A	ALL	ALL	ALL	ALL	ALL

1-1:30	O	NONE	NONE	NONE	NONE	NONE
	A	Read Gp 1,2,3 Math Gp 1,2,3	Read Gp 1,2,3 Math Gp 1,2,3	Read Gp 1,2,3 Math Gp 1,2,3	Read Gp 1,2,3 Math Gp 1,2,3	LIBRARY
1:30-2	O	NONE	NONE	NONE	NONE	NONE
	A	ALL	ALL	ALL	ALL	ALL
2-2:30	O	Jim(R3, M3) Theresa(R3, M3)	NONE	Jim(R3, M3) Theresa(R3, M3)	NONE	CHORUS
	A	Read Gp 1,2 Math Gp 1,2	ALL	Read Gp 1,2 Math Gp 1,2	ALL	individual conferences
2:30-3		Jim(R3, M3) Theresa(R3, M3)	NONE	Jim(R3, M3) Theresa(R3, M3)	NONE	individual conferences
		individual conferences	ALL	individual conferences	ALL	individual conferences

*O = students out of the room.
 A = groups/class available for instruction
 R = reading group
 M = mathematics group

Figure 1-8

By plotting which students, and therefore which reading and mathematics groups are not in perfect attendance, the teacher can plan to instruct complete groups at any given time. This also helps the teacher determine when and for how long the entire class is available for instruction. When many students are not in class, the teacher can plan this time for individualized instruction, conferences or progress checks.

DEVELOP STAFF POTENTIAL

How to Plan and Conduct Effective Staff Conferences

The staff conference is your only regularly scheduled meeting with the teachers. The effectiveness of this conference can be increased if you prepare notes for the faculty's use.

Neatly typed conference notes should be distributed to the staff on the day of the conference. The notes should include:

- a curriculum topic you will present at the conference
- any administrative details you want the faculty to know
- any important upcoming dates

The cover page of the conference notes is a good place for a quote. It's topic might be as varied as a summary of recent research or a child's poem. It gives you a valuable opportunity to draw the faculty's attention to a subject you consider important.

Once it's distributed, you can assume that the faculty will read and understand the notes. It is not necessary to review the various items included in the notes unless any topics need clarification. The conference itself is a presentation of the specific curriculum topic you've chosen. .

The curriculum topic is your vehicle to introduce or refine the area you want to develop with the faculty. Sharing is one successful way to introduce curriculum topics to the staff. Identify individual teachers who have some valuable curriculum strategy or technique that other teachers should know about. Request that these teachers present their techniques at a faculty conference. Ask them to prepare some notes that can be presented, and incorporate them in the conference notes. Then, turn the faculty conference over to the teacher who will give the curriculum presentation. At other times, you may want to involve other teachers or district personnel in other presentations.

Two examples of curriculum topics for staff conferences follow in Figures 1-9 and 1-10. One is concerned with writing skills; the other with diagnostic/prescriptive mathematics.

How to Plan and Implement
Classroom Demonstration Lessons

The classroom demonstration is an effective way to develop teachers who need help with their teaching strategies. For demonstration lessons to be effective, it is vital for the person who is going to view the demonstration to develop a positive attitude. The teacher should be encouraged to understand that the demonstration is a suggestion rather than a criticism.

The demonstrator selected must be a master teacher. If possible, review the lesson with the demonstrating teacher to reinforce the most important aspects of the lesson.

When a master teacher cannot be found to demonstrate a particular strategy, whether it involves questioning or motivational techniques, you may demonstrate the lesson yourself. However, this practice is rare for two good reasons. First, you are at a disadvantage since you do not know the class, and second, you may not have taught in a classroom for some time. So, if you are not comfortable demonstrating the lesson, don't try it.

How to Motivate Interclass Visits

The classroom chosen for interclass visits must be carefully picked because more than just the teacher is on display. An interclass visit includes all aspects of a model environment:

- the room is attractively decorated with students' work
- the atmosphere conveys purposeful activity of all students
- the teacher is involved with the students
- the students know how to conduct themselves, whether or not the teacher is in the room
- the students appear happy, calm, and interested in their tasks
- the students are able to verbalize what they are doing and why
- the students are courteous and kind to each other

Using Writing to Build Thinking and Reading Skills
—Mrs. Cassuto

The Writing Center

A. What is it?

A place in the room arranged to contain:
a. tasks designed to build and develop writing competence
b. a place to sit where the students can come to write
c. a set of proofreading symbols and a Work Plan for Writing
d. a set of folders

B. How Does It Work?

Time in the Writing Center is part of each student's prescription. A 20-minute stint at least three times a week is expected, or at least hoped for. The choice of time is flexible. Choice of selections is also flexible, but this is decided during conferences with the students.

Students are scheduled for weekly conferences. The conference day is part of their "fixed schedule."

Approximately six students are called to the Writing Center.

Purpose: A new writing activity may be introduced, and a brief lesson taught. Then each student takes his/her writing folder and works:

• to complete a writing activity previously begun
• to revise one before the private conference
• to rewrite a composition that has been corrected

Goal: To complete the conferences in 30-40 minutes.

C. What Kinds of Activities Are Used to Teach Writing?

Activities are divided into three categories:

1. Learning How

Board(s)—(sometimes two boards are used) contains a set of simple tasks that are the components of good writing such as:
• A set of words to be arranged in sentences
• A set of incomplete sentences to be completed by the students
• Word Boxes
• Directions for writing a paragraph that describes how to bake a cake or how to fry an egg
• Word Trees (New Directions in Creativity)
• Directions for writing the answer to a question in a dialogue
• Directions for selecting a synonym of the appropriate intensity

2. Showing That You Know

Board—contains composition ideas. Instructions are brief and clear. Ideas for all writing activities are available in the Media Center, and may be tailored to your design.

3. For Fun and Fantasy

Board—contains ideas that some students thrive on. Others prefer more down-to-earth expository exercises.

D. The Reasons It Works

Time in the Writing Center is part of the daily activities. It puts writing in the same category as reading and math.

Learning takes place even when there is no direct involvement with the students because the Center is stocked with directions and activities that are a result of sensing student needs in other curriculum areas.

Teaching can take place in small increments because the tasks are designed for the class. Commercial materials are used whenever possible.

E. How Writing Center Permeates All Areas of the Curriculum

1. Current Events—Students report on an event. Others are asked to write a summary sentence or a lead sentence for the article. This provides experience with the main idea; it builds from an experience with writing, and comes from within the child.

2. Using a Circle of Knowledge—Have information gathered, recorded and placed in the Writing Center to be the subject of a paragraph writing activity. Previous experience with topic sentence is used here.

3. Sequence—Sensitivity to order of events in reading material can come from asking the students to write about a sequence from his/her own life. For example, tell how you got ready to come to school this morning.

4. Higher order thinking skills for unskilled thinkers and writers—A particular activity may be "graded" to demand levels of sophisticated response.

Levels	For example, Machines
Knowledge	1. *List* the machines you have at home.
Comprehension	2. *Compare* two machines. Tell how they are alike.
Application	3. *Describe* how a machine is used.
Analysis	4. Which machine is the most valuable to your family? *Explain* your reasons.
Synthesis	5. *Create* a machine of your own. What function does it have? How is it powered? How would it contribute to your family's comfort?

Figure 1-9

Diagnostic/Prescriptive Mathematics
—Mrs. Razar

A. Determine Areas to Be Prescribed

1. administration of a diagnostic test
2. administration of a survey test
3. administration of the test available in the math kit

B. Prescribed Areas for Self-Directed Kit Work

1. Areas in which the most errors were made on the test
2. For students who make few errors prescribe enrichment areas, e.g., measures, sets, inequalities, etc., or prescribe more difficult items in such basic areas as subtraction.

C. Self-Directed Use of the Kit

1. Each student works on a card in sequential order in the prescribed area

2. Each completed card is self checked
3. Individual scores for each card are recorded on a record sheet
4. Each student takes a test after completing a block of cards on a topic
5. The test is checked by the teacher
6. On the basis of the test score, the teacher determines the pupil's understanding
7. The teacher indicates the next area of involvement for the student
8. Possible new prescriptions include:
   a. continue in the same area (this is not always advisable because of boredom)
   b. move to another prescribed area and come back to the first area at a future time
   c. further practice in the same area using other materials

D. Recordkeeping

1. Children's Notebook
   a. A series of prescriptions are listed
   b. The series includes several areas for independent work
   c. As children finish a prescribed area, the teacher makes a notation in the child's notebook
2. Record Sheets
   a. As children finish a card in the kit, they record their score on a record sheet
   b. Each test completed by the student is recorded by the teacher on a test sheet
   c. The test sheet is attached to the back of the record sheet
   d. The new area to be prescribed is recorded on the test paper
   e. The test paper is attached to the test sheet
   f. Record sheets are kept in a separate area

E. Individual Conference

1. Children ask for conferences whenever they need help.
2. The teacher may call selected students for conferences at any time to check progress.

Figure 1-10

- the students are able to positively use the resources and classroom
- the students are aware of and use routines established by the teacher

Be sure that the visit contains only exemplary components.

The visiting teacher should be given a clear set of objectives for the visit. Communicate exactly what and how the visit will accomplish these objectives. Some objectives include:

- *Classroom Management System*
   —student/teacher recordkeeping system
   —student/teacher checking system
   —teacher planning

—teacher's management of instructional groups
—arrangement of furniture and materials in the classroom
—students' use of the classroom
—alternatives open to the students

- *Teaching Techniques*
  —creative introduction of curriculum
  —unique curriculum materials
  —interdisciplinary curriculum topics

How to Develop a Staff Renewal Center

Since many schools today are faced with aging staffs, you seldom need to focus your attention on the young and inexperienced teacher. You are probably more concerned with the continued development of a mature and experienced staff.

The constant influx of new curriculum and materials into the schools demands regular attention to staff renewal since the modern teacher must understand and master new ideas. A well-developed Staff Renewal Center can help teachers become aware of new ideas and become skillful in using them.

To accomplish these objectives, carefully plan the creation of the Staff Renewal Center. The following types of materials should be available:

- *Professional Materials*
  —current professional magazines
  —current research journals
  —books on educational topics
  —educational articles from various sources

- *Curriculum Materials*
  —copies of curriculum bulletins used in the district
  —copies of new curriculum topics

- *Commercial Materials*
  —sample textbooks
  —sample workbooks
  —publishers' brochures
  —colorful giveaway materials such as posters and calendars

- *Materials for Teacher Use*
  —oaktag
  —index cards
  —magic markers
  —glue
  —laminating machine or clear contact
  —scissors
  —crayons
  —colored circles and stars
  —paper fasteners

—rexograph stencils
—typewriter
—tape recorder

The best developed center is worthless if teachers do not use it. You can suggest that teachers spend some time in the center, but it's much better to have teachers go there on their own because it meets their needs. If you plan well, this will happen spontaneously, without much prompting on your part.

Place the Staff Renewal Center in an area of the school that is convenient for the teachers. The room itself should be attractive and comfortable. Besides work space and good lighting, the room should have comfortable chairs. Have a coffee pot or hot water available in the room, and ask teachers to contribute to a "kitty" when they help themselves to refreshments.

Introduce the center at a staff conference and let the teachers know that it is their room. Ask teachers for their reactions to the room after they have seen it, and get suggestions for improvements. Provide a sign-in sheet so that teachers can show that they have used the room. You can also furnish a separate list so that teachers can jot down any materials or supplies that are needed.

ENCOURAGE CONTINUED STAFF EDUCATION

How to Plan and Implement Staff Workshops

The staff conference, while important to staff development, is often not long enough to do anything other than motivate teachers. You usually need several sessions to fully develop suggestions and ideas so the teacher can carry them over into the classroom. Staff workshops are also helpful in staff development.

Unlike the conferences, workshops should be voluntary. Teachers must have a need to understand the topic to be presented, which will motivate them to participate.

Workshops might be held during lunch hours. Invite teachers to join you for lunch and provide the coffee, tea, and cookies. Use the time to continue the presentation that was introduced at the staff conference, giving teachers the opportunity to participate and, whenever possible, create or make something they can immediately work with.

Workshops may also be held before or after school. The best time for the workshops, of course, depends upon the individual situation.

How to Develop In-Service Courses

Some topics cannot be adequately presented during the staff conference, even if you have support workshops to supplement it. These topics should then be presented as in-service courses.

When a particular topic is important to you or your staff, bring it to the attention of the district office and suggest an in-service course be planned during the next semester. If you want to encourage your staff to attend this course, offer to have it at your building. Teachers are far more likely to attend in-service courses held at their own school than at other locations.

Some topics that are currently of interest for in-service courses include:

- Education of the Gifted
- Personalized Teaching
- Mastery Learning
- Teacher-Made Materials
- Developing a Management System
- Teaching/Learning Styles

How to Encourage Attendance at Seminars

Seminars and conferences contribute to the development of the professional teacher, and most teachers are anxious to attend. When the staff is given the opportunity to attend a professional seminar or conference, several teachers will usually request permission to go. Select the teachers who will profit most from the experience—this may be a skilled teacher who needs exposure to a new idea or concept, a teacher who might someday become a master teacher, or else a teacher you have selected to develop and implement a new curriculum technique or topic. An unsatisfactory teacher rarely benefits from this type of experience.

Get the maximum benefit for the rest of your staff by inviting the teacher who went to the seminar to present the new ideas and suggestions learned at the next staff conference. Plan some follow-up workshops in which materials brought back to the school from the seminar can be viewed and discussed.

Although it is difficult to pay for the teacher to attend the meeting, the district can sometimes support the effort by providing a substitute teacher. If it is not possible to pay a substitute teacher, you may want to consider dividing the students among several other classes so that the teacher may be released. The cost of traveling to the conference is generally born by the attending teacher. If possible, the registration fee should be paid out of the school fund.

How to Help Teachers Achieve Advanced Degrees

The commitment needed to pursue an advanced degree is enormous. The benefits to the school, however, are large; teachers who are involved in university work enrich the school with new ideas and techniques.

Make the teacher going for an advanced degree a visible part of the staff. This teacher can present some information from a course he or she has taken; this would be an excellent topic for a staff conference. This type of recognition for the teacher will make him or her feel good about making this effort.

Universities are often interested in developing a working relationship with the schools. If a group of teachers is interested in a particular course, the university may agree to teach it on site at the school rather than at the university.

Sometimes universities will offer tuition credit or reduction to teachers at schools being used as field settings such as in student teaching. It is also possible to offer the school as a field setting for internship programs such as speech and hearing, reading, and administration, to name a few, in order to obtain a possible tuition credit or reduction for your staff.

2

HOW TO IMPROVE PUPIL PERFORMANCE

The instructional aim of teachers is to improve pupil performance. You can help teachers do this by helping them to understand, develop, and implement a diagnostic process of instruction.

THE RATIONALE FOR A DIAGNOSTIC/PRESCRIPTIVE PROCESS

Research shows that up to 50 percent of the time, students are taught topics they have already mastered, while others are taught topics for which they have no background skills. For example, it is literally impossible for a student to complete a long division algorithm if he or she cannot subtract. For this reason, pupil performance can be dramatically improved when students' learning needs are diagnosed and used to prescribe teacher and student-directed instruction.

If teachers know the strengths and weaknesses of individual students, instruction will be more meaningful. The strengths of the students then become the building blocks for more difficult topics to come. Students' weaknesses show which skills must be mastered before students can move on to more difficult topics.

INTRODUCE STAFF TO THE DIAGNOSTIC/PRESCRIPTIVE PROCESS

Educators have for a long time realized that many students take on a disinterested attitude when their needs are not met. Teacher awareness of this attitude helps motivate use of a diagnostic/prescriptive approach.

Diagnosis is made easier by the use of a standardized test in both reading and mathematics. Unfortunately, these tests are costly, but it is possible to buy an evaluative test that will also diagnose.

When it is impossible to buy a diagnostic test, informal diagnostic inventories may be useful. You can also consult your state or district listings of reading skills to compile your own list. These lists can then be used as checks, along with informal assessments by the teacher.

For an informal assessment, each student reads a graded selection to the teacher. During the oral reading, the teacher records phonic analysis, morphemic analysis, vocabulary skills, and fluency skills of the individual student. Following the reading, the teacher asks several prepared comprehension questions to determine the student's understanding of literal meaning, interpretation, critical evaluation, locating information, and organizing information skills. The teacher has then developed an informal reading assessment of the student and knows the strengths and weaknesses of that child.

It is also possible to conduct an informal mathematics assessment of students' skills by using a survey test. Select two or three examples of topics that should have been mastered in the previous grade, and include several on-grade skills that have not yet been taught. Students' papers are then reviewed to determine mastery of concepts from the grade below as well as new concepts on grade level. The teacher then has an informal mathematics assessment of the student and knows the strengths and weaknesses of that individual student. This information tells the teacher exactly which skills each student in the class must master in both reading and mathematics.

How to Plot the Results of Diagnosis

Developing forms related to the diagnostic instrument used will assist the teacher in plotting Mastery and Need forms (Figures 2-1 and 2-2) for each student. Teachers are then relieved of the burden of creating their own means of recording the information they have gathered.

How to Understand Class Reading and Mathematics Needs

The first steps toward improving pupil performance are administrating a diagnostic instrument and plotting the results of the diagnoses.

The results must then be implemented in a plan whose design capitalizes on the diagnostic information, using it to plan for meaningful instruction.

USE DIAGNOSTIC INFORMATION FOR INSTRUCTION

Once diagnostic information has been gathered, the results should be analyzed in two ways. First, the student's skill needs are surveyed for each topic included in the diagnostic instrument. This is easily accomplished by looking across the line next to the student's name and noting where Xs have been written to indicate skill needs. Second, group and class skill needs are surveyed by looking down the column under each item. This review of needs alerts the teacher to which students in the class require certain skills.

INFORMAL READING DIAGNOSIS—MASTERY AND NEED

TOPIC 1. a b c d e f g h i j k 2. a b c d e f g h 3. a b c d e f 4. a b c

STUDENTS	PHONIC ANALYSIS	auditory discrimination	initial consonants	final consonants	short vowels	long vowels	consonant blends	consonant digraphs	vowel diphthongs	silent letters	syllabication	accent	MORPHEMIC ANALYSIS	root words	inflectional endings	compound words	prefixes	suffixes	contractions	abbreviations	word roots	VOCABULARY	contextual clues	synonyms	antonyms	homonyms	multiple meanings	descriptive, sensory words	FLUENCY	rate of reading	scanning/skimming for details	skimming/previewing

X INDICATES SKILL NEED

Figure 2-1

INFORMAL READING DIAGNOSIS—MASTERY AND NEED

TOPIC 5. a b c   6. a b c   7. a b c d e f g   8. a b c d e f g   9. a b c d e

STUDENTS	LITERAL MEANING	stated details	main idea	following directions	INFERENTIAL	inference	drawing conclusions	context clues	CRITICAL—EVALUATIVE	cause and effect	predicting outcomes	figurative language	fact and opinion	author's purpose	propaganda	character analysis	LOCATING INFORMATION	organization of a book	table of contents	index	glossary	dictionary usage	encyclopedia	library skills	ORGANIZING INFORMATION	select material	classify information	outline material	summarize information	notetaking techniques
_____																														
_____																														
_____																														
_____																														
_____																														
_____																														
_____																														
_____																														
_____																														
_____																														
_____																														
_____																														
_____																														
_____																														
_____																														
_____																														
_____																														
_____																														
_____																														
_____																														
_____																														
_____																														

X INDICATES SKILL NEED

Figure 2-1 (continued)

INFORMAL MATHEMATICS DIAGNOSIS—GRADE 4—MASTERY AND NEED (PART I)

STUDENTS	TOPIC 1	2	3	4	5	6	7	8	9	10	11	12	13	14 15 16	17

Topic labels:
1. counting by 5
2. understanding: 3. place value, 4. numbers, 5. numeration
6.
7. sets—division 8.
9. addition of 10. whole numbers 11.
12. subtraction 13. of whole numbers 14.
15. 16. multiplication 17. of whole numbers 18.
19. division of whole numbers 20.
21. division of a whole number 22. by a fraction
23. understanding fractions 24.
25. geometry; 26. understanding shapes
27. algebraic concepts 28.
29. Roman numerals 30.
31. problem solving 32. using money 33.
34. telling time 35. how to use a calendar 36. how to interpret a graph 37.
38. problem solving 39.

X INDICATES SKILL NEED

Figure 2-2

Those skill needs that are required by one or two students can be planned as individual or peer-assisted instruction, while those skill needs that involve five to ten students can be planned as group instruction. Those skill needs that include most of the students in the class can be planned as whole class instruction during which time the few students who do not need this instruction can be assigned to other topics or content areas. The teacher is then ready to complete part two of the Mastery and Need form.

Shown in Figure 2-3, part two includes two wide columns. One column is Teacher-Directed Instruction and places each student in a teacher-directed instructional group based

INFORMAL READING DIAGNOSIS—MASTERY AND NEED (PART II)

TOPIC 1. a b c d e f g h i j k 2. a b c d e f g h

PHONIC ANALYSIS	TEACHER-DIRECTED INSTRUCTION state developmental instructional group	SELF-DIRECTED INSTRUCTION list individual objectives and materials to be used
auditory discrimination		
initial consonants		
final consonants		
short vowels		
long vowels		
consonant blends		
consonant digraphs		
vowel dipthongs		
silent letters		
syllabication		
accent		
MORPHEMIC ANALYSIS		
root words		
inflectional endings		
compound words		
prefixes		
suffixes		
contractions		
abbreviations		
word roots		

STUDENTS

TOPIC 1   2   3   4   5   6   7   8   9

STUDENTS	TEACHER-DIRECTED INSTRUCTION state developmental instruction group	SELF-DIRECTED INSTRUCTION list individual objectives and materials to be used
1. counting by 5		
2. understanding:		
3. place value,		
4. numbers,		
5. numeration		
6.		
7. sets—division		
8.		
9. addition of		
10. whole numbers		
11.		
12. subtraction		
13. of whole numbers		
14.		
15.		
16. multiplication		
17. of whole numbers		
18.		
19. division of whole numbers		
20.		
21. division of a whole number		
22. by a fraction		
23. understanding fractions		
24.		

Figure 2-3

on strengths and weaknesses. The other column is Self-Directed Instruction and includes those skills required by only one or two students in the class. In addition, the self-directed column contains a listing of specific materials and activities that complement the skill needs and strengths of each student. Those students without skill needs may continue to advanced skills or work in related enrichment areas.

Once each student has been placed in a group and has been assigned a prescription for materials and activities, a second type of instructional grouping can be prepared. These instructional groups do not focus upon the sequential, developmental program of instruction, but rather take into consideration the specific topic weaknesses of the students. Based on specific topic deficiency, the groups are necessary to the development of background skills that will be needed by students if they are to continue in a sequential, developmental instructional program, no matter how slowly that program is paced.

The Topic Instructional Groups form (Figure 2-4) is prepared by listing, under each topic number, the names of the students who demonstrate the specific weakness. The teacher then has a second set of instructional groups to include in the preparation of his or her plans.

TOPIC INSTRUCTIONAL GROUPS—READING AND MATHEMATICS

TOPICS: Reading

1.a	1.b	1.c	1.d	1.e	1.f	1.g	1.h
Tom	Tom	Fred	Tom	Tom	Tom	Tom	Tom
Jane	Ted	Tom	Juan	Jane	Jane	Jane	Jane
	Marie	Ted	Ted		Jim	Susan	Fred
	Sally	Marie	Sally		Luis	Sylvia	Louise

TOPICS: Mathematics

1	2	3	4	5	6
Larry	Barbara	Evelyn	Harry	Alice	George
Nicky	Walter	George	Isabel	Walter	Harry
Alice	Danny	Mario	Jesse	Mario	Nicky
	Frank	Claudia	Kathy	Steve	Louise
	Claudia			Gordon	Fred
					Luis

Figure 2-4

RELATE DIAGNOSTIC INFORMATION TO TEACHER PLANNING

The completed Mastery and Need forms are powerful planning tools for the teacher in helping students dramatically improve their performances in reading and mathematics. The teacher might plan to instruct at least *one* topic need group in mathematics or reading each day. However, *each* reading and mathematics developmental skill group should be instructed every day.

Of course, the daily instruction is not always possible because many students are pulled out of the classroom for various programs. Teacher-preparation periods and special school programs also intrude on possible instructional time. Since teachers may become frustrated as their instructional efforts are thwarted by other programs, good management can help the teacher clarify what instructional time is available for which groups of students. (See Figure 1-6 in Chapter 1.)

Teachers can also be helped to become more effective by thinking through the length of their group lessons. Not every lesson needs to be 40 or 45 minutes long. In fact, shorter, more frequent lessons are very helpful in allowing students to master less information at one sitting, and providing a review and reinforcement exercise before another concept is taught. This is especially true of the topic need lessons that should be 15 to 20 minutes long and aimed at one specific objective.

RELATE DIAGNOSTIC INFORMATION TO MATERIAL SELECTION

Following the review of the class' diagnostic information and the placement of students into developmental instructional groups and topic need groups, specific materials should be considered. The materials selected for a specific instructional group or topic need group should:

- be within the reading range of the group
- contain the skills that the group of students require
- address the students' interests
- be suited to the students' background and experiences

Materials must also be selected for the self-directed instructional aspect of skill or enrichment need. The materials selected for self-directed use should:

- be those a student can use without assistance
- have clearly specified directions
- require responses that the student is capable of completing
- have a system for the student to record answers
- include a means for correction of student responses
- be readily available for student use

Those materials selected for the specific needs of individual students should be listed in the self-directed column of the Mastery and Need form. In addition, each student should record his or her self-directed instructional materials in a specific place in a notebook so that the student may refer to the list when necessary, record the completion date for a particular item, and add new ones.

FOLLOW A PROCESS TO IMPROVE
PUPIL WRITING COMPETENCE

Writing is a major area of concern for all educators. But if only structure and handwriting are stressed, the student's creative expression will be stifled. On the other hand, if only creative expression is focused upon, students will not be learning about the important mechanics of writing the English language. How is a balance between the two achieved? The answer lies in establishing a dual objective program.

Objective 1: To Have Students Express Themselves Creatively

The fostering of creative written expression encourages students to express themselves freely, with the emphasis on the person and the development of original expression. Evaluation of students' written work is therefore focused on improving creative expression rather than on punctuation, spelling, and grammar, and should be accomplished by using directional comments concerning the writing's creativity. The "red pencil" indication of errors in mechanics is avoided since this will encourage students to confine their written efforts to words and phrases that they know or believe are correct.

Creative expression is also developed by helping students be confident in their ability to express themselves. Students should believe that *what* they have to say and *why* they should have the opportunity to say that in writing are important.

This self-confidence can be developed through written comments on students' work. Sample comments directed at improving creative expression are:

Help me to see the pretty snowfall.

I want to feel as frightened as your story's character.

Can you make me taste the wonderful dinner you ate?

Can you compare what you saw to anything or anyone else?

Why don't you want to return to that place?

Try to describe the beautiful garden.

Sample comments directed at improving students' confidence in their ability to express themselves are:

You chose interesting words to describe the snow.

Your work makes me think of having fun at the beach.

Now I know how you will keep cool this summer.

I think some of your predictions may come true.

Your game sounds very exciting.

I am so glad you discovered the magic of books.

Objective 2: To Have Students Write in Correct Standard English

Instruction in all aspects of written English is vital if we are to foster the development of students who are capable of writing in correct English. Thus, the most valuable diagnosis of skill need and instructional materials are the writing efforts of the students. Directing the students' attention to their errors and the subsequent correction of those errors contributes to the growth and development of a competent writer. After repeated experiences in proofreading and correcting errors as well as instruction in related skill areas, students will hopefully become proficient and competent writers.

REMEMBER: The dual objectives are not dichotomous. Rather, they require the development of an effective writing program.

DEVELOP THE TOTALLY COMPETENT WRITER

The 7-stage writing cycle discussed here is intended to develop both creative and competent writers. Each phase of the cycle developmentally builds skills and helps students to improve. Writing is a skill that must be practiced; therefore, it is neither wise nor practical to expose every written effort of the child to this process. The teacher should select one piece of written work every few weeks for the cycle.

1. Creative Expression

The writing cycle begins with instructional techniques aimed at developing creative expression. These techniques include motivation as well as instruction in creative expression.

Motivate writing by providing for a common experience such as a story or a trip, introducing an exciting topic such as the future world, selecting stimulating pictures or films for viewing, creating a topic sentence, and introducing an unfinished story.

Instruct for creative writing by teaching precise language, such as finding new words for overused ones, teaching descriptive expression such as "describe the cat," teaching descriptive comparison such as personification, similes, and metaphores, and teaching descriptive details such as describing the similarities and differences between two items.

2. Evaluate Creativity

The initial writing efforts of the students are now evaluated only for creative expression. Directional comments should be written on the students' papers for improving creative effort and developing students' confidence in the ability to write.

3. Rewrite and Proofread

Ask the students to proofread their work by themselves or with a peer, to make their creative effort as mechanically correct as possible, and to include the teacher's suggestions in the rewriting. Students may be helped in the proofreading effort by preparing a guide for them, such as the one on the following page.

4. Diagnostic Evaluation

The teacher now evaluates the written effort of the student to diagnose mechanical writing needs. The development of a form (Figure 2-5) to record these needs will save time and allow the teacher to identify similar needs among students so that instructional groups can be formed.

As you proofread your work, check for:
1. margins—on the left side, the right side, the top, the bottom
2. correct form for what you are writing
3. paragraph indentation
4. capitalization—
   first word of the sentence
   the word "I"
   names of people and places
   titles
   initials
5. punctuation—
   periods after sentences
   commas between words in a series
   quotation marks around someone else's words
6. usage—
   correctly use the singular to mean "one"
   correctly use the plural to mean "more than one"
7. spelling
8. sentence form—
   too many ideas in one sentence
   an incomplete sentence
9. ideas in order—does the story make sense to the reader?
10. overused words—have you used interesting words?
11. handwriting

5. Instruction in Mechanics

Instructional groups can be formed based upon the results of the diagnostic evaluation of the students' work. Samples of the students' work should be included. Specific assignments for review and reinforcement can be completed independently in class or as homework.

6. Rewrite and Proofread

The students are now asked to rewrite the work that was used for the diagnosis of needs, and are encouraged to proofread their work. They may do this independently or with a peer.

7. Evaluation

The students' work should be evaluated for both creativity and mechanics. A diagnosis of new or continued needs in both areas will:

- demonstrate growth in skill areas previously diagnosed as a need and provided for with direct instruction

- indicate new or recurring skill needs for future instruction

| ANALYSIS OF MECHANICAL WRITING NEEDS | | | | | |
| SKILL NEEDS | | | | | |
STUDENTS' NAMES and DATES OF WRITING	SENTENCES: incomplete run-on paragraph	PUNCTUATION . , ? ; : " ' !	CAPITALS: sentences, names, titles	USAGE	SPELLING

Figure 2-5

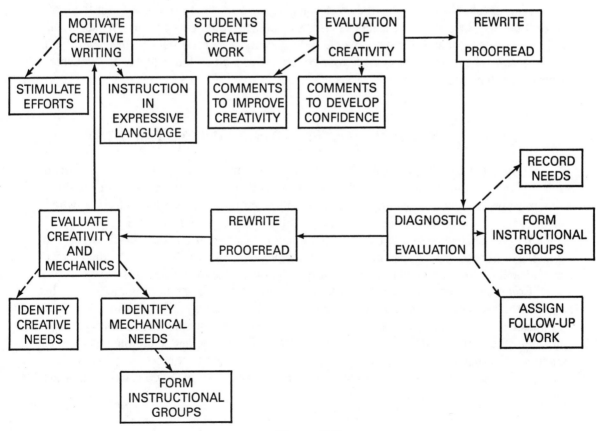

Figure 2-6

- assess the development of creative expression
- indicate the creative expression needs of groups of students or the class as a whole

EVALUATE THE SCHOOL'S WRITING PROGRAM

Schedule periodic collections of samples of student writing from each class. Group the collections between sequential grades so that you are able to compare pupil writing progress among students in different classes on the same grade, and evaluate student growth in writing from one grade to the grade above. Notify the teachers at the beginning of the school year of when student writing samples will be collected so that a sample for each youngster will be ready:

grades 5 and 6 by September 30

grades 3 and 4 by October 30

grades 1 and 2 by November 30

Continue this pattern for the remainder of the school year to evaluate the writing program.

Teachers should also be instructed to complete a cover sheet (Figure 2-7) for the set of student papers. Respond to the teacher's efforts by placing comments on the cover sheet, and noting any suggestions for improvement. Ask teachers who need help to meet with you. Make a copy of the cover sheet with your comments as well as the analysis of mechanical needs for future comparison.

EFFECTIVELY REPORT STUDENT PROGRESS TO PARENTS

Despite the fact that schools involve hundreds of students and classes involve tens of students, each student has an individual parent who is usually concerned about the child. When the progress of a student is reported in written or oral form, it is the individual who is the focus. This concept is important to keep in mind when the reporting process takes place. Each individual student should be evaluated in comparison with him- or herself rather than with his or her peers. What parents should be encouraged to look for is the individual growth of *their* child, rather than a comparison of the child with Johnny or Jean.

Communicating a written report to the parent is a difficult task. Grades, whether numbers or letters, are interpreted by parents in different ways. In addition, the areas evaluated are not always understood by the parents. Reading as a total act, for example, does not help the parent understand why the child can sound out and therefore read almost anything, but not with understanding. Thus, the development of a report to parents that is clearly understood both for the areas included and the evaluation recorded is most important.

COVER SHEET

Teacher _____

Class _____   Date _____

Motivation/Instruction in Creative Expression:

Evaluation of Creative Effort:

Attach the Analysis of Mechanical Writing Needs form. Indicate instructional groups formed in each area.

Evaluation of Students' Progress in This Writing Cycle:

Future Plans:

Figure 2-7

How to Develop an Effective Report to Parents

The report to parents should reflect the content focus of the program. It is most helpful to parents, for example, that they see the aspects of reading that are being evaluated. The development of an evaluation system that is clearly understood by the parent is another aspect that should be given attention. Thus, the evaluation system should be explained on the report itself. Figure 2-8 attempts to define the content of each area that is evaluated. This content will vary to some small degree depending on the scope and sequence of each school district

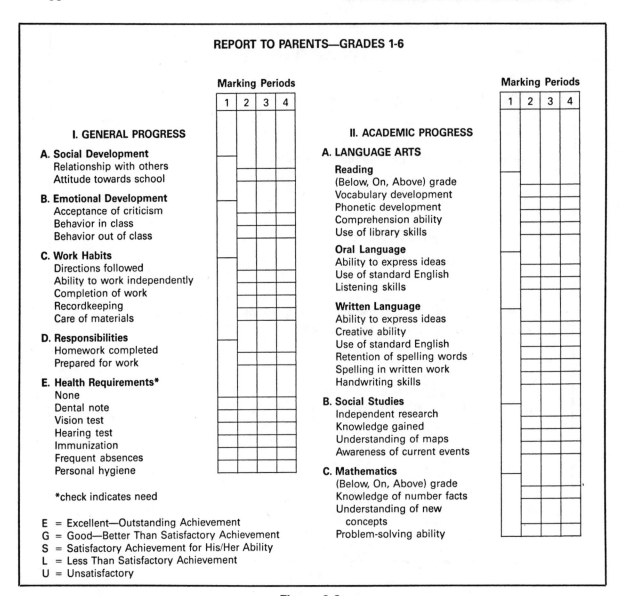

REPORT TO PARENTS—GRADES 1-6

Marking Periods

	1	2	3	4

I. GENERAL PROGRESS

A. Social Development
Relationship with others
Attitude towards school

B. Emotional Development
Acceptance of criticism
Behavior in class
Behavior out of class

C. Work Habits
Directions followed
Ability to work independently
Completion of work
Recordkeeping
Care of materials

D. Responsibilities
Homework completed
Prepared for work

E. Health Requirements*
None
Dental note
Vision test
Hearing test
Immunization
Frequent absences
Personal hygiene

*check indicates need

E = Excellent—Outstanding Achievement
G = Good—Better Than Satisfactory Achievement
S = Satisfactory Achievement for His/Her Ability
L = Less Than Satisfactory Achievement
U = Unsatisfactory

Marking Periods

	1	2	3	4

II. ACADEMIC PROGRESS

A. LANGUAGE ARTS

Reading
(Below, On, Above) grade
Vocabulary development
Phonetic development
Comprehension ability
Use of library skills

Oral Language
Ability to express ideas
Use of standard English
Listening skills

Written Language
Ability to express ideas
Creative ability
Use of standard English
Retention of spelling words
Spelling in written work
Handwriting skills

B. Social Studies
Independent research
Knowledge gained
Understanding of maps
Awareness of current events

C. Mathematics
(Below, On, Above) grade
Knowledge of number facts
Understanding of new
   concepts
Problem-solving ability

Figure 2-8

and state department of education. The areas of science, music, art, and physical education should also be included in the report and should reflect the content of the program offered to the students. An overall report for grades 1 to 6 can be used flexibly by indicating on the report that areas not marked are not appropriate for the student. The kindergarten program, however, is very different and usually requires a special report. Figure 2-9 reflects a skills oriented and academic approach to instruction at this level.

REPORT TO PARENTS—KINDERGARTEN

A = <u>all</u> of the time
M = <u>most</u> of the time
P = <u>part</u> of the time
S = <u>seldom</u>
N = <u>never</u>

I. GENERAL PROGRESS

	Marking Periods		
	1	2	3
A. Social Development			
Relates to peers in work and play activities			
Is aware of the feelings of others			
Is readily accepted by the group			
Is aware of group responsibility			
Shows leadership ability			
B. Emotional Development			
Shows self-confidence			
Practices self-control			
Adjusts to change			
Accepts constructive criticism			
Accepts responsibility for own actions			
Cares for own needs			
C. Work Habits			
Follows directions			
Works independently			
Plans appropriately for her-/himself			
Uses time constructively			
Keeps accurate and neat records of work			
Makes use of a variety of materials			
Is responsible for care of materials			
Observes safety rules			
D. Special Health Needs			

II. ACADEMIC PROGRESS

	Marking Periods		
	1	2	3
A. Reading			
Shows an interest			
Shows ability to understand what is read to him/her			
Can interpret pictures			
Can tell a story in sequence			
Shows ability to understand what he/she reads			
B. Language Arts-Oral			
Shows confidence in speaking before a group			
Expresses ideas clearly and interestingly			
Is an attentive listener			
C. Number Concepts			
Shows an interest			
Learns new concepts			
Solves problems			
D. Science			
Shows an interest in scientific experimentation			
Is able to understand basic scientific concepts			
E. Social Studies			
Is able to demonstrate knowledge acquired			
Indicates an awareness of current issues			
F. Physical Education			
Participates			
G. Art			
Uses materials creatively to the best of his/her ability			
H. Music			
Shows appreciation			
Participates			

Figure 2-9

How to Explain the Report to Parents

Despite attempts to make the report as clear as possible, some parents will still not understand what is being evaluated and how the evaluation is determined. Therefore, it is helpful to print an explanation of the report (Figure 2-10) that may be included with the report or that may appear in the school's publication at about the same time that the report is distributed to parents.

HOW AND WHEN TO CONDUCT PARENT CONFERENCES

The single most effective communication link between the student's achievement and the parent's understanding is the teacher-parent conference.

Most districts provide a specific time period for the purpose of having teachers speak with parents. However, the specified conference time frames should not be the only opportunities for communication between parent and teacher. Both parent and teacher should request conferences when there is a reason or a need to discuss the child. Those special conferences can be scheduled early in the morning, before students arrive, during teacher preparation periods, or after school. Sometimes, the teacher and the parent want to speak without the student in attendance. At other times, it may be beneficial to have the student present to answer questions or to contribute to the development of a cooperative plan. The decision to meet with or without the child should be made prior to the conference so that the child may be available if needed.

HELP TEACHERS IMPROVE CONFERENCE TECHNIQUES

The teacher is a combination of host, diplomat, planning engineer, and sympathetic ear. Be prepared to listen to the parent and try to understand the parent's point of view concerning his or her child. Remember that the parent believes in the child and speaks with the teacher from the child's point of view. Most issues are rarely black or white, right or wrong, guilty or innocent; rather, they are shades of gray depending upon perception and attitude. Most of all, the teacher should aim at gaining the parent's trust and confidence by building a sincere attitude of interest and concern for the welfare of the child.

The following suggestions will help teachers (and you) conduct successful conferences:

- Be friendly. Put the parent at ease. Picture yourself in the parent's shoes.

- Begin on a positive note. Find something nice to say about the child.

- Listen to the parent. Pay attention to the parent and be sympathetic. You will gather information that will help you to work effectively with the child.

- Sit at a student desk or a round table rather than the teacher's desk. Eliminate the artificial barrier that the teacher's desk represents. Many parents are fearful of authority situations, and the teacher's desk represents one of them. Beginning on a note of fear rather than a note of cooperation can only detract from a successful conference.

- Do not ask prying questions of a personal nature. If the parent is reluctant to respond, move to another subject.

REPORT TO PARENTS—AN EXPLANATION

Ratings:

E = Excellent— Outstanding Achievement
Both the amount of work and the quality of work that the student does are excellent.

G = Good—Better Than Satisfactory Achievement
The student does better than just average work but could possibly do even more.

S = Satisfactory Achievement for His/Her Ability
The student is really trying and doing the work asked of him/her. The work done, however, may be below grade level. See areas READING and MATHEMATICS.

L = Less Than Satisfactory Achievement
The student does very little of the work and tries only sometimes.

U = Unsatisfactory
The student does none or almost none of the work asked of him/her and what is done is usually very poor. The student does not seem to care or to try.

Marking Periods:

There are four Marking Periods during the school year.

Period I — Usually in November. You will also be notified about conference time.

Period II — Usually in January. No conferences are scheduled at this time but you may request a conference. If appropriate, holdover letters are included in this report to parents.

Period III — Usually in March. You will also be notified about conference time. If appropriate, a second holdover notice will be included in this report to parents.

Period IV — At the end of the school year this report will include the new class and grade assignment for the child.

Marking Periods—Ratings:

Period I — Ratings are made only for each area in general. No ratings are given for the topics under each area because only a few weeks of instruction have been conducted and it would be unfair to rate the students at this time.

Periods II, III, IV — Ratings are made for the various topics under each major heading. Notations are also made for Health and Attendance.

PLEASE NOTE   — If an area is left blank, a rating is not possible for that
                       area because: the child has not been in the class long
                       enough to make a judgment, the area is not
                       appropriate for the child or the grade, or the child
                       does not speak enough English to be able to
                       participate.

Definitions of Terms Used:

I. GENERAL PROGRESS

A. Social Development—A view of the child as a member of a group.
   Relationship with others—How the child gets along with other
      children and adults.
   Attitude towards school—What the child shows he/she thinks about
      the value of school.

B. Emotional Development—A view of the child's individual feelings and
      actions.
   Acceptance of criticism—How the child accepts suggestions made to
      him/her.
   Behavior in and out of class—How the child follows rules and cares
      about the rights of others.

C. Work Habits—A view of the child in his/her development of areas that
      will help the child to become a better student.
   Directions followed—Does the child do what is asked of him/her?
   Ability to work independently—Can the child work on his/her own
      without constant attention and direction from others?
   Completion of work—Does the child finish the work that is asked of
      him/her?
   Recordkeeping—Does the child write neatly and carefully the work
      that is asked of him/her?
   Care of materials—Does the child use, return, share and take care of
      the various materials that he/she uses in work?

D. Responsibilities—A view of how the child shows he/she cares that
      school is important.
   Homework completed—Does the child consistently bring finished and
      well-done work?
   Prepared for work—Does the child come to school with items needed
      for work such as pencils, a notebook, paper, crayons, etc.?

E. Health Requirements—Each area checked indicates that your child has
      a health need.
   None—There are no health needs.
   Dental note—The child needs a checkup by the dentist.
   Vision test—The school vision check shows that your child's vision is
      poor and requires a further check by an eye doctor.
   Hearing test—The school hearing test shows that your child's hearing
      is poor and requires a further check by a doctor.
   Immunization—The school records indicate that your child needs
      some immunization and should see a doctor.

Frequent absence—Your child is not at school too often and may need a checkup by a doctor.

Personal hygiene—Your child needs attention in the area of personal cleanliness.

II. ACADEMIC PROGRESS

A. *Language Arts*—The areas of reading, writing, listening and speaking

Reading

Below, On, Above grade—The level at which your child currently is able to work. An "S" rating in this area means that your child *is trying his/her best* but *may not* be able at this time to read as well as is expected of children his/her age.

Vocabulary development—Does the child learn and remember new words?

Phonetic development—Does the child know and use the sounds of the letters to help him/her learn new words?

Comprehension ability—Does the child understand what he/she reads?

Use of library skills—Does the child use and remember how to use the books and materials in the library to help him/her find information?

Oral Language

Ability to express ideas—Does the child speak clearly so that others who listen can understand what he/she wishes to say or tell?

Use of standard English—Does the child use good grammar and pronunciation when speaking?

Listening skills—Does the child listen to and understand what is said orally?

Written Language

Ability to express ideas—Does the child write so that others can understand what he/she wants to tell?

Creative ability—Does the child write in a way that is interesting and shows good use of many different words?

Use of standard English—Does the child use correct grammar, punctuation, and word forms in his/her written work?

Retention of spelling words—Does the child remember new words that have been studied?

Spelling in written work—Does the child correctly spell the words written in compositions and reports?

Handwriting skills—Does the child form the letters in a correct way and is his/her written work neat and easily read?

B. *Social Studies*

Independent research—Does the child know where to find and how to use information on a topic by himself/herself?

Knowledge gained—Has the child a basic understanding of the topics being studied?

Understanding of maps—Can the child read and understand different kinds of maps?

Awareness of current events—Does the child know about and understand the key issues?

C. *Mathematics*

Below, On, Above grade—The level at which your child currently is able to work. An "S" rating in this area means that your child *is trying his/her best* but *may not* be able at this time to do mathematics as well as is expected of children his/her age. The child may not have mastered certain skills.

Knowledge of number facts—Does the child remember and use the basic facts of addition, subtraction, multiplication, and division?

Understanding of new concepts—Does the child understand, remember, and use what was taught to him/her?

Problem-solving ability—Can the child understand what is asked in a problem and correctly find the answer?

D. *Science**   E. *Physical Education**   F. *Art**   G. *Music**

*Participation in activities—Does the child involve himself/herself in the topic?

Completion of assignments Does the child finish what is asked of him/her?	Sportsmanship Does the child respect the feelings of others Is he/she a good winner/loser?	Creative use of materials— Does the child use the materials in unusual ways?

Figure 2-10

- Be prepared to document what you say about the child. Gather records of his or her progress, examples of the student's work, test results, and diagnostic assessments and prescriptions.

- Prepare an outline of your remarks. Jot down the main points you want to get across to parents, and state those points in simple language easily understood by a parent. Try to be as specific as possible.

- Focus on solutions. Back up criticism with specific suggestions for improvement and a cooperative plan with the parent, if possible.

- Stay with the most important area(s) of concern. Do not overwhelm the parent with multiple problems that become too numerous to be dealt with at the same time.

- Listen and be tactful, and do not argue or complain. Parents are not really interested in your problems.

- Leave lines of communication open at the conclusion of the conference. Be sure to indicate that future contact between the teacher and the parent are desirable. These contacts may be made in person or by telephone.

SCREEN NEW ADMISSIONS TO THE SCHOOL

The new student admitted to the school is generally unknown. School records and test scores often take weeks to arrive, so you are faced with some immediate decisions about that student. At this time, a screening process should be initiated.

Examine Alternatives in Student Placement

First, place the new student in an appropriate class. Certain information is available to you: the age of the student and the last grade completed. The ability to speak, read, and write in English can easily be determined through an informal interview with the child and an informal reading assessment. Any graded series of selected reading passages can help in this reading assessment.

Next, the available placements in the school should be surveyed. Give consideration to the current number of students in various classes and the rationale used in the organization of those classes. The decision for placement of the new student will depend upon whether the classes are homogeneously or heterogeneously grouped, if there is a special grouping for the gifted or the learning disabled, and if there are special classes for students with limited English ability.

Identify Student Needs

At the same time that the new student is assigned to a particular class, the teacher is given an Analysis of Needs of New Admissions (Figure 2-11) with instructions that the form should be in your office within one week. During that initial week, the classroom teacher is expected to diagnose the student's needs in a range of areas, and indicate the results of that diagnosis on the form. The form is reviewed by you and then routed to the appropriate person who will formally evaluate the student in that particular area. When the evaluating special teacher returns the form to you with the results of the evaluation, you then determine if placement in a special program is desirable, and identify that program. The analysis form is then returned to the special teacher who indicates the student's program schedule. The special teacher gives the analysis form, now containing test results, program placement, and schedule, to the classroom teacher. The teacher records the information and returns the form to you indicating that the analysis process has been completed for the new student. These analysis forms should be retained by you in alphabetical order.

DEAL WITH STUDENT RETENTION

Decisions concerning student retention are always difficult and painful. No one really wants to have a student lose a year in the natural progression of his or her education, so the teacher, the parent and the child may become emotional over the prospect of retention. It is your role and obligation as principal to provide a clear rationale and explanation for the decision; retention and promotion should not be emotional issues.

In some districts and states, the decision is taken out of the hands of the principal because mandates set particular levels of achievement for promotion. In this case, your role is to communicate and explain those established mandates. When no such mandates exist, the decision should be made with the following criteria in mind:

ANALYSIS OF NEEDS OF NEW ADMISSIONS

(Return to the office within one week.)

Student's Name _____ Class _____ Date _____

Date of Birth _____

A.* Problem	Check	Initial
Non-English Language Spoken		
_____		
Reading		
Mathematics		
Learning Disability		
Behavior		
Speech		
Other		
_____		
None		

Comments:

B.* Action	Evaluate	Results
Language Level		
Reading		
Mathematics		
Learning Disability		
Speech		
Emotional Needs		
Other		

C. **Program Placement**

English Language	
Bilingual	
Remedial Reading	
Remedial Mathematics	
Learning Disability Resource Room	
Counseling	
Speech Improvement	
Other	

D.**Schedule

Day(s)	Time

Routing—Attention:	Date	Date
Bilingual Teacher		
Eng. 2nd Lang. Teacher		
Reading Teacher		
Remediation Teacher		
Disabilities Teacher		
Speech Teacher		
Guidance Counselor		
_____		

*Return to the Principal

**Return to the class teacher

Class teacher—record results and program schedule and return to the principal

Figure 2-11

- *The child's current level of achievement.* A student who is considerably behind (more than one year in reading and mathematics) will find the work increasingly more difficult in the succeeding grades. Such a student usually falls further and further behind, so retention in the early grades usually gives this child a greater chance of catching up to the grade norm.

- *The child's ability to deal effectively with the content of the next grade.* Consider the scope and sequence of the curriculum in the next grade. Evaluate the child's potential to deal with the concepts that will be presented in all the content areas.

- *The child's age.* Some children may have been retained in other schools before coming to the present school, so those records may not be available. Students who are speakers of foreign languages are sometimes placed a grade below their agemates when they enter an English-speaking school. On the other hand, the child may be young for the grade, having entered school in a state where admission was permitted at a younger age.

- *The child's social and emotional makeup.* A socially aggressive child may not function well with students who are younger, while socially immature children may perform better with younger students. Youngsters who are involved in family crises, such as divorce, are sometimes unable to give their full attention to their schoolwork, which will only add more pressure. Retention may cause tremendous emotional blows to the egos of some youngsters and cause them to feel inferior. Such children would suffer emotional damage greater than any academic gain.

- *The child's physical growth in comparison with others of his or her age.* Youngsters who are physically mature may be embarrassed by being placed with younger students.

- *The availability of supportive services for the child.* At times, the decision to promote a child may be linked to services that can assist the child. Sometimes, additional funds are provided for students who are retained, so, in this case, they would receive more services by not being promoted.

- *The parents' cooperation.* Some parents are sincere in their desire to assist the child by working with him or her at home. In such cases, the child may benefit by being promoted.

- *The student's incentive to make a personal commitment to try.* Youngsters who are serious in their desire to achieve come to school regularly, pay attention to lessons, and complete their homework. Those students, of course, have a greater chance of succeeding.

- *The student's attendance record.* Youngsters who are frequently absent will have a difficult time in reaching desired achievement levels.

- *The teacher's evaluation of the quality and quantity of the student's work throughout the year.* A student's score on an evaluation test is an indication of that child's ability on one particular day during a two-hour segment. The teacher who has worked all year with that student has a much better estimate of the student's functioning level.

The Three-Step Notification Process

Notifying parents of the child's retention should not be their June surprise. Parents must be notified throughout the school year so that they can help the child. The first notification of possible retention should accompany the first report to parents during the fall semester, and reflect the low achievement score that the child received during the spring evaluation process. The parent should be aware that the child has been promoted, but that his or her scores are below the level usually required for the current grade. Notification of possible retention may also be made by the teacher for students who are not performing well in class. Early notification may have wonderful results in motivating youngsters to take school seriously.

Figures 2-12, 2-13 and 2-14 will help you to notify parents of possible retention. Figure 2-12 is the first step, notifying the parents during the fall semester. Figure 2-13 is sent to the parents during the month of January, and Figure 2-14 is sent when the results of the spring evaluation program are received.

The Importance of Parent Notification

Frequent communications and conferences with the parents throughout the school year serve three purposes. First, they inform the parents about the work and progress of the youngster. The teacher should be specific concerning homework that has not been completed, classwork that is neglected, and test scores that are poor. The more information given to the parents, the better informed they become about the child's ongoing performance in the class.

Second, frequent communications help parents to understand the efforts that the teacher and the school are making toward helping the child to achieve. The parents should be informed of any special programs or support services that the student is receiving. Most parents are very grateful to learn about the interest of the teacher and the school in the advancement of their youngster.

Third, notifications are the teacher's opportunities for gaining the parents' cooperation and support. They should be asked to reinforce good school attitudes with the child at home, to talk with their children about school, and continuously encourage them.

Provide Alternatives to Retention

Here are four alternatives to retention.

• *Trial promotion.* When a clear decision about retention is not possible, you may elect to promote the student on trial. The teacher would then be made aware that the youngster's continued placement in the class is based on his or her work and achievement. Continuous communication with the parent of the child is vital. The parent must clearly understand that if the child does not make satisfactory progress, he or she may be placed in the grade below during the school year.

• *Trial retention.* You might test the student at future times to determine if promotion during the school year is possible. This plan may be effective if the parent intends to send the youngster to special tutoring during the summer. In that case, retesting in September may determine if the child will be promoted or retained. To allow for the student who may progress very quickly during the first half of the year of retention, you may decide to test the child in January and promote the student if his or her progress ensures that retention will not become a possibility again in June.

• *Acceleration following retention.* Some children progress in spurts. If this should happen to a student who has been retained, that child may be ready to be accelerated to his or her appropriate age/grade placement.

NOTIFICATION TO PARENTS I

Date _____

Re: _____ _____
Student's name   Class

_____
_____
_____

Dear _____,

Every effort is being made to prevent the possibility that your child may not be promoted in June. However, it is necessary for the school to alert you that at this time your child's achievement is not satisfactory.

Your cooperation as a part of a team whose aim is to give your child every opportunity to improve is essential. Let us work together for this common goal.

Sincerely,

_____
Principal

_____
Teacher

- -

(please return to the teacher)

_____
Date

I have read this letter and agree to offer my child and the school my complete cooperation.

_____
Signature of parent

_____ _____
Pupil's name   Class

Figure 2-12

NOTIFICATION TO PARENTS II

_____
Date

_____
_____
_____

Dear _____,

Kindly call to see me on _____, _____, at _____, to discuss the possibility that your child may not be promoted in June. If the date and/or the time are inconvenient, please notify me to that effect and another appointment will be arranged.

Sincerely,

_____
Principal

_____
Teacher

- -
(please return to the teacher)

_____
Date

Dear _____,

I have received your letter concerning the possibility that my child may not be promoted in June.

_____ I shall be present at the conference.
_____ Please change the date/time to _____.
_____ I cannot come for a conference but I am aware of the possibility of retention.

_____
Signature of parent

_____ _____
Pupil's name   Class

Figure 2-13

NOTIFICATION TO PARENTS III

_____
Date

_____
_____
_____

Dear _____,

    Kindly come to see me on _____, _____, at _____, to discuss the fact that your child will not be promoted in June. If the date and/or the time are inconvenient, please notify me to that effect and another appointment will be arranged.

                                Sincerely,

                             _____
                                        Principal

                             _____
                                        Teacher

                    (please return to the teacher)

                             _____
                                        Date

Dear _____,

    I have received your letter regarding the fact that my child will not be promoted in June.

_____ I shall be present at the conference.

_____ Please change the date/time to _____.

_____ I cannot come for the interview but I am aware that my child will not be promoted.

                             _____
                                  Signature of parent

_____   _____

Pupil's name   Class

Figure 2-14

• *Special class placement.* Students who require special education will not benefit from retention. The regular school usually cannot provide the services that a special education placement can give a youngster, so for students who are evaluated and found to need a special education setting, retention may be waived.

FORMULATE A JOINT PLAN OF ACTION

The school and the parent are partners in the youngster's future, and each has a specific role to play. Joint action plans are therefore logical ways to cooperatively assist the student. A home tutoring program is one example of such a cooperative plan, with the teacher supplying supplementary materials. The parent is asked to supervise this home tutoring program and consult with the teacher on a regular basis.

Some youngsters require more than can be given by the classroom teacher and the parent. Such a child may require professional services and should be evaluated for possible needs in the areas of learning disabilities or guidance. The parent's signature is usually required for this evaluation process to begin. Both the teacher and the parent then work together as each contributes information about the student.

3

HOW TO DESIGN A SUCCESSFUL ELEMENTARY CURRICULUM

Curriculum is the life's blood of the school. A discussion of curriculum begins with the question of what to learn, usually expressed as the scope and sequence of the state's or district's mandates. This definition of curriculum, however, lacks a comprehensive point of view.

BASIC SKILLS AND THE REGULAR CURRICULUM

Basic skills are the building blocks of the elementary school curriculum, forming the foundation upon which all future learning depends. As discussed in Chapter 2, basic skills should be approached through a diagnostic/prescriptive orientation.

Basic skills are best mastered when they are specifically taught in small segments, with each instructional sequence accompanied by a specific objective. The youngsters should be periodically evaluated before a new level of information is offered. In this way, the teacher is aware of which students need additional instruction before moving ahead, so that students are prevented from falling more and more behind in the sequence.

Gifted students usually absorb concepts quickly and easily, and do not require the same review and reinforcement as average or slow students. In fact, gifted students tend to become bored and uncooperative when they are forced to review work that is already understood, so these students should be permitted to move quickly through the sequence. The basic skills aspect of the curriculum should be mastered as quickly as possible so that students can become involved with advanced levels of content and thinking processes.

Extend the Curriculum

Gifted students and average students who have moved quickly through the basics require an extended curriculum, which can take two different forms. First, the skill level of the content can be expanded to the next grade level topics. No student is then held back from continuing to master content at his or her own pace and ability to absorb.

Second, the curriculum can be expanded by exposing average and gifted students to an in-depth study of topics on their grade level. In social studies, for example, these students may be permitted to explore a topic of their interest from within the unit under study. They should be encouraged to use a variety of sources and authors in research studies that take them beyond the basic concepts taught. Similarly, in mathematics these students can use their understanding of basic computation skills to explore problems or design their own problems to share with others.

Add Variety to the Curriculum

Beyond the scope and sequence of the regular curriculum lies a world of fascinating topics to explore. Every classroom should offer students the option of becoming involved in some of these topics at various times during the school year. These topics usually give the youngster an interdisciplinary approach to study and, therefore, provide a means of realistically demonstrating the relationship among various aspects of the curriculum. A list of such topics is truly endless and reflects the creativity of the teacher. Some examples are consumerism, futures, economics, careers, family life, recreational time, and a study of oneself.

Give Students a Choice in the Curriculum

The key to learning is motivation. Since students learn best when they are interested, they should be permitted some choices in the curriculum depending upon their interests, talents, and curiosity. Permitting these choices does not detract from the basic curriculum, but rather, enhances it. Reading, of course, is important, but reading a science content or a history content is no less effective in reading instruction than reading a basal reader. Similarly, writing is an essential basic skill, but allowing the student to write about what he or she wants to communicate is more effective writing practice than writing about the topic that the teacher has selected. The involved, stimulated, and challenged student is the better learner.

A RANGE OF LEVELS IN LEARNING

Content cannot be taught in isolation; it must be presented at a particular level of learning. Usually, the teacher is so concerned with knowledge and understanding that students are not asked to *use* that knowledge and understanding to expand their thinking skills.

Bloom's Taxonomy

Benjamin Bloom provides a succinct hierarchy of thinking skills that can easily be used by teachers to broaden the range of their students' thinking levels. The taxonomy is composed of six levels:

Classification	*Objective*
Knowledge	Information Gathering
Understanding	Confirming
Application	Implementing
Analysis	Segmenting
Synthesis	Creating
Evaluation	Predicting

Recognize the Content of Each Level

The lowest point of the taxonomy is the *knowledge* level. Information at this level is concerned solely with the facts and the gathering of information. "Across what ocean did Columbus sail?" "How long was the journey to the new world?"

The next level of the taxonomy is *understanding*. At this level, the student confirms an understanding of the facts. "Why did Columbus, an Italian, seek money from the King and Queen of Spain?" "Why did Columbus have difficulty in finding a crew for his ships?"

The taxonomy now moves to the *application* level. The student is expected to demonstrate an understanding by using the information. "Write a diary of the voyage of Columbus as if you were a sailor on the command ship. Include in this diary a sequence of events as well as the thoughts and feelings of the crew." (Teachers usually stop at the application level, losing valuable opportunities to expose the youngsters to a higher range of thinking.)

The next level of the taxonomy is *analysis*. At this level, students are asked to analyze the information. "Prepare a list of reasons Columbus probably had for requesting money from Spain. Prepare a second list of reasons Queen Isabella probably had for giving Columbus the money."

At the *synthesis* level of the taxonomy, students are asked to rearrange the information to create something new. "What other sources of funds might Columbus have found?" "What suggestions could you have given Columbus to help him find a crew?"

The highest level of the taxonomy is *evaluation*. Students working at this level are expected to use their knowledge and understanding to predict. "What new areas of exploration are opened to a modern-day Columbus?" "Why would people be interested in funding such a voyage?" "What fears or doubts might some people have?"

Match Levels of Learning to Students' Needs

All students should be exposed to the full range of thinking skills, beginning with knowledge and moving through the levels of evaluation. The degree and intensity of using the higher-order thinking skills will depend upon the youngsters' needs and abilities. Slower students usually need more time to learn and understand basic skills, requiring review and reinforcement to retain this knowledge. Although these students should experience higher levels of thinking skills, the emphasis of instruction is at the lower end of the taxonomy. Average to gifted students who learn and understand basic skills quickly and easily and who, therefore, do not require multiple exposures to review and reinforcement, should spend large amounts of time working with higher-level thinking skills. The emphasis of instruction for these students should be on using knowledge and understanding in activities that require higher-order thinking levels.

The following categorized list of verbs can help teachers prepare activities and questions that address each of the levels of the taxonomy.

Lower-Order Thinking Skills

Knowledge		*Understanding*	*Application*
collect	name	conclude	construct
complete	note	estimate	demonstrate
copy	omit	explain	draw
count	order	fill in	illustrate
define	place	justify	indicate
duplicate	point	rephrase	isolate
find	recall	represent	make
identify	repeat	restate	record
imitate	select	support	
list	state	transform	
label	tally	translate	
mark	tell		
match	underline		

Higher-Order Thinking Skills

Analysis	*Synthesis*	*Evaluation*
analyze	alter	argue
categorize	change	assess
classify	design	judge
compare	develop	predict
conclude	discover	validate
criticize	expand	
defend	extend	
differentiate	formulate	
discriminate	generate	
organize	modify	
present	propose	
summarize	rearrange	
support	recombine	
question	reconstruct	
	regroup	
	reorder	
	simplify	

Higher-Order Learning Levels in the Curriculum

Many opportunities exist for including higher-order levels of learning in the curriculum. Students should be given opportunities to work with higher-order thinking objectives related to all aspects of the regular curriculum. These experiences can be provided in every content area, as seen in the following breakdown. The objectives have been differentiated for the slow to average student and the average to gifted student.

Subject	Slow/Average Student	Average/Gifted Student	Taxonomy	Objectives
Consumer Education	Compare two different brands of the same item and determine which is the better buy.	Analyze an advertisement for a product and identify the persuasion aspects from the factual aspects.	Analysis	compare abstract
Health Education	Identify the systems of the human body and name the parts of each one.	Explain and justify the necessity for the interrelated nature of the systems of the human body.	Analysis	detail dissect
Art	Explain the particular style of painting of a famous artist.	Select a particular style of painting and be able to justify why you consider it superior.	Evaluation	judge dispute
Math	Classify a group of shapes into sets, each having one common element.	Organize a group of shapes into sets each having some objects that can also be found in at least two other sets.	Analysis Synthesis	detail relate
Language Arts	Explain the possible thoughts and/or feelings of each character in the fairy tale.	Add one or two characters to the fairy tale whose actions will change the outcome of the story.	Synthesis	create abstract
Social Studies	Explain the point of view of both a Tory and a Colonist during the Revolutionary War.	Relate the point of view of a Tory during the Revolutionary War to the point of view of a Northern citizen during the Civil War.	Synthesis	compare contrast

DIRECT THE INSTRUCTIONAL EFFORT

The use of higher-order levels of learning rarely comes naturally to students. The school curriculum usually focuses on the knowledge, understanding, and application levels, so when students are faced with objectives that address the analysis, synthesis, and evaluation levels, they often do not know how to approach them. Since being able to think at higher levels is a learned skill, students should be led to realize that there must be a body of knowledge to use in analysis, synthesis, and evaluation. Students can be helped to use higher-order levels of learning through a planned series of experiences. A sample plan for instruction is shown on the following page.

ENLARGE TEACHING POSSIBILITIES

None of us would willingly limit our educational possibilities by narrowing our instruction from just one person. Rather, we learn from a wide variety of people with whom we have contact. Students should also experience this variety of instructional sources.

TOPIC: Energy Sources

TEACHER OBJECTIVES:	STUDENT OBJECTIVES:
1. *Knowledge* Nature has provided sources of energy that man needs.	*Information Gathering* To identify sources of energy provided by nature.
2. *Understanding* Energy in nature is potential energy that must be converted.	*Confirming* To learn how natural resources are turned into energy.
3. *Application* Energy is a basic need of modern man.	*Implementing* To identify your need for and use of energy in your everyday life.
4. *Analysis* Natural resources are limited while energy needs grow.	*Segmenting* To learn about supply and demand.
5. *Synthesis* Solutions created by man to solve his energy problems sometimes create new problems.	*Creating* To create new but realistic and factually based solutions to the energy problem.
6. *Evaluation* Man must search for new sources of energy to fulfill his ever-growing needs.	*Predicting* To predict energy sources as a solution to the problem of lost natural sources.

STRATEGIES FOR IMPLEMENTATION:

Materials Needed for Each Step	*Instructional Methods Proposed for Each Step*
1. various texts, films, etc.	1. creation of an outline
2. multi sources, including magazines, graph paper, etc.	2. preparation of a graph
3. observation, interviews, visits	3. illustration or dramatization
4. various economic texts, prepared situations to clarify	4. small group analysis
5. resource people to present, interviews, science fiction	5. individual solutions reported for group reactions
6. source materials from major energy companies concerning future research	6. brainstorming techniques

The Teacher

All aspects of the classroom are, of course, the responsibility of the teacher. But all aspects of instruction cannot be limited to just one person. The teacher is the main instructor, spreading his or her influence by performing many different functions. Two major roles of the professional teacher are diagnostician and prescriber. As previously discussed, instruction based upon students' needs and delivered according to those needs is the most effective instruction.

Students have a responsibility in the learning process. They are not passive recipients of instruction, but rather, active participants. At times, therefore, their self-directed activities require assistance, so the teacher then becomes guide and facilitator. When the learning process becomes difficult, students need reassurance and encouragement. The teacher then becomes the motivator, counselor, and comforter. Since the total responsibility for the instructional program is the teacher's, he or she is also the evaluator.

Other Adults

There are various ways for other adults to also contribute to the instruction of students. Teacher aides can be valuable to the instructional needs of students. Although the paid teacher aides are the most dependable of all adult assistance in the classroom, they are expensive. Student or associate teachers completing requirements of a university program offer another type of dependable adult assistance. These student teachers do not create a financial burden on the school district, but their services are usually available for only short periods of time before reassignment or completion. Volunteers offer the third type of available adult assistance. Volunteers are not paid and do not have the limited calendar of university students, but since there is no commitment on their part other than the desire to serve, they may not be dependable at times.

Regardless of the type of adult assistance that is available, the teacher must be responsible for them. It is the teacher who plans the role and contribution of the adult assistant, provides the guidelines for participation, and establishes the limits of responsibility. In all instances, the teacher evaluates both the performance of the adult assistants and the students entrusted to their care.

Student Buddies

Students acting as peer helpers provide still another alternative to assisting the teacher. Teachers can use this idea in several ways. Students who perform well in particular content areas or in specific topics within content areas can assist other students. For example, if the teacher taught a class lesson on subtraction with exchange during a particular week, those students who mastered the topic could be enlisted as peer helpers for others who still require additional help.

The concept of peer assistance can also help give confidence even to the slowest student, if he or she is designated as a peer assistant for some class chore or subject that is an area of strength. Peer assistants can be of help to other classes of younger students, too. Many kindergarten and first grade teachers would gladly welcome such help. Older students should be given these opportunities to gain confidence in themselves and to understand the need to offer service to others.

In all of these instances, the teacher is in charge and has the overall responsibility to designate the nature of the assistance, the time frame for this help, and the limitations. The teacher is the evaluator of the performance of the peer assistant and the student with whom he or she works.

The Group

The group process itself can make a valuable contribution to instruction. Several specific structured group designs can offer alternatives to students in the instructional process (Rita Dunn and Kenneth Dunn, *Practical Approaches to Individualized Instruction,* West Nyack, New York: Parker Publishing Company, Inc., 1972). One such structured group instructional design is the "Knowledge Go Round." It is intended as a review or reinforcement device and provides an exciting way for students to interact with important material. For example, a Knowledge Go Round may be established to identify number sentences for ten, list new words to replace the word *good* in a story, or state ways to earn a living in the northeastern part of the country.

Another group instructional design is "Team Learning," used to introduce new material. The students in the group are provided with a written or taped presentation of new material. The material is followed by a set of questions that represent literal, inferential, and critical analysis of the information. The group works together to respond to these questions. Poetry, biographical data about a famous individual, and a passage from a text all provide good material for Team Learning.

A third type of group instructional design is "Group Analysis." In this activity, the group is presented with a situation and a problem. The group must examine the problem and determine its solution. Situations related to morality, honesty, and the benefit of humanity are good topics for Group Analysis.

The beneficial aspects of group instruction are:

- encourages students to work together and help each other
- makes students modify their positions to reach consensus
- allows students to learn to respect the ideas of others
- provides students with the opportunity to learn from and with each other

As with all alternative instructional designs, the teacher decides what and who is included in the instructional group, controls the instructional situation, and evaluates the performance of the group and the individuals.

It is helpful to create a form (see Figure 3-1) for the students to use in the group instructional process. This form states the type of group activity, the names of the students in the group, and the name of the recorder who will write the answers that the group has reached. Space is also provided for the answers to be recorded. The teacher is then given these answers with the names of the involved students for future evaluation.

The Individual Student

There are times when the student learns best by him- or herself. This decision may be made by the student or the teacher, but the opportunity should be available.

INSTRUCTIONAL DESIGNS

Date _____

1. Check activity: ☐ Knowledge Go Round
                          ☐ Team Learning
                          ☐ Group Analysis

2. Students in group: _____

_____

_____

_____

_____

Recorder: _____

3. Answers:

Figure 3-1

PROVIDE FOR VARIETY IN INSTRUCTION

With an ever-expanding curriculum content to be covered in each grade and a refined means of identifying individual student needs, the instructional responsibilities of the teacher are overwhelming. Thus, self-directed materials and instruction have become effective ways of teaching.

Use Teacher-Directed Lessons

A carefully planned and well conducted teacher-directed lesson is an effective way to instruct. The first step is to plan for that lesson.

1. Identify an instructional need of a group or the class.
2. Specify the specific aims of the lesson.
3. Select the instructional materials best suited to the aims.

4. Plan the delivery:
   a. how to motivate the lesson
   b. how to proceed with the lesson
   c. how and when the selected materials will be used
   d. how to provide for a medial summary
   e. how to provide for a terminal summary
   f. how to plan for a review and reinforcement activity
5. Use good teaching techniques:
   a. plan questions that are literal, inferential, and critical
   b. prepare instructional aids in advance
   c. encourage students to speak to the group or class
   d. actively involve the students in the learning process
   e. plan a logical sequence for presentation of the aims, moving from known material to more difficult material
   f. be sensitive to maintaining a good pace

Use Programmed Learning

Programmed materials provide a sequential, developmental presentation of material with provision for review, reinforcement, and, usually, evaluation. Some of the advantages of this type of instruction are:

- material is presented in small units
- review is continuously provided
- information is provided in sequential steps
- students can pace themselves in the learning process
- self correction provides immediate feedback
- students can work independently

Some disadvantages of programmed instruction are:

- students are isolated from other students
- the materials may become boring
- students must be motivated to use the material correctly

As with all types of instructional materials, the decision to use them should be based upon:

- the type of instruction for which it is best suited—developmental, sequential, non-critical, or evaluative information
- the type of student for whom it is best suited—self directed and motivated learners, and those who have a unique learning pace that is faster or slower than most of the others in the class
- the individual needs of the students—those whose learning needs are dissimilar from most of the other students in the class
- the use of a variety of instructional strategies instead of the use of just one all of the time or most of the time

Use Task and Activity Cards

Task and activity cards provide a different form of self-directed instruction for individuals or small groups. Some of the advantages of this type of instruction are:

- they can be tailored to suit the specific learning needs of individuals or groups of students
- they can be prepared at specific learning levels that are within the reading and understanding of the students
- they can be prepared to consider student interests, such as a reading skills card using sports as the topic
- they are motivational
- they can be used by individuals or small groups
- they require active student involvement
- they can be self-correcting

At this point, let's define task cards and activity cards. With *task cards,* the student is asked to perform a *particular task* that reviews, reinforces, extends learning, or develops thinking skills. Sample task card topics might be:

- Rewrite these sentences placing punctuation marks correctly.
- Match the name of each inventor listed on the right with the name of the invention from the list on the left for which he or she is known.
- Complete the outline map by selecting the names of the states and placing on the map the products for which they are known.

With *activity cards,* the student is asked to use the designated materials to *create something of his or her own* that is designed to teach, review, reinforce, extend learning, or develop thinking skills. Sample activity card topics might be:

- Select a picture from the box and write a story that you think may have happened or will happen.
- Use the materials in this box to create a complete circuit. Tell how or where that circuit might be used.

The following suggestions will help make task and activity cards more effective:

- Clearly state the objective on the card itself.
- Use language that is clearly understood by students and well within their reading level.
- Be sure the activity reviews, reinforces, and drills only one specific skill. A series of cards can address a topic.
- Write directions in sequential order to avoid confusion.
- If possible, keep the activity open ended to provide for student exploration.
- Whenever possible, provide for self-correction to permit immediate feedback.
- Illustrate the cards and make them attractive.

- Prepare the cards neatly by either printing or typing.
- Extend the life of the cards by mounting them on sturdy cardboard and covering them with clear plastic.
- Prepare cards on different levels to suit the learning needs of most of the students.
- Place all related materials necessary for the task or activity in a box with the card.
- When preparing the cards, label the card by content area (math, science, etc.) and topic (time, addition, etc.); number the cards in a series on the same topic in order of difficulty; provide self correction with an answer key, color or picture or shape code, overlay, tape recording, etc.; and plan for a storage container and site to locate the cards.

Use Contracts

A contract is a self-contained outline of study that clearly states what is to be learned by the student. This learning technique can be used by the individual student or small groups, and is composed of:

1. *objectives* that state in the student's language what to learn, the intensity of the learning, and how to prove that learning has taken place. For example: You will be able to list at least three inventions that have helped modern man to grow more food.
2. *resources* that give the student alternate ways of researching the information needed. For example: texts, films, tapes, records, books, and transparencies.
3. *activities* that give the student creative alternatives to demonstrate that learning has taken place. For example: write a play... construct a model of... make puppets of the characters.
4. *reporting alternatives* that extend the individual student's learning to others by sharing the information. For example: present your play about... explain your model of... make your puppets talk and explain.
5. *study plan* that guides the student through the contract. This is shown in Figure 3-2.

CONTRACT STUDY PLAN

Student _____   Date _____

Objective selected:

Information needed:

Resources selected:

Activity selected:

Approved _____
                    Teacher's signature

Figure 3-2

6. *evaluations*
   a. teacher conferences that guide the learning, direct the activity, and check the work
   b. pretest to determine if some objectives have previously been mastered
   c. medial test to determine student progress through the contract
   d. terminal test to evaluate mastery of the contract

7. *recordkeeping* for recording student's progress. Place the students' names in a list on the left side of the paper. Number the columns across the top of the page to match the number of objectives included in the contract. A check is placed under the number of the objective that the student has successfully completed and shared. An "L" is placed under the number of the objective to which a student listened. This chart, as shown in Figure 3-3, may be posted on a bulletin board or kept in the teacher's record book.

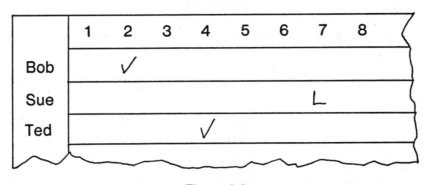

Figure 3-3

The teacher and the student cooperatively decide how many objectives must be completed for a particular contract. The contract can become an individualized tool if this decision is based upon capabilities of the student. For example:

1. Advanced students performing above grade level norms are asked to select and complete ten objectives.
2. Average students performing on grade level are asked to select and complete five objectives.
3. Slow learners or learning disabled students are asked to select and complete two or three objectives.

Another alternative is to ask all the students to select and complete any five of the objectives, with extra credit given for additional objectives completed. If the teacher believes that particular objectives are more important to the basic concept of the contract, those objectives can be assigned to all the children. The teacher decides the number of objectives to be completed and shared and the number of listening activities that each student must participate in to successfully complete the contract.

The student is usually permitted to select both the objectives and the activities which he or she wants to complete. Some students require guiding and directing to make this decision. In addition, some students require assistance in selecting appropriate resources from which to gather information.

The flow chart in Figure 3-4 will help students understand how to work through a contract.

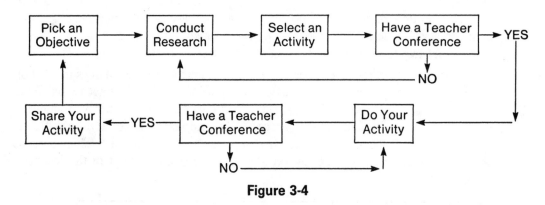

Figure 3-4

The following steps will assist the teacher in writing a contract. Each step has been previously explained.

1. Identify a global topic. "To learn about the grasslands regions." "To learn about electricity."
2. List the pre-study skills necessary for the topic. "Map skills." "Using an index."
3. List the major concepts to be learned.
4. Write the major concepts as objectives.
5. Match the objectives to activities or write activities that will suit any objectives.
6. Match the activities to reporting alternatives.
7. Locate and place related print and nonprint resources in the classroom.
8. Write the study plan. Discuss the plan and the contract process with the students.
9. Prepare the recordkeeping system.
10. Rewrite the objectives to be used as pre, medial, and terminal assessment questions.

Student-Created Instructional Materials

Students are capable of creating interesting instructional materials, whether they be task cards, activity cards, or contracts, and other students may very well profit from using these instructional activities. Students might also create instructional materials as the product of a task, activity, or contract. Give the student guidelines for constructing his or her own contract:

- Select the topic to study.
- Narrow the topic.
- List what you think would be most valuable to learn.
- Write the objectives that should be accomplished.
- Select the resources to be used.

- Select the activities to be used.
- Do the activities.
- Check your work with the teacher.

Use Assembly Programs

Assembly programs can instruct as well as entertain. There is a variety of ideas for assembly programs, including:

- culmination of class units
- original dramatizations
- panel or forum discussions
- pageants
- holiday celebrations
- quiz programs
- puppet shows
- operettas
- choral speaking
- school campaigns

Student Creativity

Student creativity and imagination can be encouraged through open-ended activities and involvements. Rather than stress the fact or the cognitive development all of the time, students should be asked to use the information in original ways to reach their own conclusions. Questioning techniques related to the higher-order levels of learning can help students learn how to analyze, synthesize, and evaluate what they have learned. Student-created activities and contracts assist students in developing new and creative topics and means of studying those topics.

Research Skills

Research skills are probably the most important learning tool. Facts are developed and infused into the curriculum at such a rapid rate today that it is difficult for any one computer, let alone individual, to store all of this information. Thus, it is important for the students to develop research skills so that they know how to search for the facts. Today's student must be able to discriminate between information sources that are authentic and those that are not verified. Learning where to retrieve the required information and from what source will develop a student with a large information potential.

DEVELOP INDEPENDENT SELF-DIRECTED LEARNERS

The self-directed learning system becomes efficient and effective when students know and use a management system. This system gives them the guidelines that will help them plan their time. The management system is designed by the teacher who then communicates to the students the following items:

1. What to learn—This is dominated by diagnosis and prescription. Within these guides, the student has alternatives related to tasks/activities and contracts.

2. When to learn—The time factor is determined by the teacher or left to the student either partially or entirely. The student may be asked to work on prescribed activities or contracts whenever he or she is not involved in a teacher-instructional group or class lesson. Requirements will help the student understand that subjects such as reading and mathematics should be worked on every day.

3. Where to learn—The classroom should be arranged to facilitate self-directed learners. Areas or centers of the room can each be equipped with materials from one content area. Students may work directly in that area of the classroom or they may bring the materials to an assigned work area or their own desks.

4. How to keep records—Students should be instructed about where to record their answers as well as the assignments, tasks, activities, or contracts worked on independently. Records may be kept in a notebook, a looseleaf, on specially designed teacher forms, or on separate sheets of paper that are placed in a folder. A set procedure will ensure that students' work is not lost.

5. Who checks students' work—An effective checking system will help students grow and master skills while allowing the teacher greater time to devote to those students who require more direction and instruction. Checking can take various forms:

   a. The student may check his or her own work with an answer key. In these cases, students must understand that the only way they have of learning if they have mastered a concept is to honestly evaluate their own answers. Most students will honestly correct their own work if they are not afraid of grades on everything they do. Student progress on independent work can be checked weekly by the teacher during a conference to determine how the student is performing.

   b. Peer checkers can be assigned to particular skill work. The student checker uses the answer key to check the work of others. Answers that are not correct are indicated by the checker. The student then goes over those answers and finds the correct response.

   c. The teacher can check some of the student's work. It is not productive for the teacher to spend time correcting answers that can be checked by the student or a peer. The teacher should check work for which there is no answer key, such as the writing efforts of the students.

6. How to get help—Students who need help during independent work may write their name on the chalkboard for the teacher, ask another student assigned as a topic helper, or ask any other adult in the classroom.

EVALUATE STUDENT PROGRESS

Application is the true evaluation of learning, the means by which the student applies what has been learned into a self-developed creation. These products assist the teacher in a true evaluation of student mastery and are more valuable than any paper-and-pencil test of facts. The fact learned in isolation is easily forgotten; but the product created as a result of learning the fact endures.

Variety of Style in Student Products

The entire process by which students learn is controlled in large measure by their cognitive and learning styles. This variation in style includes both the way in which information is processed as well as the ways in which products are produced. An understanding of student individuality in style helps teachers to allow greater options to students in the learning process and, therefore, enhance learning conditions.

Cognitive styles control the internal or processing factors of learning. The following graph lists the extremes of possible cognitive styles we all have. Most students fall between the two extremes or may vary between them in different areas. Few people are pure examples of one style.

LOCUS OF CONTROL	MATERIAL	PROCEDURE	OBJECTIVE
INTERNAL self can control self-determination	*ANALYTIC* examines topic specifics details only relevant data	*INCREMENTAL* approach chronologically sequential	*FIELD DEPENDENT* research evidence and convergent thinking looks for answers
EXTERNAL outside forces control luck, fate control	*GLOBAL* examines topic overview generalizes; looks at all data	*INTUITIVE* approach diffusive unsystematic	*FIELD INDEPENDENT* creative; intuitive divergent thinking; looks for questions

Learning styles control the external or environmental factors of learning. (Rita Dunn and Kenneth Dunn, 1972). The following graph lists a variety of external factors for which each of us has a preference. As with the internal factors, most people are not pure examples of a single style.

THE HUMAN BODY	INTERACTION PATTERNS	ENVIRONMENT	PSYCHOLOGICAL

How We Learn
  visual
  auditory
  tactile
  kinesthetic
 	
Oral Needs
 	
The Time to Learn
  A.M.
  P.M.
 	
Need for Movement
	Alone
	With a Peer
	In a Team
	With an Adult
	All of These
		Sound need/tolerance
		Illumination need/tolerance
		Heat need/tolerance
			Inclination to begin
			Perserverance to complete
			Obligation to task
			Confidence within oneself; needed from others

Visual and Artistic Products

Illustrations, graphs, drawings, murals, and timelines, are among the many visual and artistic products that students can produce.

Oral Products

The student who prefers an oral presentation might select debates, discussions, puppet shows, lectures, and songs.

Written Products

Those students who are more comfortable with written presentations might select narratives, letters, poems, articles, and scripts.

Tactile and Kinesthetic Products

Students with preferences for tactile and kinesthetic products might select presentations in the form of games, puzzles, dance, pantomime, and modeling.

A Final Word

By allowing students the greatest possible options in using and processing information, we take advantage of their particular cognitive and learning styles. Using students' style preferences can help them learn more quickly and effectively. **Remember:** The form that the product takes should be the one selected by the student. What is important when evaluating any product is the *quality* of the information that it contains.

4

HOW TO MEET
THE NEEDS OF STUDENTS

The printed scope and sequence of curriculum and the state- and district-level curriculum bulletins and teacher's guides to textbook series do not and, in many cases, cannot meet the needs of all students. Beyond what is usually required of students on a particular grade are the important considerations of the needs of the *individual* student.

HOW THE TEACHER IDENTIFIES STUDENT NEEDS

The teacher is in a perfect position to identify particular student needs, which often have a wide range. Obviously, the academic needs are the first to be considered. Teachers are usually quite accurate about identifying students who need additional help with academic needs below and above grade-level norms.

Physical needs rarely go undetected by the professional teacher. Daily evidence leads teachers to conclusions that prove correct more often than not. A child who is excessively absent may have physical problems that are greater than just the average childhood illnesses. Students who hold books too close or too far from their eyes may have visual needs that do not show up in yearly eye checks. Students who consistently reverse letters in reading and writing, confuse words with similar letters, or have difficulty in retaining certain concepts may have undiagnosed perceptual needs. Students who turn heads to listen, respond only when they are facing the speaker, or have difficulty with letter sounds may have hearing needs that have not been picked up in the audiometer tests conducted as part of the school program.

Emotional needs are also demonstrated by youngsters through their behavior. The student who is unable to deal with criticism no matter how constructive, relates poorly to peers, approaches situations with unusual patterns of actions, or is excessively aggressive or passive may have emotional or social needs.

The following checklist (Figure 4-1) may be helpful in identifying individual student needs. Although the teacher is a prime *identifier* of needs, he or she may not be able to *meet* all varying needs.

TEACHER SCREENING CHECKLIST

_____ dental checkups completed

_____ student health card review completed

_____ height and weight recorded on student health card

_____ vision screening test completed

_____ audiometer testing completed

_____ cause of absence(s) recorded on student health card

_____ referral of student(s) who indicate needs in:

       _____ vision

       _____ dental care

       _____ hearing

       _____ excessive absence

_____ anecdotal records of student(s) with atypical behavior patterns

_____ referral of student(s) who exhibit atypical behavior

Figure 4-1

HOW THE PARENT IDENTIFIES STUDENT NEEDS

The parent views the child from a different perspective and, therefore, becomes another valuable source for the identification of needs. Parents often look to the school for assistance with problems their children have that they cannot deal with or do not know how to handle. All too often, parents who have separated or divorced find that their children become problems at school. They find it difficult to fill their own as well as their children's emotional needs. At times, a family history of problems becomes the means by which a student's individual school problem can be identified. Sometimes a student's aggressive school behavior is also demonstrated at home and is unsuccessfully handled by the parent. Occasionally, the parent will come to school to discuss what appears to be a personality problem between the teacher and the student. Some of these problems can be alleviated through individual provisions for the students; others require schoolwide programs.

HOW THE PARENTS ASSOCIATION IDENTIFIES STUDENT NEEDS

The Parents Association sees the school in a global light. The Association is a valuable source of identification of needs that may involve large numbers of students. These needs may be a part of large programs, such as lunch, the yard facilities, or even the bus schedule.

The identification may involve the curriculum of the school, class trips, or the reading scores of students. At times, the needs may involve certain segments of the student body, such as the graduating class or the kindergarten program. The Parents Association is also concerned with community needs and will identify school needs that can be sympathetic to community wants, such as a site for the baseball league or a summer recreational program.

HOW THE CENTRAL OFFICE IDENTIFIES DISTRICT NEEDS

The central office views the district as a whole and will identify needs that are common to all or most of the schools. These may involve a segment of the school population, such as the gifted or the remedial reader. The needs may also be involved with such financial constraints as the closing of schools or a cutback of teaching staff. District needs that affect all schools may result in the development of solution strategies that must be implemented in all schools.

HOW THE ADMINISTRATOR IDENTIFIES SCHOOL NEEDS

The school administrator is in a position to view the school as a whole to identify needs that affect the student body. Some of these needs may be concerned with programming or administrative procedures. Other needs relate to the constraints of the school plant. Still others may be concerned with the development of the professional staff or new curriculum.

HOW TO MEET ALL THESE NEEDS

Despite who identifies the needs of the school, solutions must be developed. Some of the problems require small modifications or arrangements within the organizational structure of the school. Other problems require the development of new programs that will better meet the needs of the students. When the development of a new program is required, particular steps should be initiated to ensure the program will be successful.

Step 1: Awareness

Develop a Rationale to Support the Need for a Program. New programs are popular only among those who will be served by the program. That is why a sound rationale for the program's need should be well developed. The rationale should be concerned with meeting the particular needs of a growing population. These populations may be as diverse as students who are speakers of foreign languages, have learning disabilities, have below-level competence in reading or mathematics, or have tremendous learning potential.

All populations, including the professional staff, parents, community leaders, and student body, need to be exposed to the rationale that has been developed. The clearer the understanding for the need of a new program, the more universally it will be accepted. It is also wise to include the ways in which the new program will give the classroom teacher more time to spend with other students.

Establish Lines of Communication. The next step in selling a new program is communication and public relations. Information is a powerful tool, since a lack of it can cause misunderstandings and misconceptions. Public meetings should be held and literature distributed as widely as possible to enable the community to understand what is truly intended and why. Possible dissenters can then be directed to state their objections in relation to the needs of others.

Identify an Advocacy Group. These efforts at communications and public relations will also heighten the community's awareness to the need for such a program. An advocacy group will usually develop that can be very effective in responding to those who do not believe that funds and effort should be directed to the proposed program. This advocacy group will not only become invaluable in providing advice and support for the program, it will also be an essential power base from which to direct the program.

Incorporate the Advocacy Group into the Plan. Since the advocacy group will become a power base, it is wise to include its participation in the plan. Many different ways are possible, including being part of an advisory council or a steering committee, or actively participating in the program as assistants or office helpers. No matter how the group serves the program, its active participation will ensure success.

Step 2: Planning

Identify Who to Include in the Planning Stage. The planning stage includes a wide range of individuals. The professional staff must, of course, be involved. The most successful new programs are those in which the staff who will conduct the program believe that they have had a part in its development. Likewise, parents and interested community members need to believe they have influenced the program with their ideas. The students who will be involved with the program should also be represented in the planning stages, so that they will develop an interest in and commitment to the program.

Give Status and Ownership to Each Group. Equal status must be given to each population involved in program planning. All of the groups should believe that their contributions, thoughts, and concerns are given respect and consideration. In this way, a commitment to the program is developed among the professional staff, the parents, the community members, and the students who are involved. The more the populations believe they have had input into the development of the program, the more they each will feel they own the program and that its success is directly related to them. Nothing can offer greater insurance for program success.

Plan for All Aspects. All aspects of the program should be considered during the planning stage. If potential trouble spots can be anticipated, chances are better for a smooth operation of the new program. Aspects of the program to be considered include curriculum, programming, staffing, evaluation, articulation, and communication.

Step 3: Guidelines

Establish Criteria for Student Involvement. The program must, of course, fit the population selected, and the criteria used for identification must fit the goals and objectives of the program. Set realistic criteria for identification, and communicate that criteria throughout the school or district. Take care to search for a possible population among those who are usually overlooked, such as the handicapped and the disadvantaged. Be sure to use flexible criteria that have more than one means of identification. For example, in identifying students for a program for the gifted and talented, a measure of intelligence is only one among many other types of identifiers. In all cases, it is advantageous to use many criteria and establish a matrix. Those who are selected, then, will come from a larger pool of possible candidates. Some populations that may require special programs include students:

- with below-level reading scores
- with below-level mathematics scores
- with unacceptable writing skills
- with creative potential
- with advanced academic potential
- with ability in the performing arts
- with speech problems
- with emotional problems
- with health problems
- who are disadvantaged
- who exhibit superior ability in a particular subject

Establish Criteria for Staff Involvement. Selecting staff for the program is not usually without outside constraints. Union regulations and seniority may severely limit the administrator's office. (It is often possible to avoid union constraints when a new program is advertised as "experimental.") It is important to list the specific skills necessary for the teacher to have for successful implementation of the program. If possible, require prior university or in-service course work in the program's area. It is also possible to require training prior to and during the course of the program. If a particular teacher is desired, try to set the criteria to match the qualifications of that particular teacher. In all cases, it is important to determine the necessary teacher characteristics for program success, and then list the specific skills you believe are vital. Some general skills usually related to program success include:

- knowledge and understanding of diagnoses and prescriptions
- knowledge and understanding of various materials
- proven ability in creating teacher-made materials
- strong management skills
- ability to maintain good discipline
- ability to design a program that caters to students' interests
- ability to relate to students and parents in meaningful ways
- experience in writing questions that are inferential as well as literal
- desire to improve, including the ability to accept suggestions
- proven ability in planning skills

Identify Staff Development Needs. All successful programs have curriculum specifications and instructional strategies. To ensure appropriate implementation of both the designed curriculum and instruction, specific teacher skills should be identified. For example, a program designed to benefit students with advanced academic skills must focus on the development of critical thinking skills. Teachers, therefore, must understand what these skills are and how to incorporate them into all content areas. In addition, a program designed to improve reading ability using a holistic reading approach requires the teacher's understanding of this approach and knowledge of how to adopt available reading materials to fit this instructional strategy.

Another aspect of staff development needs relates to the emotional environment of the classroom. Good mental health conditions are always important, but favorable learning environments include another aspect—that of the teacher's expectation of student success. Several studies have proven that the single most important aspect of student success is the teacher's expectation that the student will succeed. This pre-set conclusion results in a teacher's approach of, "You can. You will. I will help you to do it." The teacher does not accept, "I can't. I will not. I do not know how. This is too hard for me."

Prepare a Staff Development Plan. Once staff development needs are identified, a plan to meet those needs should be developed. The training plan should be implemented before the program begins.

If money is available, staff development is best accomplished during regular teaching hours by hiring substitute teachers to release those teachers who will be involved. Summer training programs can also be effective in training plans, but money should be available to pay those teachers who will be attending. When no other plan is available, training sessions can be conducted after school. If teachers cannot be paid for these sessions, arrangements should be made to provide in-service credit. Lunch workshops can also be used for training sessions if no other time frame is available. The lunch session is, of course, difficult and short.

The success of the staff development plan is the responsibility of those who will actively work with the teachers. Great care and consideration should be given to the selection of the person(s), who should be motivational, realistic, and supportive. A consultant in the specific area usually will have the best developed staff development program; universities often have personnel with expertise in specific areas; and, at times, the district office has an in-house person with skill in the area. The best staff development plans actively involve teachers in doing and learning as quickly as possible the type of activities and tasks that they can easily implement.

Identify Materials Needed. Of prime consideration are the instructional materials needed for the program. It is not always necessary to purchase instructional materials because some programs rely heavily on teacher-made materials. At times, even existing available materials can be modified or redistributed to meet the needs of the new program.

It is rare to find a program that has its own materials. Usually, certain commercially available materials are recommended. It then becomes important to search for available materials that are suitable. It is advisable to inspect the materials, and ask some of the teachers to review them with you before purchasing, since advertisements do not always live up to their publicity. It is possible to be stuck with some beautiful materials that are too difficult for the student population for which they were intended.

In addition to instructional materials, the program may require other supplies. If recordkeeping is an important element in the program, be sure to order a supply of file folders and index cards. If the program requires teacher-made materials, oaktag, markers, laminating facilities, and duplicating paper may be essential. Think through what will be required of others who will be involved and who have had experience with such a program before the order has been completed.

Prepare the Budget. In addition to the materials and supplies that must be ordered, other budget considerations should be met. Be sure to include any related staff needs. School aides and paraprofessionals may be necessary to implement the program, whose salaries and related health and welfare benefits must be included in the budget.

The evaluation design is another important budget item. If formal tests are to be used, provide the funds to purchase and mark those tests. Some programs require secretarial services. If this is an important feature of the program, be sure to budget for secretarial hours or days.

Establish Communication Lines for Involved Program Staff. Throughout the life of the program, there will be a need to communicate information to the involved staff, so develop a line and form for the communication. It may be most practical for you, as principal, to communicate directly with the program staff through numbered memos. Or perhaps a program coordinator can be appointed to serve as communicator. In any case, the program staff should be aware of the person who will communicate with them and the form that the communication will take.

It is just as important for the program staff to know with whom they can communicate about any of a myriad of problems and ideas. Whether that communication link is you or the program coordinator, the means for communication and the time frame must be established. This is especially true if the program coordinator is not always available to the staff. Specific times when that person is available should be made known.

Communicate with Staff Outside the Program. The unknown is always suspect, so staff not involved in the program should receive full communication about the intent, design, and progress of the program. Program staff meetings may be opened to outside staff for information purposes; program workshops may help outside staff learn about and develop instructional techniques that they can also use within the classroom; or program fairs may help tell about the program with staff who are not involved. All of these ways are helpful in removing the mystery, developing an understanding of the program and, perhaps, building in-house staff support. It may also help arouse the interest of new teachers for future program involvement.

Define a Monitoring and Reporting System. Well-run programs can document their progress through systematic monitoring and reporting systems. Teacher plans should be collected and reviewed on a regular basis, a process that should be established at the start of the program. It is a matter of personal choice if those plans are collected weekly, twice a month, or monthly for the entire period. Just be sure to read and review those plans.

Formal and informal observations, concerned with the program specifics, should also be conducted periodically. Conferences with the teacher following the observations should focus on improvement of performance based upon the program's design.

The process must include reporting to parents about the progress of the individual students involved in the program. The reporting system can be arranged to coincide with the normal reporting periods. A separate report form can be developed that specifies the objectives of the program and the specific progress of the individual student, or it may be advisable to comment on the usual report form. In either case, the parent should be invited to a conference with the teacher to have that report discussed and explained.

Specified report periods on program progress should also be established, which can also coincide with the regular report intervals. At these report periods, the teacher should provide a program evaluation (see Figure 4-2) for each student, based on the objectives of the program. Students, too, should be required to self-evaluate their progress (see Figure 4-3) several times during the year. These evaluations can be about academic progress as well as feelings and attitudes about the program.

Create an Advisory Council. An advisory council can be of tremendous assistance throughout the life of the program. The council should be composed of parents whose children are in the program and members of the advocacy group. These people should be solicited through communications sent home either with the students in the program or by mail. Regularly scheduled monthly meetings will help the administrators of the program know how well the program is being received by the students and the parents.

Write Specific Program Objectives. Each specific objective of the program should be specified in writing. In addition, the objectives should be measurable. Objectives should include those related to academic improvement as well as those related to the affective domain and attitudes and feelings about school, learning, and oneself. The writing of specific objectives begins with a global goal to be accomplished, such as "To improve the reading ability of the students included in the program." This global goal is then supported by specified objectives:

1. to raise the level of reading at least one year
2. to improve and enlarge the reading vocabulary by at least 75 words
3. to expand the decoding skills by at least five new skills
4. to improve comprehension skills at the literal level to the degree that students can identify the main idea, sequence of events, and specified meaning of each story they can read
5. to improve comprehension skills at the inferential level to the degree that students can predict outcomes, select from among alternatives, and make assumptions
6. to improve comprehension skills at the critical level to the degree that students can discriminate between fact and fiction, sense and nonsense, detect the mood of a story, and recognize character traits

The specific objectives are supported by tasks and activities that are designed to help the student achieve the specified objectives.

REPORT TO PARENTS OF PROGRAM PROGRESS

Ratings:

0 = Outstanding (the student is trying hard and accomplishing tasks)

S = Satisfactory (the student is working and doing well)

I = Improvement (needed in both effort and results)

U = Unsatisfactory (the student is not trying or accomplishing tasks)

SPECIFIC PROGRAM OBJECTIVES

	Period	PARTICIPATION				RESULTS			
		I	II	III	IV	I	II	III	IV
1.									
2.									
3.									

Teacher Comment: Parent Comment:

Figure 4-2

STUDENT SELF-EVALUATION

Ratings:

A = Always (almost all the time)

S = Sometimes (most of the time)

N = Never (I do not)

HOW DID I DO? Period	I	II	III	IV
I follow directions.				
I keep records of my work.				
I can work by myself.				
I take good care of materials.				
I respect others in the class.				
I work well in a group.				
I plan carefully.				
I am on time.				
I listen.				

Figure 4-3

Task

1. a. to conduct a silent sustained reading period daily
   b. to focus on reading skill development in all content areas
   c. to develop an appreciation of reading as a needed skill through required reading in areas of interest

2. a. to require students to locate and learn at least one new vocabulary word each day
   b. to develop and build a class vocabulary book
   c. to review the words in the class vocabulary book at unused moments, i.e., as a means of getting clothing, getting a drink, etc.
   d. to give each student an opportunity to present to the class a new vocabulary word each week

3. a. to teach phonic sounds that are important in decoding
   b. to teach phonic blends that are important in decoding
   c. to apply the skills taught in practice and in practical situations
   d. to develop phonic games that can be used by individuals and small groups of students in review situations
   e. to play class phonic games in teams

4. a. to encourage students to write or tell their original stories after they have identified the main idea (students who listen are required to specify the main idea)
   b. to ask students to create a set of directions that others must follow to get to a prize or reward
   c. to ask groups of students to agree upon the message or meaning of a group of stories, fables, or tales they read

5. a. to present students with a series of events and ask them to predict the outcome of the story and justify their opinions
   b. to present students with a story situation and ask them to select an alternative sequence from among those presented (each alternative selected must be justified by the story situation presented)
   c. to present a series of story situations to students and then ask them to make assumptions about the main character, the sequence of events to follow, and the possible outcomes

6. a. to require students to discuss why certain story incidents are factual while others are fiction
   b. to require students to identify between fact and fiction in stories they read
   c. to require students to create stories that are factual and those that are fiction
   d. to ask students how a story made them feel and why, and to require students to state the clues to the story's mood
   e. to ask students to state and write the character traits of the main characters in the stories they read, and to require them to specify how the character is similar to or different from themselves or others they know

Establish a Timeline. Each step of the program's development should have a specified timeline to help keep the program on target. The goals should be determined before a group of professionals is asked to specify the objectives to be met. In addition, the tasks and activities related to the objectives must be written before staff development needs can be identified and planned for. A target date for program implementation will provide everyone involved with a realistic due date to be kept in mind as tasks required for implementation are conducted.

Step 4: Evaluation

Evaluation is the key to successful programs, and is an ongoing process. If properly implemented, trouble spots can be corrected before they become so large that they interfere with the success of the program itself. Evaluation should be developed in comparison with the specified design of the program, with all populations involved in the design of the program also involved in the evaluation.

At the evaluation stage, it is often too late to modify specified objectives. That is why it is important to state realistic objectives within the specified time frame. Other goals that are desirable but difficult to achieve should be postponed for later years when the program is established and well understood by all participating parties. Experience with the program will help put more difficult goals within reach.

Who Evaluates. The evaluation population is comprehensive. First, it involves the parents of the students who are in the program. Parents are in a position to observe their children outside the school situation and note if attitudes as well as knowledge are improved.

Students are a second important population to act as evaluators. They should be given an opportunity to react to the program as a source of potential knowledge and as a means of modifying attitudes about oneself and school in general.

The faculty responsible for implementation of the program must also be given a chance to react to the program. They should be able to comment on the effectiveness of the program in all its aspects from specification of objectives to materials purchased, staff development techniques, and communication plans.

Administrators must be involved in the evaluation design to determine if, in their opinion, the program has been successfully implemented and if it accomplished its intended purpose.

Consultants can be valuable in the evaluation design to determine if the true intent and design of the program has been accomplished. They may be able to spot where any trouble was and why.

Who Is Evaluated. Students, of course, are evaluated for their progress and development in both the content and affective goals of the program.

The faculty is evaluated by themselves, the administrators, and the students for successful implementation of the program's goals. This evaluation should be ongoing to be most effective.

Administrators are evaluated by the faculty and district personnel, if appropriate, to determine how well they guided and monitored the program. It is the administrators who, having a more global view, can often help the program succeed through thoughtful and sensitive monitoring of progress.

Consultants are evaluated by the faculty and administrators to determine if their participation was beneficial in actual implementation of the program. If the consultant's participation is ongoing, growth and development of the program's staff is another aspect of the evaluation of the consultant's contribution to the program's effectiveness.

What Is Evaluated. All aspects of the program are included in the evaluation plan. First, the content of the program is evaluated, including the specific objectives and tasks and activities used. Next the process of the program is evaluated, including the materials selected and the instructional strategies employed. This aspect of the evaluation cannot be left to the end but must be conducted on an ongoing basis throughout the program.

The student products—activities as well as test results—evidenced in the program are also a part of the evaluation. Both quality and quantity of work are considered.

The goals and objectives that were set relating to the affective domain of feelings and attitudes are also evaluated. Whatever aspects of this area were targeted in the design should be evaluated.

How Evaluation Is Conducted. Evaluation can be conducted in a variety of ways determined by the population to be evaluated and the objective of the evaluation. It is wise to use various means of evaluation to achieve the most comprehensive effect possible. The following list illustrates a variety of ways to evaluate different populations.

WHO	*HOW*
students	tests
	conferences
	evaluation of products
	observations
faculty	conferences
	written plans
	observations
	recordkeeping
parents	interviews
	conferences
	questionnaires
administrators	conferences with staff
	conferences with superiors
	questionnaires
	presentations conducted
	written material prepared
consultants	quality of presentations
	individual interaction with staff
	quality of written materials
	conferences with administrators
	conferences with staff
	questionnaires

When Evaluation Is Conducted. The different aspects of evaluation are best conducted at different stages of the program, with some aspects of the program, such as teacher performance and administrative details, evaluated on an ongoing basis.

Medial evaluation is important for all aspects of the program to determine the possible outcomes and the program's position in relation to the time frame that has been set. If desirable, program modifications can be made at this stage.

Evaluation at the end of the program is, of course, necessary to evaluate its effectiveness and to determine if the program will continue and, if so, with what modifications.

Why Evaluation Is Conducted. There are at least three reasons why evaluation is conducted: (1) to identify problems that have developed and to create an intervention strategy to eliminate them; (2) to improve the quality of the program as it is in progress; and (3) to assess achievement of the program's goals and objectives.

Step 5: Publicity

Publicity helps to build sympathy, support, and understanding about the need for the program. These efforts are important to those parents whose children are involved in the program, since school activities are often not understood. These efforts are also important to those who are involved in school activities but not associated with the program itself, since the work of the school should be viewed as a total team approach. The publicity efforts are important to others who are not related to the school or the program's target population since the general public should be aware of the many concerns the schools face and the ways in which solutions are sought.

Make the Program Visible. Open information meetings should be scheduled to focus on the steps taken in the development of the program: the design of the program, the process to be used, and the expected gain. The objective of the meeting is to let the audience know the school is identifying problems and working to eliminate them.

Involvement workshops actively place participants in the role of students. Participants work on tasks and activities as well as materials and equipment purchased for the program. There is no better way to truly explain the educational process to be used than to ask participants to experience that process themselves. For example, if computers are to be used as part of the instructional plan, allow the public to work on a computer as a learning experience to help clarify the instructional impact of this device and to eliminate the notion that "toys" make less work for teachers.

Fairs can exhibit the work of the students, who can explain and discuss their own work. The fair provides an opportunity to visualize what has been accomplished. It is also an opportunity for the students and the teachers to see and admire the results of their efforts.

Make the Explanation Meaningful. A visual presentation is always more interesting and better understood than one that is totally oral. One means of keeping an ongoing record of student progress is to take photos of the students working and the results of their efforts. These photos can be placed in albums and dated.

Slide and tape presentations can also carry the program's message in an exciting and meaningful way to the public. The students can make the tapes themselves to give the program even more meaning.

Videotape presentations are, perhaps, more dramatic than slides in showing the actual activities of the students. The preparation of a videotape presentation is costly and time consuming, but well worth the effort if the program's story is clearly and realistically told. Both the slide presentation and the videotape presentation have the advantage of taking the audience into the classrooms in which the programs are conducted.

Reach a Larger Audience. Interested individuals do not always attend meetings, and it is a mistake to assume that these people do not want to know about the program. Written communications can help keep this population informed. A program brochure can be developed to state the program's purpose, process, and intended results. Articles about the progress of the program can appear periodically in school, district, and community publications. In addition, parents and other interested parties should receive periodic update bulletins about the current work and meetings related to the program.

5

HOW TO ASSURE SUCCESSFUL KINDERGARTEN REGISTRATION

The national trend toward declining public school enrollment is most severely felt at the primary level, with the individual needs of parents often persuading them to seek alternatives to public education. The large group of job holders among mothers of young children has fostered the development of day care centers; but when the children reach the appropriate age, they often continue in private school. Two reasons usually support this decision: (1) private schools often offer an extended day program, and (2) the habit of private education has already been set in the mind of the parent.

The loss of confidence in the public schools has also contributed to parent's decisions to enroll their children in private schools. Therefore, administrators must *publicize* the *quality* education offered at the public school. If parents believe that the educational opportunity for their children lies within the public schools, they will make the effort to provide ways to deal with individual problems concerning child care after school hours. Thus, the task for the school is to communicate to parents that the educational needs of the children are met with quality instruction delivered by concerned educators, and there is no better place to start than with the kindergarten program.

DESIGN EFFECTIVE FLYERS

The first step in a publicity campaign is getting the word out to the community. An attractive flyer can start to tell the message to parents of kindergarten-age children. The purpose of the flyer is to stimulate interest and encourage parents to learn more about the kindergarten program.

Involve the School

The students, staff, and Parents Association of the school should be aware of the publicity effort and be involved in making it successful. Students can hand out the flyers early in the morning as people of the community leave for work. Students should take flyers home to inform parents, friends, and relatives of the informational meetings and efforts being made.

The school staff can welcome visitors on a guided tour following the information meeting. Staff members who live in the community can also make their friends and relatives aware of the kindergarten program and the meetings that will be held.

The Parents Association should be totally involved in the publicity effort. They can select a group of parents to work with school officials to plan the publicity campaign, carry it out, and, if necessary, help to finance it.

Involve the Community

Local merchants are usually delighted to help spread the word of the school's kindergarten program. Posters can be placed in shop windows, and merchants can be asked to tell their customers about the planned meetings and the school's efforts.

Local newspapers can cooperate by printing notices of the meetings. It may even be possible to convince the newspapers to write an article about the school and its kindergarten program. If the newspapers have space, several black-and-white glossy photographs of the current kindergarteners can be very effective.

Clubs and associations in the community might display flyers in meeting rooms, and may cooperate with a school request for speaking time at a meeting.

WRITE AN INFORMATION BOOKLET

The information booklet is a powerful communicator, telling the school's story in a convenient package, and can be distributed at the information meeting and during class registration. The booklet should have an attractive cover designed by a publicity group or student. If appropriate, the initial flyer can be used as the cover.

The following sample booklet pages can be modified to fit your particular school situation.

SAMPLE: A Letter of Greeting—Page 1

Dear Parents,

We are delighted to welcome you and your children to school. That first day in September will be one that you and your child will always remember. It is the first step of a joyous and never-ending adventure into a world filled with exciting and interesting things to do and learn. Now you and the school are partners jointly dedicated to helping your child grow into a healthy, happy, fully aware person.

Sincerely,

Grace Timson, Principal

SAMPLE: Introducing School Personnel—Page 2

School Workers Your Child Will Meet

Mrs. Cane, Resource Teacher

The resource room is specially designed and filled with learning materials for students who have learning difficulties. Mrs. Cane works with these students to help them develop the learning skills they need.

Mrs. Gamely, Guidance Counselor

Assistance to you and your child can be found with Mrs. Gamely. She works with students, parents, and teachers to improve the learning experiences of all the children.

Mr. Gentle, Music Teacher

Every child receives instruction in music. The children learn how to read the international language of music and how to appreciate its message. Those children interested in learning how to play an instrument or participate in vocal music also have special programs.

Mrs. Kelb, Physical Education Teacher

Every child receives instruction in physical education. The children learn how to exercise through movement and games. In addition, nutrition education is taught at all grade levels.

Mr. Lesser, Reading Specialist

Small group lessons in reading are conducted by Mr. Lesser for students who need extra help. The reading room is an interesting place to learn how to read better.

Mrs. Lind, Media Specialist

The media center houses special equipment and programs for students with special needs. These needs may be to have more review or to move ahead more quickly. Mrs. Lind helps the children to use the equipment properly.

Mr. Plyer, Teacher of the Gifted

The students in this program work with Mr. Plyer to find an area of study in which they are interested and then, by themselves or in small groups, create a project.

Mrs. Seldon, Speech Teacher

The speech of students who need help is improved by working with Mrs. Seldon in a special program.

Mrs. Stenco, Lunchroom Director

The serving of a hot, appetizing, and nutritious lunch is the responsibility of Mrs. Stenco. The school and the Parents Association have worked to constantly improve the lunch program. Special provisions are made for students with particular nutritional needs.

Mrs. William, Librarian

Every child visits the library once a week with the class, where the children learn how to find books and information. The library becomes an important learning tool. Each week the students return the books they have completed and borrow new ones to read and enjoy. Mrs. William is there to help the children learn about the library and how to use it. She also helps individual children and small groups with research needs.

SAMPLE: Hints for Helping the Child to Prepare for School—Page 3

How to Help Your Child Prepare for School

1. Talk about school with your child. Discuss happy experiences that are waiting for him or her.
2. Listen to your child. Discuss concerns that he or she expresses. Encourage your child and be reassuring.
3. Establish good routines for eating and sleeping and doing school work. Agree upon a school bedtime.
4. Provide a work and study area for your child. This area should be a private place away from distractions and siblings.
5. Establish a communication link with the teacher so that you are always informed about your child's progress.
6. Become an active member of the Parents Association and help it to work for *all* the children.

SAMPLE: What the Child Should Know—Page 4

What Your Child Should Know

Independence and self-reliance are important qualities for school-aged children. Your child should be able to:

1. state his or her name and address.
2. take off and put on his or her own clothing: boots should be large enough to slip on and off easily, shoelaces should be securely tied, buttons and zippers should be easy to use, and clothing should be comfortable and appropriate for school and the weather.
3. recognize his or her own clothing: it is helpful if everything that will be removed (hats, gloves, coats, etc.) is labeled with the child's name.
4. carry a handkerchief and be able to use it.
5. go to the toilet without help.
6. handle objects and return them properly.
7. follow instructions given by an adult.
8. stay with a group of children without Mommy or Daddy.
9. follow the best and safest way home.
10. rely on being picked up on time by someone he or she knows.

SAMPLE: What the Parent Should Know—Page 5

What You Should Know

1. The entrance and exits used by the children.
2. You will be notified about your child's placement during the first week of September.
3. Please be on time for the beginning of the school session. This will help to develop the importance of school and your child's habits of punctuality.
4. Please be on time to pick up your child. Children who are forced to wait for pick up become anxious and unhappy.
5. Read all the notices and bulletins that are sent home by the school. Promptly return the ones that require a signature.
6. If your child is fearful about school, play a "pretend" game with him or her to bring some familiarity to a new situation.
7. Listen to what your child has to say about school. Do not force the conversation, but be attentive when your child is ready to share the experience.
8. Praise the work your child brings home.

SAMPLE: The Curriculum and Philosophy of the School—Page 6

The School's Philosophy

This school is dedicated to the belief that all children can and will learn. It is also understood that children learn at different rates and have different needs. The school will work to supply the children with every learning opportunity that is possible to assist each individual student.

The goal of the school is to develop independent, self-reliant, life-long learners.

The School's Curriculum

The school's curriculum includes academic, emotional, and social areas.

1. Social Development—the child:
   a. relates to peers in work and play activities
   b. is aware of the feelings of others
   c. is accepted by a group of his or her peers
   d. can accept decisions of the group
   e. has conscientious and positive attitudes toward school
   f. is aware of group responsibilities

2. Emotional Development—The child:
   a. shows self-confidence
   b. practices self-control
   c. adjusts to change
   d. accepts constructive criticism and suggestions

---

e. accepts responsibility for his or her own actions

f. cares for his or her own needs

3. Work Habits—The child:

a. follows directions

b. is able to work independently at times

c. can plan appropriately for his or her own time

d. uses time constructively

e. can keep records of his or her own work

f. makes use of a variety of materials

g. is responsible for the care of materials

h. observes safety rules

4. Academic Process—The child:

a. shows an interest in reading

b. shows the ability to understand what is read to him or her

c. can interpret pictures

d. can tell a story in a sequence

e. shows confidence in speaking before a group

f. expresses ideas clearly

g. is an attentive listener

h. shows an interest in mathematics

i. learns new concepts

j. shows an interest in scientific experimentation

k. is able to demonstrate knowledge of the world around him or her

l. participates in the physical education program

m. uses materials creatively

n. shows an appreciation of music and art

DESIGN A PRE-ENTRANCE ASSESSMENT OF NEEDS

Conducting a screening process for the incoming kindergarteners will help you identify the specific group and individual needs of the students. It will also help you plan for appropriate programs and services that the youngsters may require. The total assessment does not have to be conducted at one time. It is possible to divide it into two parts: one conducted at registration; the other at orientation.

Pre-Reading Assessment

Many pre-reading assessments are commercially available. They can usually be administered quickly and are easily scored by hand. Be sure to examine the commercial instruments before you select one because there should be a balance among the different parts; it should provide for discrimination among shapes and sizes; it should provide an opportunity for students to identify pictures after a clue word has been provided; it should require the student to discriminate among objects to identify the ones that do not belong in the classification and those that are incomplete; and it should give students who can read an opportunity to identify words and phrases. An instrument that contains all of these parts is valuable in identifying the reading readiness potential of the individuals. Since the pre-reading assessment requires between 30 to 40 minutes to administer, try to administer the assessment at orientation while the parents are attending a presentation.

Oral Assessment of Needs

An informal oral needs assessment (Figure 5-1) will help to identify the maturity and knowledge of each youngster. Since children of this age range vary greatly in their experiences and understanding, the assessment may be helpful in grouping students with similar learning needs. This oral assessment may be completed during registration.

Rather than using an artificial grade, it may be more helpful to record the child's performance in terms of his or her ability to complete the tasks required: C = Comfortably; D = with Difficulty; N = Not at all. Such a recording system may evaluate the child in terms of the ability to complete what was asked.

A Parent Questionnaire

The parent questionnaire (Figure 5-2) asks for additional information about the youngster. It can provide clues to student needs and projections about student success with a formal school experience.

ORIENT THE PARENT AND THE CHILD

Orientation efforts are certainly worthwhile as a source of information to the parent about what to expect from the school. Orientation helps to calm an anxious parent's concerns about what is often a first separation from the child. In addition, orientation efforts leave an impression of interest in and concern for the individual child and his or her special needs.

A child benefits from orientation efforts, too, by being able to view the school first-hand. The gathering with other youngsters like him- or herself who have never attended school and current kindergarteners who are completing their first year at school can be a growing experience. Orientation also provides a second opportunity for gathering assessment information.

The Parents Association can benefit from orientation efforts by meeting and speaking with new parents. Potential contributors to the school's efforts can be identified at this meeting.

Invite the Parent and the Child to School

During registration, make an appointment for the child and the parent to attend an orientation session. Send a personalized invitation (see Figure 5-3) to the child, and give the parent a selection of dates from which to choose, and an agenda (Figure 5-4).

DEVELOP "A DAY AT SCHOOL" PROGRAM

The crucial elements in the program are timing and personnel. The students have two major participations: (1) to visit a currently functioning kindergarten class, and (2) to complete a pre-reading assessment, the timing of which will depend upon school schedules

KINDERGARTEN ORAL ASSESSMENT OF NEEDS

Last Name   First Name   Sex

Indicate the child's ability to complete the tasks asked. Use the ratings of:
C = Comfortably, D = with Difficulty, N = Not at all.

1. States his or her whole name. _____

2. States his or her address. _____

3. States his or her telephone number. _____

4. Prints his or her own name from memory. _____

5. Places pictures in sequential order. _____

6. Distinguishes left hand from right hand. _____

7. Expresses ideas in complete sentences. _____

8. Repeats four digits in forward order. _____

9. Identifies numerals. _____

10. Identifies coins. _____

11. Recognizes size __ shape __ color __ of objects. _____

12. Adds and subtracts in problem situations. _____

13. Copies simple shapes. _____

14. Erects a balanced structure. _____

15. Sits still for a reasonable time. _____

16. Appears in Good __ Fair __ Poor __ health. _____

17. Provides uses for a common object, e.g., string.
(number stated) _____

18. Draws a picture of a person.
(number of details/completeness) _____

19. Speaks English. _____

COMMENTS: _____

_____

_____

_____

Figure 5-1

KINDERGARTEN PARENT QUESTIONNAIRE

Child's Name _____

                            Last   First

Address _____

_____

Telephone Number _____

Has your child had any previous school experience? _____

If so, when? _____ For how long? _____

Where? _____

Can your child dress him- or herself? _____ Tie shoes? _____

Does your child have any special interests or hobbies? _____

What are they? _____

_____

Does your child have any special talent(s)? _____

What are they? _____

_____

_____

What kinds of activities does your child seem to enjoy most? _____

_____

_____

What are your child's feelings about coming to school? _____

_____

_____

What are your questions and concerns? _____

_____

_____

COMMENTS: _____

_____

_____

Figure 5-2

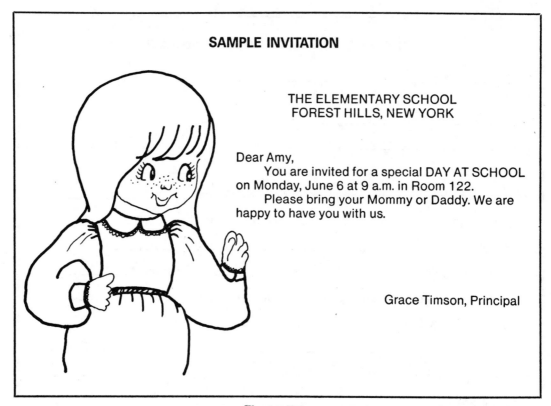

SAMPLE INVITATION

THE ELEMENTARY SCHOOL
FOREST HILLS, NEW YORK

Dear Amy,
        You are invited for a special DAY AT SCHOOL on Monday, June 6 at 9 a.m. in Room 122.
        Please bring your Mommy or Daddy. We are happy to have you with us.

Grace Timson, Principal

Figure 5-3

and available personnel. In general, conducting the visit to class first helps calm youngsters' fears about a new and strange experience. Since the parent is invited to remain in the room during the visit, most youngsters gain confidence about school.

The classroom visit should be carefully planned. Each new youngster should have a name tag, and be assigned to a current kindergartener who has the job of telling the youngster about the classroom and taking him or her to an activity. During the visit, independent activities, small teacher-instructional groups, and a whole class experience should be provided.

The pre-reading assessment can be administered after the classroom visit. Parents are asked to leave their children in a room with personnel who will conduct the test. Any child who experiences difficulty with having the parent leave may request that the parent remain. In such a case, the parent is asked to sit quietly next to the child and not to participate at all in the assessment activities.

It is advisable to have a one-to-five teacher-to-student ratio during the testing period. Any available personnel—school aides, paraprofessionals, special teachers, parent volunteers—can be trained to administer the pre-reading assessment. Those administering the assessment help to provide a warm and friendly atmosphere and assist the youngsters to follow the directions given.

ORIENTATION AGENDA (for PARENT)

THE ELEMENTARY SCHOOL

Dear Parent,

You have selected a date for you and your child to visit the school. There are several objectives we wish to accomplish:

1. To provide an opportunity for your child to participate in our current kindergarten program.

2. To give you the opportunity of seeing your youngster in a kindergarten setting.

3. To administer a pre-reading assessment to your child to help us analyze the child's learning needs.

4. To inform you about the school and its programs and to give you the opportunity to meet some of the staff and representatives of the Parents Association.

5. To involve you in a conducted tour of the school building so that you can learn more about us.

Your participation in these activities is important for both you and your child. We want to work together for your youngster's best interests.

Schedule for A DAY AT SCHOOL

9:00 A.M. — You and your youngster will participate in the current kindergarten program. Please enter the kindergarten room through the side entrance.

9:45 A.M. — your child will complete a pre-reading assessment in Room 7 across the hall from the kindergarten room.

9:45 A.M. — you are invited to have coffee and cake, followed by an orientation session and a guided tour of the school. This session is scheduled to end at about the same time that your child will complete the pre-reading assessment.

I look forward to meeting you.

Sincerely,

Grace Timson, Principal

Figure 5-4

During the administration of the pre-reading assessment, the parents are greeted in a separate room near the testing site. A short coffee and cake period allows the parents to become acquainted and to speak with school personnel. The presentation to parents should include an overview of the kindergarten program and the school's general philosophy. Slides or a film of an actual kindergarten class can add greatly to the program.

Parents should also be made aware of the special programs and opportunities available at the school for students of different needs. Throughout the presentation, the emphasis should be on assisting *each* youngster to reach his or her potential.

Involve Other Personnel

In addition to learning about what to expect from the school, parents should be informed about what is expected of them. Several members of the professional staff can provide valuable information for the parents.

The guidance counselor may be helpful in providing a non-threatening link between the school and the home. He or she is a person who the parent can always reach for assistance with problems. The school nurse can offer valuable health-related information to the parent of a young child, with nutritional and immunization information of particular interest. One of the kindergarten teachers can explain various experiences provided for the youngsters and is also a perfect respondant for parents' questions. If the school has special programs for students with special needs, such as speakers of foreign languages, the bilingual or English second language teacher may be an important addition to the orientation program.

Involve the Parents Association

Speakers from the Parents Association can also contribute to the orientation session. The members have a different viewpoint from the professionals and are able to speak about real issues and concerns within the community. It is important for new school parents to see and believe that an excellent working relationship exists between the school and the parents, too. It is therefore most appropriate that members of the Parents Association host the parents on a conducted tour of the school. The tour should include facilities used by all the students, such as the gymnasium, library, media center, auditorium, and lunchroom. Visits to selected classes and special programs may be included. If well timed, the tour conducted by the Parents Association should end at about the same time that the children's pre-reading assessment is completed.

USE THE RESULTS OF THE PRE-ENTRANCE ASSESSMENT

Each aspect of the pre-entrance assessment is important in the identification of student strengths and weaknesses. The results of the total assessment provides a view of the student from academic, perceptual, language development, emotional, social, and creative points of view. These results should be recorded in matrix form so that all aspects, not just the pre-reading assessment, are considered in placing the students into instructional groupings and providing special programs for them.

Analyze Pre-Reading Assessment

Most pre-reading assessments yield two partial scores, one for language and a second for visual discrimination. These raw scores can be converted, with the use of a table, to comparisons with normed groups. The results of this comparison yield estimates of such performances as high average, above average, average, below average, and poor. It should be remembered that these norms are based on the testing of large groups of youngsters of the same age in various parts of the country; the similarity of that norm population to the population of students being tested is unknown. The results of the pre-reading assessment is intended as an indicator of reading readiness. As one part of a total assessment, this information can be valuable, and is especially valuable when other parts of the assessment yield similar results.

Analyze Oral Data

The orally administered Assessment of Needs yields information in five different categories:

- academic (items 5, 9, 10, 11, 12)
- perceptual (items 1, 2, 3, 4, 6, 8, 13, 14)
- language development (items 1, 2, 3, 7)
- emotional development (items 15, 18)
- creative potential (items 17, 18)

Some of the items are listed in more than one category because different aspects of the item are taken into consideration.

- Items 1, 2, 3 are evaluated for oral memory and language development. Not only is the ability to remember one's name, address and telephone number evaluated, but the manner of expressing the response is also evaluated.
- Item 18 is evaluated for emotional development and creative potential. The drawing of a person is evaluated as an expression of emotional maturity depending on its completeness and proportion. It is also evaluated as an expression of creative potential depending on the number of details, such as fingers, jewelry, eyelashes, etc., included in the drawing.

Each item in a category has a value of one, and the matrix lists the score of the individual student in each category. A different type of scoring process is used for items 16, 17 and 18.

- Item 16 is evaluated as Good, Fair, Poor.
- Item 17 requires the listing of the number of uses the child was able to state.
- Item 18 is evaluated for completeness of the picture and the number of details drawn by the child.

In addition, the comments written by the evaluator on the student's form are indicated by placing an X in the appropriate columns.

Analyze Parent Questionnaire Data

The parent questionnaire (seen in Figure 5-2) yields information in five different categories:

- academic (special interests or hobbies)
- perceptual (dresses him- or herself, ties shoes)
- emotional development (feelings about school)
- social development (activities enjoyed)
- creative potential (special talents)

Each positive parent response is given a value of one. The matrix lists the score in the appropriate category under the heading of parent. Additional comments written by the parent are indicated by placing a second X in the comments line of the matrix.

DEVELOP A MATRIX

The matrix (Figure 5-5) reviews both individual scores on specific items as well as a total overview of the student. This analysis of student's strengths and needs is helpful for class groupings and assignment to special programs or services.

An analysis of the new kindergarten population as a whole will enable you, as principal, to make projections about the new semester's needs. Population trends and

---

KINDERGARTEN REGISTRANTS' MATRIX

Student Names

Items

ACADEMIC

  Pre-Reading
    language
    visual discrimination
    total

  Oral Assessment (total = 5)
    C = comfortably
    D = with difficulty
    N = not at all

  Parent Questionnaire
    total = 1

PERCEPTUAL

  Oral Assessment (total = 8)
    C = comfortably
    D = with difficulty

N = not at all	
Parent Questionnaire total = 2	
LANGUAGE DEVELOPMENT	
Oral Assessment (total = 4) C = comfortably	
D = with difficulty	
N = not at all	
EMOTIONAL DEVELOPMENT	
Oral Assessment (total = 1) C = comfortably	
D = with difficulty	
N = not at all	
Draw a Person (completeness) G=good, F=fair, P=poor	
Parent Questionnaire total = 1	
SOCIAL DEVELOPMENT	
Parent Questionnaire total = 1	
CREATIVITY	
Uses for (#)	
Draw a Person (# details)	
Parent Questionnaire total = 1	
SUMMARY	
Pre-Reading Total	
# of C's Total	
Parent Total	
Draw a Person Score	
Creativity Total	
HEALTH: Good, Fair, Poor	
FOREIGN LANGUAGE NEED	
S = severe, M = moderate	
COMMENT (X) evaluator	
parent	

Figure 5-5

changes also become easier to identify. Projected needs may be an important consideration in district plans for services to a particular school.

MAKE DECISIONS BASED ON THE DATA

The availability of the assessment data makes it possible to group students based upon need rather than by age or random assignment. Even at this age, students demonstrate marked differences in background, experiences, and readiness to profit from a formal school setting.

Some tentative identification of needs among the children will help to form class groups that can realistically be addressed by the teacher assigned. The following groups of students with similar needs will usually be found.

- High Academic—students who achieve a high score on the pre-reading assessment. These students may be reading at this time, may know many letter names and sounds, and may have a well-developed visual discrimination.

- Reading Readiness—students who are ready for experiences that will prepare them to learn how to read. These students may need repeated experiences with visual discrimination and letter names and sounds.

- Perceptual—students who appear to have perceptual needs at this time. These students may have difficulty in identifying sounds and discriminating among shapes and objects. The instructional program for these students would naturally stress the development of perceptual strengths.

- Oral Language Development—students who appear to have difficulty in expressing themselves. These students require an instructional program that will build experiences about which the children can be encouraged to speak, describe, and explain.

- Speakers of Foreign Languages—students who need to develop an understanding of English and the ability to communicate orally before they can be expected to learn to read English. These students require repeated language experiences with objects familiar to them and the opportunity to practice beginning skills in oral English.

Once the need groups have been identified, it is possible to assign groups of students to classes so that each class will contain a number of students with similar needs that the teacher can meet. However, it is unwise to assign all students with one particular need to a single class. This practice tends to isolate those students with others like themselves so that the opportunity to learn from peers is lost. Foreign language students would be particularly deprived in such a situation since there would be no speakers of English from whom they could learn. This same problem would exist with students who need to develop oral language skills. They need to be with others like themselves for instruction as well as with others who have good oral language skills from whom they can learn.

On the other hand, it is wise to form instructional groups within each classroom. The teacher can then realistically personalize instruction for each group assigned. In addition, high academic students may well be a potential pool from which gifted and talented students may later be identified. These students need the stimulation of minds and abilities like theirs to grow and develop to full potential.

Understand that this initial grouping of students by need is tentative. At this age, students grow and develop quickly and change markedly. The variety of need groups within each class enables the teacher to group the students flexibly so that as children develop they may be regrouped with others.

PROVIDE FOR OTHER VARIABLES

In addition to need groupings, other variables should be kept in mind to provide the classes with a healthy mix of students. One variable that may become a problem is bus transportation. Under certain circumstances, some children may be entitled while others are not. Thus, the availability of the bus may influence the decision of class placement as a priority. Program availability is another factor important to class placement. Students who require special programs must be assigned to classes that are in session when those services are available.

No class should be deliberately constructed without consideration for balance by sex and ethnic composition. Although need is the primary consideration, and bus transportation facilities and program availability are the next most important considerations, sex and ethnic balances are also important factors in the total composition of the classes.

COMMUNICATE DECISIONS TO PARENTS

These are times when school allocations are sometimes tentative in June, so drastic revisions may be necessary during the summer when additional or less funds are available. With these factors in mind, try to delay parent notification of class placement until late August or early September. The addition or subtraction of staff may also make a decided difference in the availability of classes into which students can be placed.

In any case, class assignment cannot be made until there has been an opportunity to analyze the collected data. Therefore, it is helpful to provide each parent with a preprinted, self-addressed postcard. The postcard (Figure 5-6) can be filled in once class assignments are determined and mailed to the address that has been written on the other side. The date for mailing the postcard will depend upon your school's circumstances.

POSTCARD
The Elementary School

Child's Name _____

Class Placement _____

Room Number _____

First Date of Class _____

Time of Session _____

Entrance to Be Used _____

PLEASE BE PROMPT FOR PICK UP AT _____

Figure 5-6

6

HOW TO PREVENT DISASTER WHEN TEACHERS ARE ABSENT

One of the most difficult and seemingly unresolved problems you face is the absent teacher. That class of 25 to 30 unsupervised youngsters is probably the largest headache of all. At times, the need to find someone, *anyone*, to cover that class results in finding a warm body and nothing more! Of course, the teacher's plans should be on the desk, but all too often they are in the teacher's hands at home. This is especially true if the absence occurs on a Monday.

When the teacher's plans are not in the classroom, the substitute's competence is the key factor for a possible successful day. Many substitutes are competent and come to work prepared with a bag of tricks or prepared lessons that can be modified for different age/grade groups. All too often, though, this is not the case, and the class becomes a nightmare. Although the learning sequence is disrupted, physical control of the students is often the real issue. Thus, a planned support system for the substitute teacher can be extremely helpful and may just save the day.

PREPARE A SUBSTITUTE'S FOLDER

Since the preparation of a substitute folder creates an additional task for the classroom teacher, a strong rationale for the folder must be established. Teachers should be made to understand that in helping the substitute, they are helping themselves.

No teacher wants to return to a classroom to find it in a state of chaos. Thus, the better prepared the substitute teacher is, the greater the possibility of the regular teacher finding everything in good order. The teacher should remember that a group of youngsters who have been successful in making a substitute ineffectual may try the same strategies when he or she returns; discipline and control then become more difficult to reestablish. Too, the planned sequence of instruction has been disrupted, and the regular teacher must then revise predetermined planned activities to "catch up."

NOTIFY TEACHERS ABOUT THE FOLDER

Teachers should be informed about the establishment of a substitute folder at the first staff meeting following the summer break. The form and content of the folder should be given to the teachers in writing, along with a due date for its completion because it is in the teachers' best interests to have the folder completed as soon as possible. On the other hand, the start of a new academic year is always a time of heavy paper work, so a reasonable due date should fall no earlier than the first two weeks of school but certainly no later than September 30.

You should review the completed substitute folder for two reasons: (1) to be assured that the folder has been prepared, and (2) to determine the quality and completeness of the information. After you have reviewed the folder and are comfortable with its contents, return it to the teacher to be placed in the center drawer of the teacher's desk.

CONTENTS OF SUBSTITUTE FOLDER

A file folder that has been labeled "To the Substitute" should contain:

- a class list of names
- the teacher's guide to the substitute
- a contingency plan for the day in the event that the teacher's plans are not available

The attendance book, cards, or register is placed under the folder. If the teacher does not want the substitute to make entries on the attendance documents, a suitable note should be attached to the attendance forms and the class list can be used for attendance purposes.

NOTE: As the student population of the class changes and the activities of the content areas progress, the contents of the substitute folder should be updated. Teachers can be periodically reminded at faculty or grade conferences to update the folders. This can be done on a monthly basis or every other month.

Guide the Substitute

The Teacher's Guide for the Substitute (Figure 6-1) is a valuable support because it contains important information that may be otherwise unavailable to the substitute. The Guide first tells the substitute who and where the grade leader (or department head) is as the natural resource person to contact. Other information such as the school time schedule for the grade and the special activities' time schedule for the class are also included.

The Guide also allows the substitute to maintain control over the individual students who may have special assignments or needs. These include students who use the bus, students who are responsible for escorting younger children in the school, and students who are monitors in charge of particular activities.

The Contingency Plan (Figure 6-2) is used by the substitute in the event that the teacher's plans are not available. This Contingency Plan gives the substitute an overview of the class and the instructional program, the names of the reading groups and the location of the readers, what mathematics concepts can be reviewed and reinforced, the current social studies topic being covered and a resource for leading a discussion or conducting an activity,

TEACHER'S GUIDE FOR THE SUBSTITUTE

Class_____   Teacher _____

1. The grade leader is _____ Room ____
2. Assembly day is _____ Time ____
3. Gym Periods are: Day _____ Time _____
   Day _____ Time _____
   Day _____ Time _____

4. Special Periods are: _____ Day _____ Time __ Rm __
   _____ Day _____ Time __ Rm __
   _____ Day _____ Time __ Rm __
   _____ Day _____ Time __ Rm __

5. School Session:
   Begins at _____ Students arrive _____
   Lunch period is from _____ to _____
   Students leave _____
   Afternoon session begins at _____
   Students are _____
   School session ends at _____
   Students leave _____
   The exit for this room is _____

6. The following students use the school bus:

   _____   _____
   _____   _____
   _____   _____

   They arrive at _____ They are dismissed at _____

7. The following monitors leave the room:
   _____ at ____ _____ at ____
   _____ at ____ _____ at ____
   _____ at ____ _____ at ____

8. The following students pick up younger children:
   _____ at ____ _____ at ____
   _____ at ____ _____ at ____

9. The following children are picked up by older students:
   _____ by _____ class _____
   _____ by _____ class _____
   _____ by _____ class _____

Figure 6-1

CONTINGENCY PLAN

Class_____ Teacher _____

Date _____ Update _____ Update _____ Update _____ Update _____

Reading Groups:

Name*_____ Book _____

activities _____
_____

Name*_____ Book _____

activities _____
_____

Name*_____ Book _____

activities _____
_____

Mathematics Groups:

Name*_____ Book _____

activities _____
_____

Name*_____ Book _____

activities _____
_____

Social Studies Topic _____
activity _____
materials _____

Additional Activities suitable for:

class __ group __ Topic _____
                      Material _____
class __ group __ Topic _____
                      Material _____
class __ group __ Topic _____
                      Material _____

Special Programs (Remedial Reading, Speech, Gifted etc.)

Student _____ day __ time __ Teacher _____ Rm __
Student _____ day __ time __ Teacher _____ Rm __
Student _____ day __ time __ Teacher _____ Rm __
Student _____ day __ time __ Teacher _____ Rm __

_____
*See attached lists of students' names for each group.

Figure 6-2

and several other possible and worthwhile class activities in creative writing, vocabulary building, and reading comprehension.

If the structure of the class is based upon an individualized program, state this in the Contingency Plan.

The students plan their own day.
Each student has his or her own prescription in reading and mathematics.
You should assist the students by...
Conduct a small group reading lesson with the _____ group on the topic of _____ using the _____ material.
The following activities are suitable for the entire class: _____, _____, _____.

The Contingency Plan also contains the names of the students involved in special programs with other personnel and the times that they are to report to other rooms or are to be picked up.

ADDITIONAL INFORMATION

In addition to The Teacher's Guide to the Substitute and the Contingency Plan, there are several other important pieces of general information that should be available to the substitute teacher. This information prepares the substitute for such school activities as the collection of lunch money that are usually taken for granted. The better informed the substitute, the greater the possibility for his or her successful performance.

Secretary's Communication with Substitute

The first steps in providing for the substitute teacher are taken by the school secretary. When a teacher is reported as absent and a substitute is secured, the secretary should complete the top portion of the Information for Substitute Teachers sheet (Figure 6-3).

The first person the substitute sees is usually this secretary, who provides the initial orientation. It is the secretary's responsibility to give the sheet to the substitute teacher, answer any questions that may be asked, and be sure that the substitute receives the correct set of keys for the room and directions to the room.

This is an important process. The substitute teacher should be received with a smile and good cheer, a greeting that sets the tone for the school and may well influence the mood of the substitute for the rest of the day.

Substitute's Communication with Teacher

All too often, the regular teacher returns after an absence and has little or no idea of what happened. He or she is then faced with asking the students in the class, questioning colleagues, or just forgetting about the whole thing and pretending that nothing happened at all during the absence!

It is far more effective to maintain a reporting system so that the regular teacher knows what instruction took place and how the students reacted to the situation. This can be done through the Substitute's Report to the Teacher (Figure 6-4).

INFORMATION FOR SUBSTITUTE TEACHERS

Name of Substitute _____

Serving For _____ Class _____

Room _____ Key No. _____

Duty _____ Location _____ Time _____

1. Be sure you understand your responsibility for the duty of the teacher for whom you are serving.
2. Locate the Substitute's Folder in the center drawer of the teacher's desk. This folder should contain The Teacher's Guide, Contingency Plan, and Class List.
3. Locate the attendance documents and teacher's plans. IMPORTANT: If there are no teacher's plans, use the Contingency Plan in the folder.
4. Before the students arrive, see the grade leader (or department head). That person's name is listed on the top of The Teacher's Guide to the Substitute.
5. Read The Teacher's Guide to the Substitute carefully. Be familiar with:
   - where and when students report for lunch
   - special arrangements for inclement weather
   - procedures for bus arrival and departure
   - students who have monitor responsibilities
   - students who have pick-up responsibilities
6. Read the Contingency Plan carefully. Be familiar with:
   - the reading groups of the class
   - the mathematics groups of the class
   - students who go to other teachers for special programs
7. Allow five minutes before dismissal times for clean up and getting clothing.
8. Allow all students to use the bathroom before the lunch hour. Send the students in pairs.
9. Students are to be supervised at all times. Good discipline is expected both in the classroom and in the halls.
10. Lunch money is collected on Wednesday morning. Paid lunch costs $3. Reduced lunch costs $1. Some children receive free lunch. Prepare the collection envelope carefully. If the lunch money envelope is not collected by 9:30 a.m., send it to the office with a monitor.
11. Attendance sheets are collected on Friday morning. These sheets must be totaled before they are collected. If you are unfamiliar with the sheet, see the grade leader.
12. Please be sure to lock the classroom door each time you leave the room with the class. When you clock out at 3 p.m., be sure to hang the keys in the cabinet on the correct hook number.
13. If you need help during the day, send a note to the office.

Figure 6-3

SUBSTITUTE'S REPORT TO TEACHER

Substitute's Name _____ Class _____

Absent Teacher's Name _____ Date _____

(Please return this report to the secretary before you leave today.)

Please record a summary of today's program with the class. Include all curriculum areas. Indicate if the content was your plan or the plan the teacher left.

READING State: 1. Group Name 2. Lesson Content 3. Materials Used

MATHEMATICS State: 1. Group Name 2. Lesson Content 3. Materials Used

LANGUAGE ARTS State: 1. Group or Class 2. Lesson Content
3. Materials Used

    Spelling

    Creative Writing

    Mechanics of Writing

    Handwriting

SOCIAL STUDIES State: 1. Group or Class 2. Lesson Content
3. Materials Used

HOMEWORK ASSIGNED

Attendance *Boys* *Girls*
absent A.M.

absent P.M.

COMMENTS

Figure 6-4

Instruct the substitute to leave the report with the secretary before leaving for the day. It is once again the secretary's responsibility to request the report if the substitute teacher does not hand one in. The report is then placed in the regular teacher's letterbox for review upon his or her return to school.

In addition to providing information to the regular teacher, the quality and accuracy of the report provide you with valuable information when faced with a future teacher absence. It is human nature to try harder when you know that you are being evaluated or that a report is expected from you.

The students and the regular teacher all benefit from the efforts of a substitute teacher who attempts to continue the instructional program and record what those efforts were. Even if the substitute teacher was only partially successful, the *trying* attitude is far more effective than an attitude of "Why should I care? The teacher will never know." This will come across in the report, and when there is a choice among available substitutes, the ones who performed best in prior situations would naturally be selected first.

7

HOW TO DEAL
WITH DISCIPLINE

Your day is usually filled with numerous interruptions of varying degrees of importance, with a large number of these interruptions involving a disruptive student. Keep in mind that you should not be the first recourse in attempting to deal with this student; rather, your time and energy should only be reserved for the more serious problems that cannot be resolved by others.

The disruptive child is the single most frustrating element in the teacher's day, so the establishment of a specific process for dealing with this student will offer the teacher some relief and prevent him or her from immediate soliciting your assistance.

MAKE THE TEACHER THE FIRST CONTACT

When a problem arises from any source, whether the teacher, the student, or the parent, the first contact is usually with the teacher. If the teacher brings the problem to you, ask, "Have you spoken with the parent?" If a parent brings a problem to you, ask, "Have you spoken with the teacher?" You should not become involved at this initial stage. The teacher lives with the student during the day and is well aware of the student's actions throughout that time; the parent also lives with that child and is well aware of the child's feelings and actions at home. There are no two people better prepared to discuss the child than the parent and the teacher. Usually, the problem—which is often concerned with a lack of communication—can be resolved at this level.

ESTABLISH A COMMUNICATION LINK WITH THE PARENT

One important outgrowth of the parent/teacher discussion is the understanding that both the parent and the teacher have a mutual interest—the success of the child. An ongoing communication link between the parent and the teacher can help guide the student through a successful school year, so have your teachers use a Daily Report (Figure 7-1) to parents.

DAILY REPORT

Student's Name _____

Class _____ Date _____

E = Excellent	G = Good		F = Fair	P = Poor	U = Unsatisfactory
BEHAVIOR	A.M.	P.M.	WORK	A.M. P.M.	PARENT SIGNATURE
_____	___	___	_____	___ ___	_____
_____	___	___	_____	___ ___	_____
_____	___	___	_____	___ ___	_____

Figure 7-1

The student holds onto the form and is responsible for asking the teacher to fill out the appropriate columns before lunch and at dismissal time. The form is divided into a.m. and p.m. sections to give the child smaller sections of time to remind him- or herself of responsibility for both actions and work. The parent is responsible for asking to see the form each day and for signing in the last column to indicate that the form was seen. If the teacher is absent, the student is responsible for asking the substitute teacher to fill out the form.

The effectiveness of the report is dependent upon the teacher's willingness to complete the evaluation and the parent's continued interest in viewing it on a daily basis. In general, the report helps the youngster remember that he or she is responsible for both work and actions during the school day. When the marks of "fair," "poor," or "unsatisfactory" frequently appear on the form or if the form is no longer effective, the next step in the process is necessary.

INVOLVE GUIDANCE PERSONNEL

The guidance counselor is the next natural resource when the discipline problem may be more severe than originally anticipated. The teacher should refer the student to the guidance counselor, who then sees the teacher to discuss the student and the problem. Generally at this point, two pieces of information prove helpful to the guidance counselor. The first is the Brief Report on Pupil Progress (Figure 7-2), which gives the counselor some insights into the child's behavior.

The second piece of information is an ongoing anecdotal record (Figure 7-3). The notes state exactly what the child said or did in concrete situations, and are devoid of interpretation or the personal reaction of the observer. Anecdotal records are valuable because they help develop a picture of the child's behavior patterns and growth, interests, attitudes, strengths and weaknesses, as well as problems over a period of time.

BRIEF REPORT ON PUPIL PROGRESS

Name _____ Class _____ Room _____ Date _____

Teacher's Name _____

Academic Progress: Reading Score _____   Functioning Level __
                     Mathematics Score _____   Functioning Level __

CHECK THE APPROPRIATE COLUMN:

	Good	Fair	Poor
Ability	____	____	____
Achievement	____	____	____
Attendance	____	____	____
Work Habits	____	____	____
Relationship with Teacher	____	____	____
Relationship with Children	____	____	____
Maturity	____	____	____
Physical Care	____	____	____

CHECK ANY OF THE FOLLOWING THAT APPLY:

_____ aggressive   _____ indifferent   _____ disliked

_____ attention seeker   _____ hostile   _____ neglected

_____ hyperactive   _____ sullen   _____ immature

_____ nervous   _____ withdrawn   _____ isolate

**ADD ANY BRIEF COMMENTS YOU FEEL WOULD HELP REFLECT THIS
CHILD'S CLASSROOM PERFORMANCE:**

_____
_____
_____
_____
_____
_____
_____
_____

**PLEASE RETURN THIS REPORT TO THE GUIDANCE COUNSELOR AS
SOON AS POSSIBLE.**

Figure 7-2

ANECDOTAL RECORD

Student's Name _____

Class _____ Teacher's Name _____

1. Be brief and objective.
2. Be accurate in describing the behavior.
3. Include positive as well as negative incidents.

Date (Month, Day, Year)	Place of Occurrence	Description of the Behavior	Recorder's Signature
_____	_____	_____	_____
_____	_____	_____	_____
_____	_____	_____	_____

Figure 7-3

Anecdotal records consist of concrete evidence and do not rely on memory, so any entry should be recorded as soon as possible after the particular incident. These records are never used to punish or embarrass a student, and should be as objective as possible and free from bias or interpretation.

At this point, let's see the difference between subjective reaction and objective reporting:

- subjective—Johnny deliberately picked up his textbook and hit Tom over the head as hard as he could. Johnny liked doing this. It gave him great pleasure.
- objective— Johnny picked up a textbook and hit Tom over the head. After he had hit Tom, Johnny smiled and returned to his seat.

An anecdotal record includes the date, name of the child, recorder's name, activities engaged in at the time of the incident, and a description of what *actually* happened. No opinions are given.

After the guidance counselor reviews the information supplied by the teacher and his or her own personal discussions with the child, several different alternatives may be considered.

Telephone the Parent

The counselor may decide that a close and constant communication with the parent is necessary as a motivator for the student and as a monitor for the parent. Since many parents work, the telephone can become that important personal and constant communication link. The telephone offers several benefits over the written form of communication: (1) it allows both the counselor and parent an opportunity to express feelings and recent incidents, and (2) it permits immediate response to questions and problems. Specific telephone appointments can be prearranged so that neither the parent nor the counselor are faced with difficulty in reaching each other.

The telephone is also an important communicator between the counselor and any therapist. If a youngster is under the care of an outside individual or agency, it is vital that the therapist who is working with the student communicate with the counselor on a regular basis. Only in this way can the personnel in the school work along with the therapist. In addition, the therapist should be able to receive updated information concerning the student's progress to evaluate the effectiveness of the course of treatment.

At times, the telephone may become an important communication link between the parent and the teacher of the youngster. The parent must fully understand what has happened in school and what has been asked of the child. The telephone can help to promote a close and personal understanding between the parent and the teacher as each works to help the individual student.

In-Person Interview with the Parent

Some situations require a face-to-face meeting with the parent, a need that may be determined by the teacher after the Daily Report has been tried and not proven to be effective. The failure of the Daily Report may be because the parent is not cooperating or because the use of the report is not sufficient to assist the child in working out his or her problems.

In this case, the counselor may meet and speak with the parent to discuss a different course of action for the student. The counselor may want to suggest formal evaluation of the student by the school's psychologist, or an outside agency. These suggestions are delicate and require sensitive handling that can only be accomplished by an in-person interview with the parent. The parent's signature is required for these services, so the forms and their meanings must be explained to the parent.

INVOLVE THE ADMINISTRATOR

As principal, you usually become involved with a particular case at the request of the teacher or the guidance counselor when the parent is uncooperative or unable to accept the suggestions of the professional staff. When a parent does not respond to the request of the teacher or the guidance counselor, a letter or phone call from you may be the necessary action to bring the parent to school. At times, your intervention is necessary to reach a mutually acceptable solution to a current situation between the child and the school. In any case, your intervention should be delayed until all other avenues have been exhausted.

USE FORMAL PROCEDURES

In all cases, the informal procedures previously discussed are used first. Only when those strategies fail are *formal procedures* set into motion.

Letters to Parents

It is usually the teacher who requests formal procedures, beginning with the sending of the appropriate letter (Figures 7-4, 7-5, 7-6, 7-7) to the parent as notification of the student's specific action. The letters are important in documenting the student's unacceptable actions and lay the groundwork when future, more serious action may be taken. When a form letter is sent to a parent, a copy should be kept by the teacher and yourself for future reference. Ask the parent to sign the letter as an indication that he or she has received and read it, and have the teacher keep the signed copy.

BUS SAFETY
The Elementary School
Office of the Principal

Date _____

Re: _____
Student's name

Class _____

Dear _____,

    Your child was reported by the bus driver for unsafe conduct on the bus. We are concerned for the safety of your child as well as the safety of all the other children.

    Please speak with your youngster regarding proper conduct on a bus. If there is no improvement, your child will be deprived of the priviledge of riding the bus.

    Thank you for your cooperation.

Sincerely,

_____
                                          Principal

cc: principal's file
    class teacher

I have read this letter. _____
                                          Parent's Signature

Figure 7-4

LUNCH BEHAVIOR

The Elementary School
Office of the Principal

_____
Date

Re: _____
Student's name

Class _____

Dear _____,

   Your child does not behave properly during the lunch period. If there is no improvement we shall be obliged to ask you to come to school to sit with your child during lunch.

   Your youngster has already been told of the specific violations involved. Please discuss these with your child with a view towards bringing about an improvement.

   Thank you for your cooperation.

                                        Sincerely,

                                        _____
                                                                Principal

cc: principal's file
    class teacher

I have read this letter. _____
                                                     Parent's Signature

Figure 7-5

SCHOOL BEHAVIOR

The Elementary School
Office of the Principal

_____
Date

Re: _____
Student's name

Class _____

Dear _____ ,

Your child does not behave properly in school. If there is no improvement, we shall be obliged to ask you to come to school.

Your youngster has already been told the specific violations involved. Please discuss these with your child with a view toward bringing about an improvement.

Thank you for your cooperation.

Sincerely,

_____
                                    Principal

cc: principal's file
     class teacher

I have read this letter. _____
                                    Parent's Signature

Figure 7-6

SCHOOL PROGRAM BEHAVIOR

The Elementary School
Office of the Principal

Date _____
Re: _____
Student's name
Class _____

Dear _____ ,

    Despite repeated warnings, your child continues to be extremely disruptive during the
_____ program. We are therefore
forced to remove him/her from the program until such time as there is a marked improvement in
attitude and behavior.

    Please speak with your child toward achieving this improvement in attitude and behavior so
that the removal will be of short duration.

                Sincerely,

                _____
                                        Principal

cc: principal's file
    class teacher

I have read this letter. _____
                                          Parent's Signature

Figure 7-7

Suspension

When informal procedures and letters fail to solve the problem, suspension may be the next alternative.

Notification to Parents. Suspension procedures begin with a notification (Figure 7-8) to the parent that a formal interview is necessary. This interview (or pre-suspension hearing) alerts the parent that a serious situation exists.

The Pre-Suspension Hearing. The pre-suspension hearing has two objectives: (1) to inform the parent that this conference is the last step before a formal suspension, and (2) to plan a course of action that will eliminate the need for a suspension.

At the pre-suspension hearing, you, the parent, the class teacher, and the guidance counselor should review all documentation that has been gathered about the student. The documentation should include:

- a record of the meetings between the parent and the teacher
- a copy of the Brief Report on Pupil Progress
- any records of referral for psychological evaluation or work with an outside agency
- the copies of all letters that have been sent to the parent

Invite the parents to openly discuss the problem without the student in attendance. This procedure allows the parent to express any hostile feelings or attitudes that may be targeted at school personnel, the child, or the spouse, so it is often advantageous for the youngster not to hear this part of the discussion. The serious nature of the problem should be fully discussed and explained to the parent, with the parent given ample opportunity to react to the information and discuss his or her point of view.

A specific plan of action should be decided upon and recorded in the notes taken at the hearing. This plan must be agreed upon by both the school personnel and the parent. The youngster is then asked to join the group.

When the student is present, discuss the student's actions with him or her, and encourage the student to state in his or her own words *what* the problem is and *why*. Ask the student for ways to change the specific actions that are causing the problem. The student's suggestions are then related to the plan that has been developed with the school personnel and the parent. At this point, the specific plans may be modified or altered completely. The student must understand and agree to comply with the plan that is finally decided.

A Formal Suspension. When the problem continues to persist following the pre-suspension hearing, a formal suspension is the last alternative. This removes the student from the school for a specific period of time, usually not more than five school days (Figure 7-9). Then conduct a hearing with the parent before the youngster may return to the school. The formal suspension usually requires the superintendent's approval since this action is recorded in the student's permanent file. The suspension should only be *a last resort* when all other steps have been taken and have failed.

The Suspension Hearing. The two objectives of the suspension hearing are: (1) to inform the parent of the serious nature of suspension, and (2) to plan a course of action that will permit the student to return to school. The parent should also be informed that following a

POSSIBLE SUSPENSION NOTIFICATION

The Elementary School
Office of the Principal

_____

Date

Re: _____
Student's name

Class _____

_____

_____

_____

Dear _____ ,

I am very anxious to meet with you to discuss a serious problem that your child, _____
_____ , is having. Would you please come in to see me on _____
at _____ so that we can plan ways to solve this problem.

I must stress the urgency of our arriving at a joint solution so that we may avoid suspension or
other alternatives. If the time or the date is inconvenient, please call the office for another
appointment.

Sincerely,

_____
                                                                              Principal

cc: principal's file
    class teacher

Figure 7-8

SUSPENSION NOTIFICATION

The Elementary School
Office of the Principal

_____

Date

Re: _____
Student's name

Class _____

_____

_____

_____

Dear _____ ,

    I regret that it has become necessary to suspend your child from school from _____ to _____ because of the following action that occurred.

_____

_____

_____

    During this period of suspension, your child should be kept at home during school hours.

    It is important that you meet with me on _____at _____. At that time you will have the opportunity to examine and discuss the relevant facts with all the parties concerned so that we may plan together for your child's return to school. If you want, you may bring two persons who may be attorneys but may act only in the capacity of advisors.

                  Sincerely,

_____
                                       Principal

cc: district superintendent
    principal's file
    guidance counselor
    class teacher

Figure 7-9

third suspension action, the student may be referred to the superintendent for further action and possible permanent removal from the school.

At the suspension hearing, review all documentation concerning the specific reason for the suspension. The student's actions must be of a serious nature that involve the health and well being of the student and/or others in the school. All parties involved with the actions of the student should be present at the hearing, too, as well as the class teacher and the guidance counselor. The procedure of the suspension hearing is the same as the one used at the pre-suspension hearing; the plan that is agreed upon, however, may be more drastic in nature.

Seek Solutions. Finding solutions that will cause a change in attitude and behavior on the student's part is not always an easy task. Some creative thinking about possible alternatives that will fit into the school program may be of great help. In this respect, keep the individual youngster in mind, analyzing his or her strengths and weaknesses, interests, and preferences. It is far more beneficial for all involved to attempt to meet the student's weaknesses through an area of strength and interest than through a traditional approach that may in itself be the sore point that is creating the problem.

For example, the student may rebel in the remedial reading class, but may actually enjoy learning to read using an art content. Some of the solutions selected may require the cooperation of additional school staff, so it is your responsibility to create a type of professional atmosphere among the staff that will encourage the teachers to help each other.

DEVELOP A PLAN

The plan developed and agreed upon may simply offer one alternative or, more usually, contain several different aspects. One possible plan is to develop special programs for the youngster. For example, assign the student to additional periods with the remedial reading teacher, with the resource teacher, or with the art, music or physical education teachers. Base this decision upon the student's interest in these areas and his or her relationship with the particular teacher. Such a plan is of great help if the regular class situation is not comfortable for the student and actually contributes to the problem.

Another plan may include changing the student's class. This is a drastic move and usually not what the student wants. There may be friends in the regular class with whom the students wants to remain, but these friends may be causing the problem. Another factor to consider is the relationship between the regular class teacher and the student. It is possible that the situation has reached a point where the student and the teacher no longer communicate. If the relationship between the two is at a low level, it may be beneficial for both to work with others. It is possible that the personality of another teacher may be better suited to the particular youngster.

Many problems are involved with the decision to change the student's class: (1) the size of the classes, (2) the academic composition of the classes, and (3) the teacher of the other class who does not want another problem. One way to deal with these is to ask the new teacher to select his or her most difficult student and switch the two youngsters. If this move is decided upon, the parents of the children must be informed. Switching the two students will help to maintain the numbers of students in the class but will not necessarily affect the academic composition of the class. The teachers may have to design an instructional program for the student being placed in the class, or may need new materials and a peer help or buddy system. The teachers should be assisted in both receiving the new materials and in developing a suitable instructional system.

The truncated day is still another option, which removes the student from school for the afternoon. The decision to use this approach should be made very carefully because, in essence, the student would receive only three hours of instruction each day—a loss of about forty percent each day. It would appear ludicrous to try to help the child to improve academically by offering him or her fewer hours of instruction. On the other hand, if the expectation that he or she may go home at lunch time enables the student to fully participate and perform during the morning hours, far more may be achieved than was formerly in a whole-day program.

This drastic plan usually requires the written consent of the parent and the approval of the superintendent (Figure 7-10). The truncated day plan is set for a specific period of time, usually one month or 20 to 30 school days. However, this option may be renewed at the end of the period of time if it is considered advisable.

The student who benefits most from the truncated day plan is one who cannot sustain a positive attitude and good behavior for a five-hour period of time. This student may be able to demonstrate better self-control if he or she knows that a shorter period of time is required. However, students have different needs and the time factor may not be the important point for all youngsters. Some children lose self-control in particular situations or as a result of a problem at home; for these youngsters, a truncated day may not be effective.

Another type of partial instructional program that may be more effective involves an informal agreement between the parent and the school personnel, requiring the cooperation of the parent and a desire to be available whenever the child has a problem. The student attends school for the whole day, but at any time that the youngster loses his or her self-control, the child is sent to the office and the parent is called to school to take the child home. This request may be made at any time of day—be it 9:30 in the morning or 2:15 in the afternoon. The advantage of this plan is that a specific and immediate action—removal—results from a specific unacceptable action of the child; thus, direct consequence is a valuable learning tool. It is especially helpful with younger children who do not always understand what is appropriate and inappropriate behavior. The major disadvantage to this plan, of course, is the possible unavailability of the parent during working hours.

IMPLEMENT A BEHAVIOR MODIFICATION PROGRAM

A modification program depends completely on the cooperation of the parent. This plan is similar to the Daily Report previously discussed, but includes a reward system that the parent must agree to follow.

Each "good" or "excellent" mark earned by the student is worth a reward. The particular reward and its value depends upon the child's age, interests, and needs. For example, two "goods" or "excellents" may warrant a quarter. The child may prefer to save up five to eight "goods" and "excellents" for a special treat, such as a movie or a visit to the zoo. Or, perhaps the student wants to accumulate thirty to fifty "goods" or "excellents" to get a new bicycle. The particular reward system is decided upon when the behavior

TRUNCATED-DAY NOTIFICATION

The School District
Office of the Supertindent

Date _____

School _____

Re: _____
      student's name

To: District Superintendent _____,

   I am requesting that my child _____ of class _____,
date of birth _____, attend school from _____ to
_____, no less than three hours of instruction, beginning
_____ and terminating _____.

   I understand that I am responsible for transportation from school to home and for supervision after dismissal as indicated above.

_____
Parent or guardian

_____
Address

- -

TO BE COMPLETED BY THE PRINCIPAL

Reason for the request: (documentation must be attached, when appropriate)

Submitted by: _____
                  Principal

Approved by: _____
                District Superintendent

Figure 7-10

modification program is designed with school personnel. It is, of course, vital that the parent keep the promise of the rewards that are offered.

Behavior modification follows a particular psychology that actions can be modified by the subject's desire to achieve something of value. Some subjects respond to such intrinsic values as good marks or praise. Others rely more heavily on such extrinsic rewards as money or special events. In this type of program, only the positive "good" and "excellent" marks are noted and commented upon. Neither the parent nor the teacher reacts to the "fair," "poor," or "unsatisfactory" marks on the Daily Report. In line with this concept, no attention is drawn to negative behavior, which is often a difficult task for the teacher and the parent but essential to the development of the child. Rather than call the student to order, the teacher should acknowledge and praise the positive actions of the particular student or other students. Likewise, rather than call attention to a number of "fair," "poor" or "unsatisfactory" marks on the Daily Record, the parent should count the "goods" and "excellents" and offer a suitable reward. The student should gradually begin to understand that his or her positive behavior is worth more than the attention being offered for the negative behavior.

DEAL WITH ANGER AND FRUSTRATION

Many students get angry for reasons that are seldom heard, and feel they are not listened to or are wrongly accused of actions. Unfortunately, many teachers look to the troubled student as the cause of the disruption rather than find the real cause. You can play a vital role in allowing the student a place to express his or her anger and talk about it. Very often, what is needed by the troubled student is a person with whom the student feels safe, and who will listen without placing a punishment on the student's actions.

If a problem arises, the student may tell the teacher that he or she wants to see the principal. Having a place to go to allows the troubled student to leave the class and the problem and to go speak with someone who will allow him or her to speak about the problem. If you are not available, just sitting quietly outside the classroom may have a very calming effect on the troubled student.

Your gentle touch can develop into a powerful bond, with the student realizing that someone *does* care. The student's desire to please this someone may become a driving force that just might be what he or she needs. Keep this communication link open and available to the student; it is a safety valve that may prevent aggressive actions on the student's part. You must develop a position of support, interest and sympathy, so that as the student's confidence develops, he or she may begin to accept your suggestions.

PREVENT DISCIPLINE PROBLEMS

Of course, the best cure for any problem is prevention. Good guidance techniques in the school can assist all of the school personnel in preventing possible problems.

Behavior Symptoms

The first principle of good guidance techniques is to be aware of the clues in students' behavior that signal a possible problem.

1. aggressive behavior symptoms
   a. The child refuses to obey rules and resists authority.
   b. The child destroys the property of classmates and the school.
   c. The child appears to enjoy hurting other children.
   d. The child bullies or teases classmates.
   e. The child follows his or her own wishes without regard for others.
   f. The child exhibits stubborn behavior with temper tantrums.
   g. The child is often involved in fighting and quarrelling.
   h. The child appears to crave risk and adventure.
   i. The child often lies rather than tell the truth.
   j. The child takes things that do not belong to him or her.
   k. The child appears to want to injure him- or herself or others.

2. withdrawn behavior symptoms
   a. The child is excessively shy, timid and quiet.
   b. The child frequently lapses into daydreams.
   c. The child appears tense and is usually tearful.
   d. The child appears unhappy and worried.
   e. The child usually prefers to sit alone.
   f. The child refuses to take part in group activities.
   g. The child does not resist attacks by peers.
   h. The child follows other children from a distance.

3. learning and physical problems
   a. The child has severe learning difficulties.
   b. The child does not achieve despite good potential.
   c. The child does not meet the developmental expectation for his or her age in language development, motor skills, spacial concepts, group participation, and speech patterns.

4. home problems
   a. The child appears to be neglected by the parent.
   b. The child has little or no supervision after school.
   c. The child is frequently absent or late.
   d. The child appears to be physically ill or dirty or in need of medical or dental care.

Suggestions

Disruptive youngsters can destroy a teacher's carefully formulated plans and happy disposition. Although there are many types of disruptive behavior and various causes for that behavior, there is no magical cure. There are, however, suggestions that may work well with some students.

1. General Suggestions
   a. Do not embarrass a child by talking about him or her in front of others.
   b. Set and reinforce rules and limits. Keep the rules simple and involve the students in identifying them.
   c. Find time to speak informally with the student about non-school matters.

    d. Avoid reacting to misbehavior with anger and a loss of professional dignity.

    e. Learn about both the cultural and individual backgrounds of the student to help you understand any problems.

    f. Get to know the parents of the child. Develop a communication link in writing or by telephone. Make both positive and negative comments about the child.

    g. Handle each individual student differently. Students do not all require the same behavior reminder signal.

    h. Find something to praise about every child.

    i. Be professional. Do not hold a grudge or insist upon an apology.

    j. Avoid creating situations that will trigger misbehavior. Sometimes it is better to look the other way.

    k. Be alert to symptoms of problems and try to gain the child's confidence and support before incidents occur.

    l. Be "in charge" at all times no matter what task both you and the students are involved with.

2. Specific Suggestions

    a. Do not react to obscene language with shock or disgust. What is mumbled should not be noted. What is stated aloud should be discussed quietly and privately with the child.

    b. Isolate the over-aggressive child. Change the child's seat whenever the unacceptable behavior erupts.

    c. Give a restless child specific reasons to leave his or her seat, such as to sharpen pencils or to clean the chalkboard.

    d. Share the interests and/or hobbies of the child and provide materials and activities that will further this interest.

    e. Do not scold a child in front of others. Let time pass and tempers cool before speaking with the child privately.

    f. Recognize a child's anger and tell him or her that you understand and would like to help.

    g. Try to give some special attention to the child each day by saying something nice, or just reaching out to pat a shoulder.

    h. Set personal goals with the child and make them very short range, such as for an hour or for the morning.

Activities

The more that is known about each child, the better able the professional is to help the child. Youngsters reveal their attitudes, wants, desires, fears, hopes, and dreams in many ways. Some of the following guidance techniques form a broader picture about individual children.

1. Turnabout—A student's expectations and attitudes about others can be revealed by asking the child to pretend he or she is someone else.

If I were my Father, _____.

If I were my Mother, _____.

If I were the teacher, _____.

If I were my brother, _____.

If I were my sister, _____.

If I were the oldest child, _____.

If I were the youngest child, _____.

2. Incomplete Sentences—The responses to incomplete sentences often offer clues to behavior.

I feel happy when _____.

I feel proud when _____.

I feel ashamed when _____.

I feel frightened when _____.

I was happiest when _____.

My worst worry is _____.

I feel that school _____.

People think that I _____.

The thing I like least is _____.

The thing I like most is _____.

My friends are _____.

3. Suggestion Box/Complaint Box/Letters-to-the-Teacher Box—Some children are unable to speak about what is most troubling to them. They can, however, put something in writing. Notes that are signed should be answered privately. Notes that are not signed should be discussed with the class or a group of youngsters to find possible answers for the problems.

4. Time Schedules—Understanding how children use their time outside of school is extremely useful in understanding an individual child's attitude and behavior.

5. Bibliotherapy—Reading a book about a youngster who has similar problems may be very helpful to a troubled child. The troubled youngster may identify with the hero or heroine in the story or find out, at the very least, that others may have similar problems. The child may then be able to make a better adjustment to his or her own problems.

MAKE HAPPYGRAMS

The positive approach is always more beneficial than the negative. It is wise for the teacher to go out of his or her way to praise a child. If this praise can be in writing so that it can be brought home for the parent to see and, perhaps save, the desire to gain more praise usually results. The use of the HappyGram (Figure 7-11) is an easy way for the teacher to give praise and to personalize it for the student.

HappyGram

_____
date

To: _____
Fr: _____

Your child, _____, has demonstrated
outstanding

_____ work   _____ behavior   _____ attitude
_____ effort   _____ cooperation   _____ other

The child is to be complimented!

Figure 7-11

MAKE COMPLIMENT CALLS

All too often, a parent is called to report a negative activity or action of the youngster; never for positive comments about the child. Making compliment calls can be a very rewarding experience for you for two reasons: (1) the parent is delighted to hear something good about his or her child, and (2) the parent will usually react by saying how very nice of you to take the time to call. Parents are left with the impression that the principal really cares about the children.

It is easier to find the time to make the calls if it is prearranged, so set a particular day and time aside on your calendar each week. (That particular time and day may change each week depending upon your schedule.) Ask each teacher to identify one different child each week whose parent should receive a compliment call. You might keep a list of the names and classes of the youngsters who have received compliment calls and post that list in a prominent place.

ESTABLISHING A FLEXIBLE SCHOOL STRUCTURE

The most successful schools are ones in which the staff is not afraid to try new ideas and techniques, an attitude developed by your flexibility. Teachers are extremely creative and will develop some very interesting approaches if they feel secure about what you think of them and if they trust you.

Just as the teacher is always "in charge" of the classroom, you are "in charge" of the school. A flexible school structure is one in which the teachers and staff will come to you with problems and concerns for which they seek advice, ideas that are new and challenging to them, and news about successes as well as reports of failures. Your role is to react to and guide the staff with respect and a genuine interest in their efforts to help the youngsters.

8

HOW TO COMMUNICATE EFFECTIVELY

Communication is the key to successful administration because what is *said* has little meaning if it is not *heard* by the people to whom it is important. In turn, an overflow of communication can have a numbing effect since countless messages of little importance will have no effect on staff. Instead, the staff will probably not even read written communications.

What is too much and how much is too little become the problem. Keeping the school personnel informed is important, but daily memos can become a bore.

DETERMINE WHEN TO USE WHAT

Information must first be sorted into four theoretical piles: (1) information that is of immediate importance, (2) information that should be communicated but has no deadline, (3) information that is of little importance and should not be communicated, and (4) information that is of importance to selected personnel.

These theoretical piles are sorted when reading the mail and when talking on the telephone.

Information of immediate importance is usually the kind of communication that has a deadline. This includes contests, position vacancies, a visiting group that will perform, a conference that will take place in the near future, an emergency situation that requires an extra effort, and a report that has an immediate deadline.

Information that requires communication but has no definite deadline includes new resources that have arrived at the school, a new procedure that requires discussion, a new curriculum bulletin that must be reviewed, a long-term project, and a forthcoming event such as a testing period.

Information that is of little importance and should probably not be communicated includes announcements of travel groups during the school term, advertisements for items that are outside of the school's field of reference (such as trips that are too far away), and advertisements for items that should not be endorsed by the school.

Information that is of importance to selected personnel includes brochures for particular resources, conferences on particular topics, and requests for information in a specialized field.

Of the various forms of communication available, you must consider the one most suitable to each piece of information. The importance of the information and the speed with which it should reach significant people will determine which communicator is best suited to each piece of information.

The Bulletin Board

The office bulletin board can become a powerful communicator if it is well organized. Topic headings on different sections of the bulletin board will enable you to post particular items in certain places. One such heading should be "Read Now." This communicates to the staff an item of immediate importance that should be read before leaving the office in the morning. The item posted in this section is one that must be known by the staff that day: a reminder that the gym may not be used today because primary elections are taking place, a reminder that a budget report is due, or a reminder that a conference or workshop is to be held that day. Post an organization sheet with the notice and request that each teacher initial it after he or she has read the notice. You can then look at the organization sheet and find which persons have not initialed and therefore have not read the notice. The notice can then be sent to those persons to be read and initialed after classes have begun.

A second heading might read, "Special Programs." These items would announce particular television or radio programs that may be of interest to the staff or the students, courses being offered to students in a wide variety of areas, or the formation of a scout troop or 4-H Club. These announcements are meant to be read and transmitted by the staff to the students.

A third heading for the office bulletin board might be, "Professional Courses." These announcements might include university courses offered for the fall, spring or summer, or in-service courses currently soliciting participants.

A fourth heading would state, "Vacancies." Items posted under this heading might include all advertised vacancies for school positions or after-school openings.

All items on the office bulletin board should be updated frequently. The bulletin board should never become overcrowded with papers, as this will diminish its effectiveness as a communicator. If each item is dated, it is easy to remove those that are no longer current.

Hold the school staff responsible for reading the office bulletin board daily. The notices are for their information, so expect them to know what has been posted. Rather than being sent to the classroom, notices that are not of immediate importance can be placed in the teacher's letterbox for signature and returned to your letterbox.

The Grade Leader

Assign a leader to each grade and then use this person as a communicator with the school staff. Selection of the grade leader is an important consideration, as this person should have experience teaching the grade and have knowledge of procedures and school policy. The person should also be highly regarded by the others of the grade and be considered a leader by them. If possible, the grade leader should also be a person who strongly supports you as principal, transmitting all messages with *your* original intent and not his or her own interpretation.

Grade leaders' meetings should be held each month. Prepare an agenda for the grade leader and supply him or her with enough copies for the other members of the grade. During the grade leaders' meetings, discuss and clarify the items on the agenda (Figure 8-1). For example, you may request a response from the grade on what topics would be of interest to the school staff for faculty conferences to be conducted during the year.

Other items of interest to the grade might include announcements of contests, schoolwide programs such as a Science Fair, and new personnel in the school. Each grade leaders' meeting should include a curriculum item of focus. This curriculum item, such as writing, should be discussed by the grade for the purpose of sharing ideas.

Ask each grade to hold a meeting among its members and to prepare a written report of the discussion of the agenda items. The written report should be due in your office by the last day of the month. Grades that have not sent this report by the last week of the month should receive a memo reminding them that the report is due soon.

The grade leaders' meeting can be held at any time of the day that is convenient to both you and the teachers who represent each grade. If no other time is available, try the lunch hour. Even though time is limited during the lunch hour, it may be the only time frame possible. If meetings are held during lunch, be sure to have coffee and tea and perhaps some cookies available for the staff, with everyone bringing his or her own lunch.

The Memo

The memo is intended for a short message with an immediate need. In some cases, the message relates a specific piece of information, such as a parent has made an appointment to see the teacher at a particular time. In other cases, the memo requests that the teacher see you or another particular person, such as the secretary, to resolve a problem or answer a question. The memo may also make a direct request of the staff member to send a report that is overdue, or to communicate with others about a special event.

The memo (Figure 8-2) is a personal communication that can also be used to begin a process of inquiry or improvement for a particular staff member. It is the first gentle touch before the formal written letter, which will be placed in the staff member's file.

The Formal Letter

The formal letter, of either a positive or a negative nature, is intended for inclusion in the teacher's file. As such, the letter becomes a part of the teacher's permanent record in the school.

The letter may commend the teacher for a particular effort that was made, such as coordinating an art exhibit which was viewed by the community. The letter (Figure 8-3) may also be used to note a staff member's action that was beyond the activities of the normal school day, such as attending a Parent Association meeting.

AGENDA OF GRADE LEADERS' MEETING

The Elementary School
Office of the Principal

February Grade Leaders' Meeting
Wednesday, February 2, 19XX

Agenda

1. Curriculum Focus—Mathematics

   • strategies for instruction
   • teacher-directed lessons
   • small group skill instruction

2. Attendance Books

   • The attendance books of only selected teachers will be collected this month. When notified, please send your attendance book to the office on February 18.
   • All attendance books will be collected on April 15 and June 17.

3. New Programs

   • All-day kindergarten
   • Special education classes for language handicapped students ages 3-5 (known as ECLC I)
   • School program modifications
     —combination of the media center with the primary media center
     —teacher review of materials in the Teacher Center, Room 217
     —modification of the kindergarten time schedule

4. Report Requested

   • For grades 1-6 students who appear to be experiencing difficulty with reading, please send their names to the office by 3 P.M. February 18.

5. Contests

   PAL—Illustrated Poetry Contest
        Theme—My Favorite Pastime
        Contest deadline—March 25, 19XX.
        Please send all entries to the office.

   AAA—Safety Poster Contest
        Theme—Safety While Crossing the Street
        Contest deadline—February 25, 19XX.
        Please send all entries to the office.

Figure 8-1

MEMO

Office of the Principal

TO: Mrs. Rice   10/13/XX
RE: Room appearance

Please see me on Monday, October 17 at 8:30 A.M. to discuss ways in which I can assist you to make your classroom a more attractive and effective learning environment.

Thank you.

Figure 8-2

LETTER OF PRAISE

The Elementary School
Office of the Principal

September 23, 19XX

Carol Ingber
Teacher, Class 5, Room 203

Dear Mrs. Ingber,

On Tuesday evening, September 20, after a long and difficult day, you attended a meeting of the Parent Association of The Elementary School. You made yourself available to the parents both during the meeting and afterwards at the coffee and cake social.

This type of activity contributes to the public relations image of the school. It gave the parents of the community an opportunity to meet you and speak with you. You have helped us to impress the parents with our outstanding programs and staff.

Thank you for your efforts.

Sincerely,

Carol James, Principal

I have read this letter and understand
that it will be placed in my file.

_____
        Teacher's signature

cc: Mrs. Ingber

Figure 8-3

The letter (Figure 8-4) may also be of a negative nature. It may document an action, or lack of action, on the part of the teacher. A letter of this nature should usually be the last step in a series of actions that you have undertaken.

LETTER RE: LACK OF ACTION

The Elementary School
Office of the Principal

December 9, 19XX

Elizabeth Rice
Teacher, Class 4, Room 207

Dear Mrs. Rice,

We have met several times for the purpose of improving the appearance of your classroom. Beginning on October 17, mutual plans were established for specific ways in which you could better organize and maintain your classroom both to improve its general appearance and effectiveness as a learning environment. We met twice again on November 3 and November 17 following planned visits to review the improvements.

Despite these meetings, plans and visits, I find no improvement in either the appearance or organization of your classroom. The students in your class are learning habits of disorder both for their own learning process as well as for school property.

This situation cannot continue. Your classroom must show a marked improvement as outlined in our discussion of October 17 or I will be forced to take further action. If you no longer have a copy of the notes of our October 17 meeting, an additional copy may be obtained from the secretary.

I sincerely hope that you will be able to take the necessary actions to make your room acceptable so that further action on my part will not be necessary.

Sincerely,

Carol James, Principal

I have read this letter and understand
that it will be placed in my file.

_____
      Teacher's signature

cc: Mrs. Rice

Figure 8-4

Secure the teacher's signature before the letter is placed in the teacher's file. The signature only shows that the teacher has read the letter and has received a copy; it does not document that the teacher agrees with the letter.

If the teacher refuses to sign the letter, an observer (usually the secretary) may sign the letter to document that the teacher has received the letter and read it.

A Program Liaison

School programs that involve particular students or cross over grade levels should be coordinated by a particular person. It is far easier to communicate with one person who probably will have the information you require than with a variety of people.

The program liaison is responsible for communicating your directions to all other persons involved. The program liaison is also responsible for such administrative details as reminders and calendar changes that are involved with the program.

The person selected as program liaison should be well organized and efficient as well as thoroughly familiar with the program. A written set of directions concerned with the program should be given to all involved personnel. The liaison can then perform the daily or weekly tasks concerned with program maintenance.

Programs that require a liaison might include:

- reminders for weekly lunch, yard, and bus duty
- update for students involved in funded programs
- rotation of students in special area programs
- notification of due dates for contests
- verification of accuracy with attendance data
- accurate listing of students involved in released time for attendance at religious school
- after-school recreation or student-help programs
- procedures to be followed during the lunch program
- receiving and returning available gym equipment
- community speakers for classrooms or assembly programs
- club or special interest programs

Reminder of Weekly Lunch, Yard, Bus Duty. Each Monday morning a written notice (Figure 8-5) should be placed in the letterboxes of those teachers who are responsible for duty that week. The notice should include the place to report, the time to report, the time to leave, and the responsibility for maintaining student behavior.

Update for Students Involved in Funded Programs. When a student is discharged, place the name in the liaison's letterbox and check this name against the master list of students who are receiving services from funded programs. Write a notation of the date and discharge next to the student's name. In addition, when new students who are screened are placed in a funded program, place the name, the program, and the schedule in the liaison's letterbox. Add this student's name, under the appropriate class, to the existing list of students receiving services, and complete the program schedule and test scores.

GOOD MORNING

_____
(teacher's name)
You have the following duty this week of

_____
(date)

Check one:

_____ yard   from   8:30- 8:45 outdoors/gym
_____ lunch   from 11:55-12:55 cafeteria
_____ bus   from   8:30- 8:45 exit 3

Thank you for your help in maintaining the health
and safety of our students.

Figure 8-5

Rotation of Students in Special Area Programs. Students in the special arts program might rotate areas every six weeks, following this sample pattern:

art students go to drama class

drama students go to music class

music students go to voice class

voice students go to art class

The dates of transfer of the students to new classes are:

October 18   February 21

November 29   April 4

January 10   May 16

The liaison is to notify each class teacher and special arts teacher of the date of transfer and the names of the new students in the class. The notification (Figure 8-6) should be sent on the Friday before the Monday when the change is to take place.

NOTIFICATION OF ROTATED STUDENTS

Special arts program areas will change on Monday, _____.
Please expect the following students who have just completed the
_____ area.

_____
_____
_____

Figure 8-6

Notification of Due Dates for Contests. Have the liaison notify (Figure 8-7) teachers of the due dates for entries for contests at least five days before the contest entries are due to allow time to receive and mail the entries.

CONTEST DUE DATES

Entries for the _____contest
are due in Room _____on _____,
so that they may be checked and mailed before the due date of
_____.

Figure 8-7

Verification of Accuracy with Attendance Data. Attendance records should be collected and checked each month. The liaison should notify (Figure 8-8) teachers to send attendance records on the Monday nearest to the fifteenth of each month.

ATTENDANCE DATA ACCURACY

Attendance records are collected each month. Please send your records to
Room _____on Monday, _____at 9 A.M. They will be returned by
3 P.M. that day.

Figure 8-8

Students Attending Released Time Religious Instructional Programs. The liaison should ask the teachers every second week if there has been a change in the students who are involved in the released time religious instructional programs. (Figure 8-9.)

RELEASED TIME

Please indicate any additions or deletions of students who attend the released time for religious instruction.

Students to be deleted:

Students to be added:

Teacher _____ Class _____

Figure 8-9

After-school Recreation or Student-help Programs. Ask the liaison to maintain a class listing of students who attend the after-school programs. Request from teachers once a month an updated number of students who attend the program (Figure 8-10).

AFTER-SCHOOL PROGRAMS

Please ask students if they attend the after-school programs. Record the number of students who attend.

Teacher _____ Class _____
No. attending _____

Figure 8-10

Procedures to Be Followed During the Lunch Programs. The liaison should monitor the following procedures sent to all teachers and report to you any problems or lack of conformance.

1. No class is to arrive before the second bell.
2. Students are to line up outside the cafeteria.
3. Students are to take appropriate seats.
4. First and second grade teachers are to seat students.
5. Students are to be called by tables for lunch.
6. Students will be called by tables to empty trays.
7. Students will be called by tables to line up for:
   recess in the yard
   return to class
   pick up by first and second grade teachers

Receiving and Returning Gym Equipment. A master list (Figure 8-11) of available gym equipment is to be kept by each grade leader. Requests for equipment are to be made by the individual teacher and checked off and dated on the list. The liaison should collect the lists every two weeks and check the current listing against the actual available equipment. Any missing equipment should be reported to you.

AVAILABLE GYM EQUIPMENT				
Item	Number	Borrowed by	Number	Date
basketballs	10			
volleyballs	7			
softballs	8			
bats	5			
gloves	10			
Indian clubs	12			
jump ropes	12			
large balls	10			
ring toss	5			
small balls	12			
badminton sets	5			

Figure 8-11

Community Speakers for Classrooms or Assembly Programs. The liaison should send a letter home with each student asking for community speakers who would be of interest to the youngsters. Such speakers may be from any profession or occupation or may have an interesting hobby or talent. The liaison collects the names, contact addresses, and topics, and then meets with you to discuss appropriate use of the talent pool.

Club or Special Interest Programs. The liaison requests (Figure 8-12) from each teacher the topic for a club or special interest program, and discusses with you the list of topics. The liaison then asks each student to state his or her first and second choices for a club or special interest program.

CLUB OR SPECIAL PROGRAM REQUEST

We want to continue our Special Interest/Club Program. Please indicate a topic that you would like to conduct that would be of interest to students.

Teacher _____ Class _____
Topic _____
_____

Figure 8-12

HUMANIZE STAFF RELATIONS

Regardless of age or gender, you will find yourself at various times in the roles of parent, sibling, friend, religious counselor, analyst, medic, advisor, marriage counselor, financial advisor, travel consultant, teacher, supervisor, secretary, babysitter, bus driver, repairer, and on and on. The nature of your position is direct responsibility for everything that is involved with the school and school life. Your day is filled with people who are important to you and for whom you are of paramount importance. To be effective, you must be a good communicator, but of equal importance is your facilitating the needs and efforts of others to communicate with you.

Because of the length of time involved in close relationships, you become a natural ear for listening and a shoulder for leaning. This need is perhaps one born of tradition, or perhaps because the work of the school is closely involved with children. It has come to be an expected part of your job as principal. The effective principal communicates three attitudes to all populations—including staff, parents, the community and students—with which you are involved. These attitudes are (1) the time to listen, (2) the interest in listening, and (3) the desire to help.

This reaching out to people who have such diverse needs is well worth your time and effort. Often, it is nothing more than a good morning smile or an extended hand. Sometimes a question about the health or well being of a loved one is all that is necessary. On other occasions, time will have to be set aside to just listen, or a teacher will have to be released at perhaps an inopportune time. Extending this time and effort will help build your image of trust and caring. Others will then be more likely to respond to you with loyalty, commitment, and sincerity.

Make Administrative Assignments

Teachers can be of tremendous assistance in helping you monitor a myriad of administrative details as well as certain aspects of the curriculum and instructional programs, within the school. This assistance is accomplished by making administrative assignments. These assignments should be spread among a large number of teachers so that no one teacher is overburdened and as large a number of teachers as possible feel responsible for something outside of their particular classroom.

The monitoring of students and providing for their safety and well being when they are outside of their classrooms is a professional responsibility. Whether or not the teacher must be in physical control or just "in charge" will depend upon the provisions of individual schools and districts.

Duty schedules should include all situations that occur during school hours when students are not directly supervised by the class teacher. Some of these activities include early morning lineup, bus arrival and departure, lunch hour, recess, and dismissal.

Consider several points when creating duty schedules:

1. Avoid giving teachers the same type of duty each time unless there is no other possibility.

2. Equalize the number of times each teacher will have duty during the year. Fairly distribute duty so that no one or few teachers suffer while others carry a much lighter load. Duty is not a punishment you give to teachers; it is a professional responsibility. If it is impossible to equally distribute duty assignments for the year, keep a

record of those who had additional duties and try to give those people fewer duties the following year.

3. Count the number of days in a duty assignment. Whether the duty is a week's term or a one-day-a-week assignment for a longer period of time, consider the number of holidays in that assignment. A week's lunch duty during the week when Thanksgiving occurs is very different from a week's lunch duty in which there are no holidays. When additional duty must be assigned, those who served during a holiday week may be considered.

4. If your district is one in which changes may occur in February, complete the duty schedule for the fall semester only. Changes in the organization can then be included in the spring duty schedule.

5. Publish a complete duty schedule (Figure 8-13) that includes all types of duty for all of the staff. Distribute the schedule at the beginning of the school year. Allow the teachers to compare their duty responsibilities with the others on the staff to observe the equality of the assignments.

6. Instruct teachers to note duty assignments in their plans for the week.

The Elementary School
Duty Schedule - Fall 1983

Week of	Bus Arrival 8:30-8:45 Exit 3	Morning Line 8:30-8:45 Outdoors/Gym	Lunch Hour 11:55-12:55 Cafeteria	Bus Dismissal 2:55-3:15 Auditorium
9/7	Kames	Ebbman	Moster	Ingber
9/12	Carlson	Romero	Razor	Singer
9/19	Linder	Turns	Budner	Spano
9/26	Rice	Windner	Valesco	Rosner
10/3	Lieb	Fischer	Karner	Windly
10/10	Prusser	Feramo	Weltner	Hames
10/17	Ingber	Kames	Ebbman	Moster
10/24	Singer	Carlson	Romero	Razor
10/31	Spano	Linder	Turns	Budner
11/7	Rosner	Rice	Windner	Valesco
11/14	Windly	Lieb	Fischer	Karner
11/21	Hames	Prusser	Feramo	Weltner
11/28	Moster	Ingber	Kames	Ebbman
12/5	Razor	Singer	Carlson	Romero
12/12	Budner	Spano	Linder	Turns
12/19	Valesco	Rosner	Rice	Windner
12/26	Karner	Windly	Lieb	Fischer
1/2	Weltner	Hames	Prusser	Feramo
1/9	Ebbman	Moster	Ingber	Kames

Figure 8-13

PROVIDE FOR YOUR ABSENCE

If there is no assistant principal in the school, your absence may create a situation in which no one is in charge. Usually, this is not a problem. But for those few isolated occasions when there is a need for someone to make a decision, it is wise to plan ahead.

Designating your alternates can be done in several different ways. Teachers without class responsibilities who have a record of long standing in the building may be the best first candidates. Such personnel may be administrative assistants, resource teachers, or support personnel. (Each district gives a different title to this type of support position.)

Where no support personnel exist, or as second and third alternates, select teachers with seniority. Usually the list of alternates begins with the most senior teacher in the building.

Post this list of alternates in the office in a prominant place. It leads to staff security and stability.

SELECT A TESTING COORDINATOR

Selecting a teacher to serve as testing coordinator may go a long way towards relieving you of mundane chores. The testing coordinator should be an individual who is concerned with detail and who is able to read and interpret directions well. Some of the responsibilities of a testing coordinator include:

- counting tests that arrive in the building
- reporting to you any missing tests
- distributing the tests to teachers
- writing directions to teachers for administering the tests
- writing instructions to teachers for collecting the tests
- counting and checking test sets received after the testing period
- collecting and reporting to you the names of absentees
- preparing the tests for shipping
- ordering tests for the next testing period

You, of course, are responsible for the administration of the testing procedure. Consult with the testing coordinator and review any directions and instructions to teachers before tests are distributed. In general, it takes less time to review the work of the coordinator than to write the instructions yourself. The work of testing coordinator is a very important job, so you should be very careful to select someone in whom there is confidence. If possible, additional released time should be allocated to this person to compensate for the extra effort extended in the many details necessary for completing a successful testing period.

SELECT A SCHOOL TREASURER

The school treasurer should also be someone in whom you have complete trust. This person should be good with figures and, if possible, have some bookkeeping or accounting background. Some of the responsibilities of a school treasurer include:

- accounting for funds allocated
- recording lunch money collected
- accounting for funds spent
- writing checks for bills
- monitoring funds received from donations
- keeping an updated balance
- reporting to you concerning the state of the school's financial situation

Selecting the school treasurer is an important consideration because your reputation and the financial condition of the school may well depend upon this person's ability. Make the decision carefully and reward the treasurer's efforts with extra released time, if possible.

PINPOINT RESPONSIBILITY FOR COLLECTIONS

Schools are often asked to collect money for different philanthropic organizations, such as the Red Cross. Place these drives in the hands of a particular teacher, who has the responsibilities of:

- informing teachers of the collection period
- designing a collection method
- motivating teachers and students to contribute
- collecting the funds
- counting and sending the funds to the appropriate agency
- reporting to you about the success of the drive
- posting a notice to teachers and students about the results

ASSIGN A DIRECTOR OF SCHOOL MONITORS

School monitors can be of tremendous assistance to the running of a school building. Traditionally, they lead younger students to the classrooms, help teachers of younger students with classroom chores, assist students to cross the school streets safely, hold doors for classes during entrance and dismissal times as well as during fire drills, and assist with the audio-visual equipment during assemblies.

School monitors can also be a large headache for a school if the youngsters involved do not do an effective job. At times, an ineffectual monitor is a greater bother than no monitor at all. This is why the selection of a director of school monitors is very important to the efficient and effective work of the monitors' squad. The person selected should relate well to students and be able to command their respect. He or she should also be a good manager and be able to revise schedules and assignments as the need arises.

COLLECT TEACHERS' PLANS

If teachers' plans are collected on a regularly scheduled basis, it is helpful to have those plans collected for you. Principals should collect only those plans which he or she has the time to thoroughly review and comment upon. If teachers believe that their plans are not read, their efforts in preparing them will suffer.

Try to monitor teachers' plans without collecting them weekly. Divide the grades of the school into weeks, and collect plans on a three-week basis from particular grades. At that time, review the plans of the teacher for a three-week period. This can have a very beneficial effect if the plans are reviewed with consideration for continuity and progression of instruction.

The teacher in charge of collecting teachers' plans can be given a schedule for collection (Figure 8-14). Have the plans of particular grades collected each Monday morning. The schedule is returned to you with the collected plans. That schedule can then be returned to the collecting teacher each Monday morning as a reminder.

SCHEDULE FOR COLLECTING TEACHERS' PLANS

Grades K, 1, 2	Grades 3, 4	Grades 5, 6 and Special Teachers
9/7, 9/28, 10/19,	9/14, 10/5, 10/26	9/21, 10/12, 11/2,
11/9, 11/30, 12/21,	11/16, 12/7, 1/4,	11/23, 12/14, 1/11,
1/18, 2/8, 3/1,	1/25, 2/15, 3/8,	2/1, 2/22, 3/15,
3/22, 4/19, 5/10,	3/29, 4/26, 5/17,	4/5, 5/3, 5/24, 6/14.
6/1.	6/7.	

Figure 8-14

PROVIDE FOR COMPOSITION COLLECTION

If you want to monitor the creative writing efforts of the students, collect compositions on a regularly scheduled basis. Teachers should know in advance that compositions will be collected and what the requirements for the compositions are. A schedule for composition collection (Figure 8-15) should be given to the teacher in charge of their collection. These compositions should then be collected and left in your office without request.

SCHEDULE FOR COLLECTING COMPOSITIONS

Grades 5, 6	Grades 3, 4	Grades 1, 2
10/4, 1/4, 4/5	11/2, 2/1, 5/3	12/1, 3/1, 6/7

Figure 8-15

APPOINT ASSEMBLY COORDINATORS

An assembly coordinator should be assigned for each assembly period. If there is a senior assembly for grades 5 and 6, there should also be a junior assembly for grades 3 and 4. The assembly coordinator is responsible for notifying the teachers of special events and their times. The assembly coordinator also assigns seats to all classes involved in the assembly.

Have the coordinator open the assembly period, call for the color guard, and introduce the play, special performance or music period that is to take place. With the assistance of all the teachers in the auditorium, the coordinator is responsible for the behavior and attitude of the students during the assembly. The coordinator also provides for rotation among the classes of the color guard.

Try to assign a different person as music director for the assembly. This person should be able to play the piano, or prepare the music for the entrance of the students and the color guard.

DEFINE THE ROLES OF SUPPORT STAFF

The support staff of the school plays a very important role in the completion of particular tasks for the teachers and the students. In general, these tasks are better performed if each individual is very sure about his or her schedule and function. Sometimes all that is necessary is a statement of what to do and when.

School Aides

School aides provide vital support services for you, the teachers, and the students. However, they are usually an untrained group and require specific responsibilities and tasks. If they are well organized and secure with what they are to do and when, aides can be very effective. The responsibilities of the school aides include:

- distributing books and supplies
- assisting with office chores
- assisting with lunch room procedures
- assisting the safety patrol
- assisting with yard control of students
- picking up bussed students
- using the rexograph and mimeograph machines
- writing absentee notices
- assisting with library procedures
- providing for repair of machines and equipment

Paraprofessionals

Paraprofessionals work directly with youngsters. These individuals usually have some training but are not prepared as teachers should be. Paraprofessionals require assistance in the following areas:

- identifying students' learning needs
- identifying learning materials
- keeping accurate records of student progress
- preparing evaluation reports
- administering tests
- preparing a schedule for students
- picking up assigned students for special programs

School Secretaries

School secretaries should possess a certain degree of expertise and knowledge about the performance of their roles; however, this is not always the case. Prepare a role definition and be prepared to monitor reports as well as other work before placing your trust in the competence of the secretary. The role of the school secretary includes:

- answering the phone properly
- greeting parents and community members who enter the office
- monitoring teacher absence and arranging for substitute teachers (unless this is centrally controlled)
- distributing substitute information
- collecting substitute information for the teacher
- providing for the pick up of students who are ill
- opening and sorting the mail
- preparing your mail
- completing attendance reports
- completing payroll reports
- checking payroll received
- answering correspondance
- typing reports, letters and memos
- completing reports requested by the district
- admission and discharge of students

Lunch Workers

Although lunch workers usually do an excellent job, discuss your expectations for their continued good and, perhaps, improved performance. The well-functioning lunch program includes attention to the following:

- maintaining a clean and cheerful lunch room
- arranging lunch tables efficiently
- arranging food for efficient service
- maintaining an effective procedure for food pickup by students
- maintaining an effective procedure for food removal by students
- positioning refuse cans to facilitate clean up
- ordering and maintaining a sufficient supply of lunch-related supplies
- ordering and maintaining a sufficient supply of food and drink
- preparing food in the required quantity
- ordering food with consideration for the preferences of the students
- ordering food with consideration for the standards of nutritional requirements
- ordering food to provide for the special needs of individual students
- preparing food with regard for the time schedule of the school

COMMUNICATE ROLE DEFINITIONS

Each of the role definitions discussed here should be presented to each particular group and talked about. During the discussion period, answer all questions and take care of any items that require clarification or modification. Also distribute these role definitions in writing so that there is a permanent record of the discussion. The written form of the role definition also serves as a reminder to the staff of their daily assignments. Substitute staff can also be quickly made aware of their role for the day by reading the distributed definitions. Keep a copy of the individual role definitions on file for future reference or modification.

9

HOW TO MAKE THE BEST USE OF YOUR BUDGET

When money is tight and availability is limited, it is essential to have a sound budget program, with preplanning built into it. One approach to budget planning is to identify current and future budget needs and spread available funds accordingly.

PROVIDE FOR PROGRAM DEVELOPMENT PLANS

Keep new programs uppermost in your mind when preparing the budget because their success will depend on your being able to get particular items and personnel. New programs do not always require funding, but when they do, it is foolish to attempt them without financial support.

When money is in very short supply, it may become necessary to sacrifice other budgetary considerations for the new program. On the other hand, if the necessary funds are not available to support the new program, it may become necessary to modify the new program and begin in a more modest manner, or modify the new program plans to capitalize on existing personnel and equipment. Base the decision upon what will best benefit your school and the students. A new program that would be very valuable to the student body as a whole or in part may be worth sacrificing part of other existing programs.

PROJECTING PUPIL POPULATION NEEDS

Another important consideration when forming a budget is the pupil population. Current needs may only be a part of the picture; it is unwise to assume that the needs of the pupil population will be the same each year. Rather, it is important to monitor student progress to determine what new needs may be anticipated the following year. For example, the current year may have focused on the improvement of reading using materials and supplies ordered the year before. Rather than reordering those same types of reading materials, a survey of students' progress in reading may show a marked improvement that no longer requires a concentration of funds. It would be better, then, to consider other areas for focus, such as mathematics. If students in the school show a deficiency in this area, use funds to help improve the subject.

As another example, funds used to purchase materials for foreign language students may have been very successful. It would be unwise, however, to reorder these same types of materials for students who have now made a year's progress in learning to speak, read, and write English. Obviously, these students will require either new materials at a higher level, or may have progressed sufficiently to be able to use existing materials in the school. An assessment of the progress of these foreign language students and a projection of their future needs would certainly be helpful in making budget decisions about what to order.

Continuing programs in a building are still another consideration. No program is so good that it should remain static and only repeat what was done the year before. New materials and supplies may contribute greatly to the effectiveness of an existing program. It is also important to consider what new topics and areas an existing program may branch into.

PROJECT STAFF NEEDS

Constant staff renewal and professional development are important elements in a successful school. During the school year, identify staff needs so that particular equipment and literature can be purchased to meet those needs. The purchase of these items are just as essential, if not more essential, than any other items because the development of a more effective staff reflects in student achievement. Thus, staff-development items should be given important budgetary consideration.

ANTICIPATE POPULATION CHANGES AND RELATED NEEDS

To be a successful principal, maintain a watchful eye on the community and its population; walk the streets of the community and go into the shops. This monitoring process will help to keep you aware of changes in the population of the community, changes that will directly involve the school within a short period of time. Being aware of these changes enables you to prepare for a possible new population with unique needs. A part of the budget may then be used to provide the materials and supplies that the new population will require.

As an example of anticipating population changes, give careful consideration to the ordering of readers for the first and second grades. The usual series used in the school may be perfect for the existing students, but may be unsuitable for a new population moving into the community who have a different language or culture. It may be a good idea to order a smaller number of the usual series and provide for a different reader that could be used more successfully with the new population.

Population changes usually begin slowly and quietly, but tend to grow very rapidly. So, once a new population begins to take residence in a community, its numbers may increase far faster than was anticipated. Keep this in mind when planning your budget.

BE AWARE OF CURRENT UNSATISFIED NEEDS

A continuous monitoring of student progress by inspecting test results and products may reveal existing needs that have still not been satisfied. In an effort to use existing funds to satisfy particular problems and concerns, other needs may be overlooked. At times, these needs are delayed year after year and may never be met.

Unsatisfied needs are often in areas that are important but not a first priority, such as creative writing, critical thinking, and science discovery. But these unsatisfied needs cannot be continuously delayed; there comes a time when even a very limited budget must address some of its attention to these needs.

Unsatisfied needs may also be priority needs, such as outdated language arts textbooks, but the high price of these books may prevent them from being included in the budget every year. Perhaps it would be possible to purchase some of these expensive textbooks if only a limited amount were ordered. In other words, instead of ordering a full set for each class, order one set for a grade and give each teacher ten or twelve books to use with a group of students. Or, ask the teachers of a particular grade to share the books. If an additional set is purchased each year or every other year, a sufficient supply will be available in a short period of time.

INSPECT EXISTING EQUIPMENT, SUPPLIES, AND MATERIALS

It would be wonderful if what was purchased would last forever, but unfortunately this is not the case. Even the most expensive equipment can break beyond repair or become outdated. To prevent not having what is needed *when* it is needed, inspect all equipment and media and keep in mind the number of available machines at budget time. If possible, try to order two or three new tape recorders, phonographs, and projectors each year to compensate for older equipment that may become unuseable during the next year. Do not count on this year's equipment and machines being sufficient for next year.

Rather than order the same amount of supplies each year, survey the use of the supplies that were ordered last year. Perhaps the paper was not used in the amount ordered. Pencils, tape, and index cards often walk out of school with the teachers and can be found in abundant supply in their homes. A visit to the supply closet may be a surprise, too; it may not be necessary to order any construction paper for the next two years!

Curriculum materials may also be in greater supply than was anticipated. One way to find out what books are actually available in the school is to ask the staff to take an inventory of what is in classroom closets. Teachers sometimes store books away from year to year rather than send them to the supply room because they would rather have the books on hand instead of worrying about getting them at a future date. Teachers are reluctant to give up materials that they are storing; the books become their's rather than the school's.

A request for this inventory will uncover some of the materials, but not all of them. You may have to conduct a personal inspection of classroom closets when the classroom is empty, and then privately and quietly approach the teacher about sharing materials with others.

Three strategies will help combat this hoarding tendency of many teachers: (1) an efficient inventory system of available materials in the school; (2) a sign-out system for materials taken by the teachers; and (3) a collection of materials, such as reading and mathematics books, that will vary in classrooms from year to year depending upon student needs. Other texts that are particular to a grade and will remain the same each year, such as social studies texts and dictionaries, need not be collected. Some principals use a very simple, but effective, procedure to combat teacher hoarding: they require every teacher to change rooms each year. This is a bit drastic, but there is something to say about the need to clean closets when a room is changed.

KNOW WHAT IS AVAILABLE FOR PURCHASE

The variety of needs facing schools today require suitable commercial materials to assist with their solution. No teacher can possibly prepare all of the materials that would be required by diversified students, so it is very important for you to know what the market can offer the teacher. (Chapter 10 explains this in more detail.)

You can keep up to date about the availability of commercial materials in several different ways. Since salespeople often visit schools, talk to them, or assign a responsible person to talk with them. Ask each salesperson what the company can offer for particular needs of the school and also inquire about new products that have been developed. If possible, obtain samples of the materials in which you are interested. Most companies will be very glad to send these samples to the school. Request those topics and grade level materials that will be beneficial, and send the samples to selected teachers whose opinions you value. The materials should be considered valuable by most of the teachers before they are actually ordered.

Keep up-to-date about commercial materials by attending book exhibits. Some companies invite supervisors to special meetings to discuss particular products that have a wide and general appeal. If you are unable to attend, send someone whose judgment you trust. NOTE: Conferences and conventions presented by a variety of professional organizations usually include book exhibits. In addition to gaining valuable information at the meetings, you can benefit from a visit to the exhibits.

RELATE THE BUDGET TO REALITY

There are at least two kinds of budgets that can be prepared. One contains all of the materials you would like to purchase. The other contains actual materials that are essential and can be covered by available funds. Everyone would certainly prefer the former rather than the latter budget, but reality always prevails. There are several alternatives, however, that may help you move a step or two closer to the utopian budget.

Set Priorities

List materials to be purchased in priority order. It is then possible to determine just how far down the list the available funds will stretch. Of course, the particular priority order would vary for individual schools, but the following list includes most of the materials:

1. reading texts and student practice books for the primary grades
2. mathematics texts and student practice books for the primary grades

3. additional reading texts and student practice books for all grades in which the numbers of students have grown

4. additional mathematics texts and student practice books for all grades in which the numbers of students have grown

5. materials for students with needs that are new to the school (i.e., speakers of foreign languages)

6. materials necessary to implement new programs

7. materials/equipment to replace old or damaged ones

8. additional sets of texts to complete a series previously ordered

9. limited quantities of a new series to be implemented

10. new materials/equipment that have become available

There are times when unusual pressing needs may take priority over all other needs. These include:

1. materials to implement a newly mandated curriculum revision

2. materials (tests) necessary to implement a mandated instructional program

3. materials (tests) necessary to evaluate a mandated instructional program

4. materials (tests) necessary to implement a mandated screening program

Find Corners to Cut

The first corner to consider cutting is the expense involved with replacing destroyed or damaged materials. Certainly, some books and materials, such as hardcover books and sturdy equipment, will provide several years of good service. But even paperback books should last more than one or two years. The key to maintaining the life of these materials and equipment is a preservation policy and campaign. When limited funds must be spent on replacing destroyed items rather than on new materials, everyone in the school suffers.

There is a great difference between materials and equipment that are worn out after repeated use and those that are destroyed because of carelessness. The students, staff, and parents should be made aware of the need to preserve all school materials in an effort to make those instructional aides last longer. The specific policy of the school should be cooperatively developed with the staff, students, and parents, and should have the support and approval of the Parents Association. Although the specifics will vary with the needs of the individual school, the effort should be wholehearted and consistent throughout the school year. Following the cooperative development of a policy, a written statement of that policy (Figure 9-1) should be presented and discussed with the staff, as well as with students and parents (Figure 9-2).

Student workbooks provide another way to cut budget corners. It is really unnecessary for upper-grade students to write their answers in workbooks since these fourth-, fifth-, and sixth-graders are capable of recording the answers on a separate sheet of paper. This approach has several other related benefits, too. First, the workbooks can be used again by other students, thus doubling or, in many cases, tripling the life of those books. Second, standardized tests usually require the use of an answer sheet, so the recording of answers on

MATERIALS PRESERVATION POLICY

**The Elementary School
Office of the Principal**

MATERIALS PRESERVATION POLICY

The following policy has been developed by a committee composed of teachers, parents and students. Please help all of us to maintain our existing resources by following the policy.

Please discriminate between destruction and normal wear and tear. Students will not be held responsible for damage resulting from normal use.

I. Schedule

A. September (before September 30th)

1. students informed of accountability

a. students sign the form letter of understanding
b. prices of particular items are listed in the letter
c. one copy of the form letter is posted in each classroom

2. students' signed letters are sent home for parents to also sign

3. the letters signed by students and parents are to be filed by the teachers

4. teacher's copy of inventory records of all materials received is to be retained and updated as needed

B. Ongoing

Teachers keep ongoing check

1. monitors assigned to check all kits on a continuing basis

2. request a copy of any "lost" kit card
include the name, level and number of the card on your request
include the money collected for the replacement of the card

II. Accountability

A. Pupil Accountability

Pupils observed destroying any material will be charged for the material.

B. Group Accountability

The group is held responsible for materials used and damaged by the group.

C. Class Accountability

The class is held responsible for materials destroyed by the class or persons unknown.

D. Accountability for Shared Materials

Materials lost or damaged by classes sharing materials will be the responsibility of both classes.

III. Disbursement of Funds

A. Kits—containing paperback books

Teachers will use the money collected to replace the books.

B. Other

Money collected for other materials will be sent to the principal with an indication of the item lost or destroyed. Replacements will be purchased on a schoolwide basis.

Figure 9-1

another sheet provides good practice in a valuable test-taking technique. Third, in a diagnostic/prescriptive program, not every student requires the skill presented on every page of the workbook. Skill review and reinforcement can therefore be selectively assigned according to student need. The practice of not writing in workbooks helps to discourage teachers from a sequential, page-by-page approach to instruction and encourages a prescription-by-need approach.

Since composition paper is a very expensive item, eliminating this item from the budget will save a great deal of money which can then be used to purchase other necessary instructional materials. Ask students at the beginning of the school year to bring in one package of looseleaf paper, understanding that the packages are for the use of the class as a whole. Even with only a partial response to this request, the teacher should have at least 15 to 20 packages of looseleaf paper to store for use throughout the year.

Sharing materials is still another way to cut budget corners. It is often unnecessary, and sometimes beneficial, to avoid buying one book per child for each class. Supplying teachers with multiple copies of one text encourages whole class instruction and discourages small group and independent attention to students' needs. Attention to individual and small-group needs can better be accomplished by identifying particular resources suitable for meeting those skill needs and supplying those resources in the number needed by the group of students. At those times when a set of texts is required for a whole class lesson, the teacher might borrow the needed number of books from another class.

Field testing new materials for a publishing company is not only an excellent way to cut corners on budgets, but is also the means by which new materials can be evaluated with the school's actual population. Publishing companies wanting to field test a new product will usually provide a free class set of materials for each grade for whom the materials are appropriate. By spreading that class set among three or four classes, their use with small groups of students can be encouraged. Using the books in several classes will also enable you to get the evaluation of the materials from several different teachers. A field-testing project usually also includes the services of the company's consultant who will work with the teachers to maximize the effectiveness of the new product.

Accepting a field-testing offer from a company also requires a responsibility on your part. There is usually an agreement to complete an honest and frank evaluation of the

MATERIALS PRESERVATION MEMO

The Elementary School
Office of the Principal

Fall 1983

To: Students and Parents
Re: Materials Preservation

In these days of limited funds, it is essential that we get maximum use of those learning materials that we have been able to buy. We are therefore requesting the cooperation of every student and parent.

Students in the class will be held responsible and be asked to pay for the loss or abuse of materials (including books) that they use. They are asked to treat the materials with care and consideration. You can help by reminding your child to care for books and materials taken home for homework. No book may remain at home. It must be brought to school the following day.

In addition, please keep younger children and pets away from the materials. A price list follows for your information.

A. Machines—part replacement
   1. tape recorder $5.00
   2. filmstrip projector $5.00

B. Textbooks
   Softcover $2.00
   Hardcover $5.00

C. Kit—card replacement   25¢

D. Scholastic kit $1.00 per book

E. Math lab materials and games $2.50

F. Filmstrips $5.00

G. Cassettes $5.00

_____

Student's signature

_____

Parent's signature

Figure 9-2

materials. It is also understood that if the materials prove beneficial with the students, an order for additional copies of the books/materials will be made the following year.

ALTERNATE SOURCES OF MONEY

There are many ways to find money to buy what the school needs. These sources of additional funds are almost always involved with fund-raising efforts conducted either by the school, by the parents, or as a joint venture involving both.

Some popular forms of fund raising include: student/class photographs; candy sales; cake sales; book fairs; plant sales; school-monogrammed pen, pencil, T-shirt, or tote bag sales; flea markets; showing popular movies after school; and raffles. Most of these fund-raising ventures are conducted by contracting with a commercial company who shares a percentage of the profit with the organizing school or Parents Association. Some fund raisers offer incentive prizes to students who sell the largest amounts of the item and raise the most money.

There are several important concerns to keep in mind when engaging in a fund raising effort. First, is the item offered for sale worth the price being asked? Remember that the school sale price is higher than the commercial price to allow for a profit margin. Second, is the item offered for sale harmful to the students? Many schools will not become involved in candy sales, for example, because the school personnel believe that candy causes tooth decay, even though such sales usually raise the largest sums of money. Third, is the possible profit to be gained worth the tremendous effort and work involved? Fund raisers take time and organization. Personnel must be assigned to the various aspects of the project, beginning with the contact of the commercial company and ending with the distribution of the items ordered. This role is usually effectively fulfilled by the Parents Association. One last and most important concern is the use of the money raised. This is especially important when the Parents Association is involved with the fund raiser. Parents usually resent having to raise money for items such as texts, workbooks, and other instructional supplies and equipment, that they believe should be provided for in the school's allocation. On the other hand, parents generally will gladly raise money to buy other equipment such as computers, copy machines, tape recorders, language masters, etc., that the school's budget usually cannot afford.

INVOLVE THE SCHOOL STAFF IN DECISIONS

All instructional materials are ultimately used by teachers, so their effectiveness is directly related to the teachers' opinions of the materials. That is why teachers should be involved in decisions concerning the purchase of new materials in every subject area.

Involving teachers in this decision making can be done in several different ways: (1) materials can be sent to grade leaders to be circulated, viewed, and then discussed at grade conferences; (2) sample materials can be sent for examination and evaluation to selected members of the staff in whose judgment you have confidence; or (3) a committee of teachers can be appointed by you or solicited as volunteers from among the staff. It is also possible to use each of these approaches by selecting the approach that best suits the particular material under consideration. Materials suited to one particular grade level would, of course, be examined and evaluated only by those teachers for whom the material has importance.

Although teachers are involved in the decision concerning the purchase of particular materials, they do not usually make the *final* decision unless you want this to happen. It is not difficult to involve teachers and then for you to make the decision since there will usually be a difference of opinion among the teachers as to which one particular material should be purchased. When the teachers are in agreement about a material, however, you should honor their opinion even if it differs from your own.

INVOLVE PARENTS IN DECISIONS

Parents' trust and confidence in the school are heightened and reinforced when they believe their feelings and opinions are actively solicited and respected. Generally, parents do not want to make the final decision in the selection of materials, but they usually do want to be consulted and advised.

Ask the Parents Association to select a committee of parents to serve on a selection committee with teachers. Parents can then view at first hand the teachers' professional discussion of the materials. Parents also have an opportunity to view the sample materials and ask questions about them. Since many parents are concerned with ethnic or sex bias contained in some texts and materials, a review of the proposed material and a discussion about it may prevent future problems.

10

HOW TO SELECT PUBLISHED MATERIALS

Publishers and principals have the same objectives for instructional materials: to provide the most effective means possible to teach students. Publishers do this by understanding and providing for future needs, and principals by recognizing the value of newly published materials and using them to their best advantage.

COPE WITH CATALOGS

The publisher has two primary means of reaching its audience: (1) the salesperson who visits the school from time to time, and (2) the mailing of information to the school. This information may be in the form of an announcement of a new product or as a total catalog of the company's products. Since you will find a multitude of catalogs and announcements in the daily mail, it is difficult—if not impossible—to read and store in your memory all of the items that are offered. One way to deal with catalogs is to develop an inventory system.

A box, bookends, or an empty drawer can help you make sense out of the mountain of catalogs that come in the mail. The catalogs can be filed in several different ways: (1) by the publisher's name in alphabetical order; (2) if the name of the publisher is not familiar, by topic or subject (for example, some catalogs deal with media and can be filed under M, and others deal with books and may be filed under B); or (3) by category, such as social studies or math. A filing system will help you find the desired catalog when looking for a particular item to order.

MAKE CATALOGS WORK FOR YOU

The filed catalogs will work for you at ordering time when the particular items you want are accessible in full description, complete with prices. This saves you countless hours of searching for a publisher.

Catalogs and brochures also serve another purpose. They often contain sample activities and colorful diagrams that are valuable in constructing activity or task cards. The publications can be cut apart and glued onto posterboard.

MEET WITH COMPANY SALESPEOPLE

Speaking with company salespeople is well worth the time involved because no written description of a product is as comprehensive as the verbal explanation. The discussion provides an opportunity to ask questions that may well lead to a decision about what to order.

Salespeople are also very informative about new products that will soon be available so that they can help school personnel form future ordering plans. Publishing companies collect data about their products and the variety of alternative approaches that different schools use with them, so it is also possible to learn about products that can be used with different populations in new ways. In speaking with salespeople, you can discuss a particular problem in the school and explore products that may be used in solving that problem.

The personal touch with the salesperson also helps to rush the order. At times, the salesperson may also be able to supply the school with extra teacher's editions.

USE SAMPLE COPIES

Besides using sample copies for examination by groups of teachers, these copies have another purpose. If a particular material is not to be ordered, the sample copy may become a new and different instructional tool. The copies should be given to the teachers of the particular grade for whom they are important. Those teachers may then pull apart the sample copy and use the pages in a variety of ways: (1) as additional individual assignments for review and reinforcement; (2) as part of a set of independent task or activity cards; or (3) as a resource book to which students may be referred when the need arises.

MAKE THE PUBLISHER A HELPING PARTNER

Publishers are partners in the education of the students and help in many different ways.

Budget Stretcher

Publishing companies can sometimes help to stretch your budgets. If, for example, your school has sets of new and unused books that are no longer a part of the instructional program, the company may offer to take those unused books and credit the school towards a future purchase, or exchange them for the purchase of a new series. In this way, materials of no value to your school may be turned into new and desired materials. Different parts of the country often use different materials and what may not be of value to one school may well be an important part of the instructional program in another.

A Consultant

The publisher's educational consultant is a valuable and free asset, with most publishers offering the services of the consultant as long as necessary. With the help of the consultant, your teachers learn to use the materials in the most desirable manner. Teachers also become more confident about new materials when they have had a good orientation to them by a professional and when they have an opportunity to ask questions. Ask the consultant to return after the material has been in use for three or four months because the consultant may benefit from the teachers' comments and criticisms concerning ways in which the materials are useful and ways in which they might be improved.

ESTABLISH GUIDELINES
FOR SELECTING PUBLISHED MATERIALS

All too often, materials are purchased from a publisher's written description only to find that they are inappropriate for the school's student body for one reason or another. Even when the materials to be purchased are inspected and a sample copy is distributed among the teachers, a lack of attention to certain details may again cause a purchase that is not suitable. Pay attention to the following specifics to save your school countless dollars on wasted, unused materials.

For Whom Is the Material Intended?

Most materials are specifically designed for and work best with particular populations. Consider the difference between rural and urban populations. Although most materials today attempt to address universal populations, it is not always successful. Materials focused on the inner-city child, for example, may be just as difficult for a farm child to understand as pictures of a rural community would be for a city child. The identification of the student with the materials and his or her previous experiences are important contributors to learning. Of course, it is the school's goal to expose students to new and unusual situations and experiences, but this learning is valuable when it is the focus of instruction. When the focus of instruction has another objective, such as reading, materials that are within the experience and understanding of the youngster often bring the best results.

Consider, too, the placement level of the students. This category includes primary, intermediate, upper elementary, junior high school, senior high school, college, and adult. Most materials are written at a particular level or span one level above and below the level for whom they are intended, so are therefore used most effectively with the intended level.

Using materials out of level, however, is a popular practice. For example, intermediate and upper elementary level students who are speakers of foreign languages often use primary materials to learn to read and speak English. When this strategy is used, it is important to consider the appeal of these materials to an older student both in story content and appearance. Well-meaning efforts with inappropriate materials may be more destructive than beneficial. Another example is junior high school and senior high school students who are remedial readers and given elementary level reading materials with which to work. The same consideration of appropriateness and appeal should apply. Materials developed specifically for beginning speakers of English at various levels as well as high-interest, low-reading-level readers are available. The better alternative may be to search for those more appropriate materials than to use out-of-level materials.

A third consideration involves ability levels. This category includes the remedial learner, average student, gifted youngster, and student with a language difficulty. Within the same age/grade level, students have vastly different needs that require the use of differentiated materials. For example, slower learning students may be more successful with shorter, clearer explanations and illustrations than gifted youngsters who require an in-depth understanding of a topic. Find texts and materials that convey the same topic at different levels of depth and intensity, appropriate for students with different ability levels.

What Instructional Approach Is Used?

The importance of attention to individual student learning styles has been previously discussed. Briefly restated here, you must consider addressing the variety and diversity of learning styles through appropriate learning materials. Remember that instruction may be approached through visual, auditory, kinesthetic, and tactile appeals, with materials often incorporating more than one instructional approach. Recognize the particular instructional approaches offered by each material and attempt to acquire materials that offer a great variety of approaches.

How Is the Content Presented?

Consider several important factors when reviewing the presentation of a given material's content. First, consider the number of concepts included. Examine the material by comparing it with the scope and sequence of the curriculum structure of the state and district. The material should include most, if not all, of the concepts appropriate for the subject on the particular grade. Then consider the rate at which those concepts are developed within the content of the material. Determine if the rate and sequence of the introduction of concepts seems to be in logical sequential order and paced to encourage student understanding.

When reviewing rate and sequence of the introduction of concepts, also consider whether provision is made within the material for review and reinforcement of those concepts. Each new concept presented should be immediately followed by reinforcement to accommodate both the rapid and slower learner. Periodic review of concepts previously introduced will contribute to long-term retention of those concepts. How the material provides for both student (self) and teacher evaluation of the mastery of the concepts is still another important consideration. Evaluation measures should be spaced throughout the material as guides for the teacher to determine pupil progress and need for further instruction or reteaching.

Materials should also be reviewed in terms of their relationship to other curriculum areas. Some materials lend themselves to an interdisciplinary approach to content, especially valuable when teaching reading through other content areas.

The presentation of the content should also be considered in terms of its relationship to the development of healthy or detrimental social/emotional experiences. Some content may emphasize social and emotional situations that could be considered important or harmful for the students. Reviewing the content with these considerations in mind will help you make decisions concerning the appropriateness of the material for the particular student body and the community as a whole.

What Support Material Is Available?

Publishing companies often provide support materials for basic texts they have published. These support materials may enhance the basic text and help enlarge instructional possibilities when they are used. The support materials may assist students who are experiencing difficulty with the basic text, and may provide additional enrichment activities.

Support materials might take the form of ditto masters, supplementary workbooks, activity or task cards, cassette tapes, records, filmstrips, and games. Each of these materials should have a clearly stated educational objective and should define the population for whom they are intended. When considering the purchase of supplementary materials, also think of the necessary additional supplies, such as paper for ditto masters, needed for their use.

How Can the Material Best Be Used?

Consider materials with regard to their intended application. Some materials are best suited for whole class instruction, while others work best with small groups. Still other materials are intended for individual use, or for out-of-classroom use as homework or with ancillary personnel. When evaluating materials for possible purchase, consider their best application compared with the needs of the school. As an example, one company provides ditto masters as a supplement to a basic mathematics series, with the ditto masters coordinated with the text pages. These masters are best used as homework review and reinforcement for those students who require additional practice.

What Is the Long-Range Outlook?

It is important to take a step back from an instant desire to purchase a material that appears wonderful and to look at it in the cold light of practicality.

Consider the initial cost of the material. Is it within the normal range of expense for your school? If the material is more expensive than those normally purchased, is the material worth the extra money, as well as its ongoing expense? Schools may be willing to exceed usual expenses for the initial purchase, but may not be in the position to support this type of expense year after year. Are the necessary parts of the materials consumed and replaced yearly? If so, determine the ongoing upkeep costs.

Calculating the per pupil cost is an excellent way of placing a possible purchase in perspective. A particular material may appear very desirable initially but after determining the cost of the material with regard to the number of students who will use that material, it may change in its appeal. Compare the per pupil cost with the number of students who will not be using the material before making a decision.

Other considerations involve the ability of the materials to be reproduced or reused. Both of these can save a great deal of money for your school.

Size, shape, and weight of materials are important considerations because some materials create storage problems. Materials that are so large and bulky or small and fragile that they cannot be stored within the classroom are usually not maximally effective.

Easy use of the materials by students without the constant intervention of the teacher is another important factor to be considered. Materials that students can handle with ease are usually preferred and trusted by teachers. Remember that materials should be sturdy enough to withstand normal use by children. Fragile material requiring constant teacher supervision is rarely used.

How Effective Is the Material with Students?

There are several factors that make some materials more effective with students than others. One of these factors is the materials' visual appeal. The size, shape, color, and general format should encourage student use.

Motivation is another factor when evaluating effectiveness. The format and content of the material should be constructed so that students are interested in working with the material and doing that work to the best of their ability, especially if the material is to be used over a period of time. Those materials that are well constructed and provide students with satisfactory experiences usually maintain their interest and desire to continue working.

Materials selected for purchase should document good evidence of pupil skill growth and development, and must accomplish a stated purpose within a time frame that can be demonstrated in student growth. Materials that have long-range goals are fine so long as they also have short-term smaller gains that are visible to both the student and the teacher.

The teacher's opinion of the possible effectiveness of the material is a very important factor. Teachers who are forced to use materials in which they have little faith or which they do not like will usually not do a good job with those materials. At times it may appear that the purpose of the teacher's use of the materials is to demonstrate how ineffective they are!

How Much Training Is Required for Use?

Materials that are so complex that they require countless hours of teacher, student, or auxillary adult training before they can be used may be abandoned before they are ever implemented. If extensive staff development is required before a material can be used, be sure that the money, the time, and the teachers' cooperation can be secured before the material is purchased.

How Are Materials Corrected and Records Kept?

Consider correction of student responses and recordkeeping if the materials are to be used in an individualized program. Some materials hold particular appeal for teachers because they can be self- or peer-corrected, saving the teacher large amounts of time that might be taken from active instruction. Student responses that lend themselves to self- or peer-correction are usually easily recorded by students in a simple recordkeeping process.

USE A SCALE TO EVALUATE
MATERIALS BEFORE PURCHASE

Figure 10-1 is designed to compare the materials being considered for purchase with the instructional requirements of the student population of a particular school. The categorized list is accompanied by two different graphs: the first should be completed to reflect the purpose for which the material is being purchased; and the second should be completed to reflect all aspects of the proposed material.

A SCALE FOR EVALUATING MATERIALS BEFORE PURCHASE

Using the scale: 0 = nonexistent, 1 = very low, 2 = low, 3 = acceptable, 4 = high, 5 = very high

1. Plot the intended purpose of the material on each item of each category.

2. Plot the attributes of the material(s) proposed on each item of each category.

Then compare the intended purpose of the material(s) with the attributes of the materials proposed.

ITEMS INCLUDED IN THE EVALUATION

I. Population for Intended Use	INTENDED PURPOSE						MATERIAL PROPOSED					
	0	1	2	3	4	5	0	1	2	3	4	5
urban												
rural												
primary												
intermediate												
upper elementary												
junior high												
senior high												
college												
adult												
remedial												
average												
gifted												
language difficulty												

II. Instructional Approach	0	1	2	3	4	5	0	1	2	3	4	5
visual												
auditory												
kinesthetic												
tactile												

III. Presentation of Content	0	1	2	3	4	5	0	1	2	3	4	5
rate of concept development												
number of concepts included												
amount of reinforcement												
amount of review												
amount of evaluation												
relates to other curriculum												
relates to social learning												
relates to emotional learning												

IV. Relevant Classroom Application	0	1	2	3	4	5	0	1	2	3	4	5
whole class												
small group												
individual												
settings outside the classroom												

Figure 10-1

V. Support Material Available	0	1	2	3	4	5	0	1	2	3	4	5
books												
tapes												
records												
films												
duplicating masters												
activity cards												
games												
media for materials												

VI. Logistics	0	1	2	3	4	5	0	1	2	3	4	5
initial cost												
ongoing												
per pupil cost												
ability to be reproduced												
ability to be reused												
destructability												
storage requirements												
ease of use												

VII. Effectiveness with Students	0	1	2	3	4	5	0	1	2	3	4	5
appeal to pupils												
motivation for pupils												
continued interest												
pupil growth												
time factor in growth												
teacher opinion of material												

VIII. Degree of Training Required	0	1	2	3	4	5	0	1	2	3	4	5
for teachers												
for pupils												
for auxiliary adults												

IX. Correction and Recordkeeping	0	1	2	3	4	5	0	1	2	3	4	5
self correction												
teacher correction												
use of auxiliary adults												
use of peers												

Figure 10-1 (Continued)

Each item on the scale should be rated on a scale of 0 = nonexistent, 1 = very low, 2 = low, 3 = acceptable, 4 = high, and 5 = very high. After each of the two graphs has been completed, compare them to determine the degree of their similarity. This comparison will then answer the question, "Does the proposed material fulfill the purpose for which it is intended?"

For example, your school wants a material with a maximum approach to visual, auditory, kinesthetic, and tactile learning, but the material actually offers only a visual approach. (See Figure 10-2.) Your school also wants that material to need only limited training of teachers, pupils, and auxillary adults before use, but the material actually requires a high degree of teacher and student training before use with no provision for auxillary adults. Clearly, this material would be a poor choice for your school.

PARTIAL SAMPLE

Instructional Approach

	INTENDED PURPOSE						MATERIAL PROPOSED					
	0	1	2	3	4	5	0	1	2	3	4	5
visual						x						x
auditory						x	x					
kinesthetic						x	x					
tactile						x	x					

Degree of Training Required

	0	1	2	3	4	5	0	1	2	3	4	5
for teachers		x									x	
for pupils		x									x	
for auxillary adults		x					x					

Figure 10-2

ESTABLISH A SYSTEM
FOR EFFECTIVE USE OF MATERIALS

Having materials available in the school does not guarantee that teachers will use them, nor does it guarantee that the materials will be used with care and returned when they are no longer required for instruction. At times, materials are not used by teachers because they are unaware that the materials exist, do not know that an order has arrived, do not know for whom the materials are intended, or do not know how to get the materials. So, establish an effective system and communicate this system to teachers to help resolve these problems.

The School Inventory

Conducting a schoolwide inventory of instructional materials and recording those resources in an organized manner is no easy task. But when the work is completed, the materials will be used more completely and effectively because teachers will know what is available in the school. The materials will be used more efficiently because those particularly suited to the instructional needs of the youngsters will be selected from among the available alternatives.

Finding the personnel to conduct the inventory depends upon the individual school. Usually, the library media specialist is responsible for conducting this type of inventory with the assistance of school aides. Parents can also play an important role in this work.

Once the inventory is completed, it should be recorded in a logical manner and given to teachers. The system of recording the materials listed in the inventory will depend upon the instructional process used in your school; but the best way is usually to list the materials by subject and then categorize by skill, level, or grade. One effective way to categorize subject matter, such as reading materials, that may be used by several different grades is to categorize the materials by skill, listing the level of difficulty in sequential order. A second way of categorizing instructional materials in the areas of reading and mathematics is to relate them to the diagnostic instruments used by the school. The materials may be listed next to the particular skills that were tested by the diagnostic instrument, for which their use is recommended. (See Figures 10-3 and 10-4.) This procedure assists teachers in analyzing the diagnostic information about each student and then selecting instructional materials with which the youngsters will work.

A school inventory is also important for you. This inventory, however, is different from the one which is given to the teachers because a comprehensive recording allows you and those working with the school's resources to know what the school owns. This inventory should not be kept in a list form because new materials must easily be added according to subject classification and alphabetical order. For this reason, an index card system is better. Of course, if the facilities of a computer are available, that is the best possible system for storing inventory information.

PARTIAL SAMPLE

STANFORD DIAGNOSTIC READING TEST (Level Red/Green)
Resources Matched to Diagnoses

Group 4: COMPREHENSION

4.0   Barnell-Loft Level B and up
   (a) Getting the Main Idea
   (b) Locating the Answer
   (c) Drawing Conclusions
   (d) Following Directions
   (e) Getting the Facts
   (f) Detecting the Sequence
   (g) Understanding Questions

4.1   Scott Foresman Levels 9 and up
   (a) Reading Systems Pupil Books
   (b) Study Books
   (c) Read and Check
   (d) Masters

4.2   Continental Press
   (a) Reading Thinking Skills 2^2 and up

4.3   Skillpacers—Random House
   (a) Yellow, Red, Blue

4.4   Cornerstone Readers
   (a) Alphabet Soup

(b) Bakers Dozen
(c) Crackerjacks

4.5   Macmillan Reading Spectrum

(a) Reading Comprehension Levels 2 and up

4.6   Building Reading Power—Blue

4.7   McCall Crabbs A-D

4.8   All in a Days Work—Career Education 2.0-4.0

(a) Main Idea
(b) Inference
(c) Sequence

4.9   Reading in Social Studies

(a) Dolphins to Dunes Level 2
(b) Skyscrapers to Squirrels Levels 2 and 3

4.10 Turning Point Levels 2-3.5

4.11 Reading for Concepts Levels A-D (grades 1-4)

4.12 Field Series

(a) Deep Sea Adventures (see samples M.C. for levels)

4.13 Stranger Than Fiction Level 2-3

4.14 All in a Day's Work Level 2-3

4.15 Sight and Sounds Book I—Grades 2 and 3

4.16 Legends for Everyone Grades 2 and 3

4.17 Profiles Grades 3 and 4

4.18 Modern Curriculum Press

(a) Increasing Comprehension D
(b) Working with Facts and Details D
(c) Organizing Information D
(d) Using References D

4.19 Oceana

(a) Critical Reading A, B, C
(b) Detecting Sequence of Events A, B, C
(c) Use of Context Clues A, B, C
(d) Following Directions A, B, C
(e) Main Idea A, B, C
(f) Drawing Conclusions A, B, C
    (A = 1.5 - 2.5)
    (B = 2.0 - 2.9)
    (C = 3.0 - 3.9)

Figure 10-3 (Continued)

PARTIAL SAMPLE

STANFORD DIAGNOSTIC MATHEMATICS TEST Level Purple/Green
Resources Matched to Diagnoses

TEACHER DIRECTED SKILLS-GROUPS	PRESCRIPTIONS
Test 2: Computation	Cyclo Teacher programs
	Flash cards
2.8 **NUMBER SENTENCES**	McCormack Mathers Math Kit
a. Simple Addition and Subtraction	Random House Math Kit AA (Gr. 2-3)
b. Simple Multiplication and Division	BB (Gr. 3-4)
c. Parenthetical	Tachistoflasher Program (M.C.)
	Language Master (Arith Prog. I, II)
2.8 a. Quizmo Add and Subtract	(M.C.)
Studyscope B—Kit 203—4	
Addition—Subtract	
HBJ Improving Your Ability to Add	
HBJ Improving Your Ability to Subtract	
Activity Cards Sports 'N Things Add and Subtract	
b. Quizmo Multiply and Divide	
Studyscope B—Kit 206—Mult. and Div.	
HBJ Improving Your Ability to Multiply	
Improving Your Ability to Divide I	
Improving Your Ability to Divide II	
Act. Cards—Sports 'N Things—Mult. and Division	
c. Sadlier Drill for Skill Orange (Gr. 3)	
Drill for Skill Olive (Gr. 4)	
3.3 **GEOMETRY AND MEASUREMENT**	McCormack Mathers Math Kit
a. Geometric Shapes and Properties	Random House Individualized Math
b. Time and Money as Measurements	Measurement K-3
c. Metric Units of Measure	
3.3 a. C1053 Mini Systems—Geometry	Attribute blocks + activity cards
C1069 Mini Systems—Geometry	Tangrams + activity cards
Study Scope Level D Kit 208	Geoboards + activity cards, rexographs

b. The Money Game
   Quizmo—Tell Time
   C1054 Mini Systems-
     Measurement (Gr. 3)
   C1070 Mini Systems-
     Measurement (Gr. 4)
   Study Scope Level A Kit A 201-2

c. Metric—rulers, measures, weights, meter sticks Filmstrips—Introducing the Metric System	Random House—Meters, Liters and Grams—Gr. 2 Scott Foresman—Activities to Go Metric A Gr. 2-4 Invicta—Think Metric Activity Cards Rexos—Metrics Using Cuisenaire Rods Vol. I—Meter Vol. II—Liter Vol. III—Gram Harcourt Brace—Measure Metric A Gr. 1-4 Metric Drill and Practice Kit Sidney Cylinder—Metric Math Lab Continental Press—Learning the Metric System—Gr. 3, 4
Situational Math Using the Metric System Think Metric Milton Bradley—Metric Measurement—Length Milton Bradley—Metric Measurement—Weight The Metric Box Projects in Metric Measurement The Metric Mice Pkg Game—Milton Bradley—Path to Metrics Trundle Wheel	

Figure 10-4

Assuming that most elementary schools do not have computers suitable for retaining the information, each material should be listed on a separate card (Figure 10-4), with each card showing the publisher's name, the date of puurchase, and the number of books, tapes, films, etc., borrowed and returned. These index cards are then arranged first by subject and then in alphabetical order by name.

INVENTORY CARD

Material _____
Publisher _____ Date Purchased _____
Number Purchased _____

DATE BORROWED   TEACHER'S NAME   # OF COPIES   DATE RETURNED

Figure 10-4

When a teacher receives materials, the date and the teacher's name including the quantity received are recorded on the inventory card. In addition, each teacher has a name card (Figure 10-5) kept in a separate area. Those materials received by the teacher are also recorded on the teacher's name card. This cross-reference system has an important purpose: at times, especially if there are a limited number of materials of one type available in the school, you or the librarian may want to know who has taken a particular material for use with students. This information is available by looking for the kit listed in the inventory by subject in alphabetical order. At other times, it may be important for you to check what materials are being used by a particular teacher. The teacher's name card will then be helpful in easily finding what each teacher is using for instruction with the students.

TEACHER'S CARD

Name of Teacher _____

MATERIAL	# OF COPIES	OUT	IN

Figure 10-5

The cross-reference inventory system is also effective at the end of the school year when materials are collected and stored for the following year. The process of collecting and storing the materials prevents teacher hoarding of materials and fosters the new selection of materials based on student need. It also helps to direct accountability for materials that have been lost or destroyed.

Inform Staff of Materials Availability

Once teachers have been given typed and categorized lists of materials available in the school, they have a written resource to which they can refer each time they need an instructional material. But these lists will not inform teachers of what new materials have arrived, so there are two other steps that should be taken concerning newly arrived materials. First, issue a typed addenda to the teachers that lists the materials by subject, category, and level or grade. But teachers are busy and do not always read what is given to them, so a second step is to place in the next set of conference notes distributed to teachers a listing of materials with a notation concerning for whom the materials are intended. In addition, prepare a display of the new materials at the faculty conference where teachers can examine the materials before or after the meeting.

PROVIDE FOR A STAFF SELECTION PROCESS

Inventory lists distributed to teachers, even those matched to diagnostic instruments, inform teachers about what is available, but may not be sufficient for teachers to make decisions concerning which materials may be suited to the student's instructional needs and teacher's use. So, establish an area where the materials may be viewed and examined by teachers.

The best place to establish a Teacher Selection Center is a room that is accessible, has sufficient space, and contains shelves, bookcases, and tables. The materials are first categorized by subject area and then by topic. In reading, for example, the skill books should be organized by skill title and arranged sequentially by level; the readers should be arranged by series in sequential order; the language arts books should be arranged similarly, separating English texts from books for individual skills. One sample copy of each text and skill book available in the school should be on display in this center. Inform teachers that the Center is for examination only and no books/materials may be removed. What the teacher can do is record the titles and levels of the books selected and then order the quantity needed.

Media of all types can also be displayed in the Teacher Selection Center, categorized by subject and topic: book and record or tape combinations should be grouped together; language arts games, tapes, films, and activities should be separately grouped next to the book and record combinations; math games, kits, activities, tapes, and films should also be grouped and placed next to each other in another part of the room.

A material that is a single copy may be borrowed directly from the Teacher Selection Center. The center should have a specific sign-out system that is supervised by particular people, such as the library media specialist, aides, or parent volunteers. The Center supervisor records the materials taken in the school inventory both on the teacher's card and on the inventory card.

ESTABLISH AN ORDER/RETURN PROCESS

After the teacher selects the materials that he or she wants to use with groups and individual students, the order is written on a Materials Request/Return (Figure 10-6) and placed in a designated area. The order is prepared by school aides by pulling the number of copies ordered from the shelves of the book room where texts are stored. The process of filling teachers' orders is made quicker and easier if the book room is properly organized and the materials are neatly categorized and arranged.

Once the order is filled, the request form is sent to the Teacher Selection Center where both the inventory cards and teacher cards are kept. The supervisor of the Center enters the materials sent to the teacher on both cards, and a check next to the materials listed on the request form indicates that those materials were sent. If a material is not checked, the materials were not sent either because it was not available or there was an error in the order. Those materials not checked are not entered on the inventory cards.

The Materials Request/Return can also be used to order supplies. Those items needed, such as chalk, pencils, and paper, are listed on the form and placed in the same designated area as a materials request. School aides fill the order in the same manner as the materials requested.

MATERIALS REQUEST/RETURN

Materials Request _____ Return _____ (check one)

Teacher's Name _____

Room _____ Date _____

CURRICULUM MATERIALS			SUPPLIES
Name	Level	#	

Figure 10-6

The Materials Request/Return also serves as a return form. The teacher indicates if this is an order or return by checking the correct line at the top. When materials are returned, they are also listed on the form; those materials and the completed form are then sent to the book room. The school aides receive the return form and the materials and check that what is listed has been sent. The returned materials are then placed on the shelves of the book room and the return form is sent to the Center supervisor, who records the date of the return of materials on both the inventory and teacher's cards.

DESIGN A DELIVERY SYSTEM

The particular system used for delivering materials to teachers depends upon available personnel and the time of the year. At the beginning of the school year, school aides are very busy filling orders, so everyone available should be involved in helping teachers receive their materials as quickly as possible. School aides and student monitors can help deliver teachers' orders after they have been prepared and checked. Later in the year when teachers' orders are less frequent, school aides may be able to deliver all of the orders. During those less busy times, the book room should be straightened and rearranged, if necessary, to provide space for new materials that arrive. This is also a good time to note which materials are out of stock so that they may be considered for future orders when funds are available.

11

SUCCESSFUL BUILDING OPERATION AND SAFETY

A well functioning and maintained school building contributes to the educational development of children. Many hours of the day and many days of the year are spent within that structure by both students and teachers, so a clean and appealing building contributes to the performance and spirit of both the staff and the youngsters.

The key factor is the working relationship between you and the custodian. As principal, you are "in charge" of the building and, as such, the custodian is a member of the staff and under your direction. But custodians also fall into another category of employees of the district and usuallly have a separate allocation of funds. In addition, the work of the custodial staff is usually not within the area of your expertise, so the custodian must be relied upon to conduct his or her efforts with efficiency and effectiveness. Because of this reliance upon the custodian for the identification and completion of tasks, a good relationship between the two of you will prove to be the most important factor in maintaining a physically well-run building.

ASSESS BUILDING STATUS

You are responsible for knowing about the current and ongoing condition of the school building—from the need for electrical work that will take time to complete to a stuffed sink that must be fixed immediately.

The status of the building, which should be updated monthly, is best accomplished through meetings between you and the custodian. At these monthly meetings, a listing of repair needs should be made, including what actions have been taken by you and the custodian to complete those needs (Figure 11-1). The monthly conferences provide the opportunity to update the repair needs list by eliminating needs that have been completed and adding those that are newly discovered. A written record of these conferences should be kept

PRINCIPAL/CUSTODIAN CONFERENCE, October 1984

JOB NEED	LOCATION	DATE NOTED	ACTION TAKEN	ACTION PENDING
1. Sheet metal work	3 roof exhaust hoods	5/2/84 P.O. 18 #31757	Job order #526152	Awaiting action to date.
2. Painting and plastering	Various areas around building	P.O. 18 submitted 12/83, 3/84, 7/84, 10/84	Request to General Supervisor of School Maintenance	Awaiting minor improvement program allocation.
3. Missing and cracked ceramic tile	Several bathrooms on first floor	P.O. 18 submitted 11/18/84	Plaster applied to surface	Awaiting action to date.
4. Window guards	Perimeter of building	10/27/83, also as per request in letter of 5/30/84	District bulletin No. 2	Awaiting action to date.
5. Additional radiators	Main lobby & corridors	6/12/83, resubmitted 6/1/84	Minor Improvement Program	Letter from Mr. Griffin dated 1/2/84.
6. Toilet stall partitions	Rooms 13, 110, 210	6/12/83	M.I.P.	Awaiting action to date.
7. Concrete work and trench drain grating with covers	Various areas around building	6/1/83	M.I.P.	Survey taken 3/21/83, 4/9/83 (none further to date)
8. Hardware and shades	Room 209	6/26/84	M.I.P.	Awaiting action to date.
9. Repair rolling grills to piano alcove	Gym and lunchroom	P.O. 18 submitted 5/23/83	Job Order #579062	Awaiting action to date.
10. Gates leading to playground need repair, including benches in Kindergarten yard	Outside Kindergarten entrance and school garden	9/24/83, 9/11/83, 3/3/84	Sent in P.O. 18 to Area Office on date noted	Awaiting action to date.
11. Remove and reset window	Room 22	10/13/84	Sent in P.O. 18 to Area Office	Awaiting action to date.
12. Caulking	Building exterior	10/14/84	Sent in P.O. 18 to Area Office	Awaiting action to date.

Figure 11-1

by both you and the custodian, and the proper person at the district office should be notified of the school's needs by forwarding a copy of the monthly conference.

ESTABLISH A MONITORING SYSTEM

Everyone in the school plays a part in the continuous monitoring system of the school building: you constantly observe conditions while making daily rounds with either the custodian or alone; teachers report existing conditions of both an immediate or repair-needed nature; and the custodian and his or her staff note needed repairs and conditions during their daily routine work.

An accurate daily monitoring system helps to catch problems before they reach an emergency condition and contributes to the maintenance of a well-functioning school. Everyone in the school should be a partner in this constant watch.

PROVIDE COMMUNICATION LINKS

Once a problem in the school building has been noted, an effective communication link must be established. The objective, of course, is to correct the problem as quickly as possible, an objective more realistically met if the report is properly made.

Establish a policy that directions for work and reports of building problems be directed to the custodian. On the other hand, the pedagogical staff is your responsibility, so directions for actions and reports of other problems are directed to you. This procedure will eliminate possible problems that could develop from teachers directing custodial workers or custodial workers telling teachers what should be done.

With this procedure in mind, the communication link becomes logical and effective. Reports of problems emanating from custodial workers are directed to the custodian, who can then direct his or her staff to correct the problem; reports of problems emanating from teachers or other members of the pedagogical staff are directed to you, who can inform the custodian of a problem and expect him or her to take actions to correct it. In all cases, the custodian should make you aware of a problem, the steps taken to correct the problem, and when the problem has been corrected.

Immediate Needs

At times, problems of an immediate nature occur—a child who has become ill in a classroom, an overflowing sink in the art room, the smell of smoke in the building. These emergencies cannot wait for the usual communication links, so they are best handled through a systematic procedure. The first step is to contact the custodian. Since most custodians usually spend little time in their office, using the school intercom will not be effective. The alternative, then, is to pre-establish a bell system signal via the public address system. Once the custodian is aware of the immediate need, he or she can direct a member of the staff to take action.

Several people may be directed to contact the custodian besides you; however, in each case of an immediate need, you should be notified even if someone else has actually contacted the custodian. Available personnel in the office, such as the secretary or an aide, may be instructed to do the actual contacting. You should inspect the scene of the immediate need as soon as possible, but certainly following the action to ensure that a safe condition results.

Minor Repairs/Needs

Minor repairs that do not represent an immediate need can be handled differently. These requests for minor repairs, usually made by teachers, should be placed in your letterbox so that you have control over the general condition of the classroom and the length of time required for those repairs to be completed.

The use of a repair request (Figure 11-2) will assist teachers in making these requests and will enable you to process them quickly. When a request form is found in your letterbox, initial the request, date it, and then post it on a specific bulletin board in the office. By mutual agreement, the custodian or a member of the staff reviews the bulletin board periodically during the day and removes the request. The repair is then made as soon as possible.

The Elementary School   _____ (initial)
Request for Repair   _____ (date)

Teacher _____   Room _____   Date _____

_____ broken shade   _____ plugged sink

_____ light bulb   _____ leaky faucet

_____ ripped window shade   _____ closet door

_____ torn shade cord   _____ wardrobe door

_____ broken window   _____ broken lock location

_____ radiator malfunction   _____

_____ other _____

Figure 11-2

BEAUTIFY THE SCHOOL BUILDING

Maintaining a well-kept school is everyone's job, so teachers, other personnel, and the custodial staff must work together. The following suggestions will contribute to beautifying your school building.

Effective Use of Bulletin Boards

Each bulletin board in the school should be numbered and each teacher assigned to a particular board. The teacher is then responsible for a display of students' work on that bulletin board, changing the displays periodically. You should note new bulletin board displays as you walk through the halls and present the class with a commendation card (Figure 11-3).

COMMENDATION CARD

Class _____ is to be commended for an outstanding
bulletin board display about _____

_____

_____

_____
Principal

Figure 11-3

You will be able to keep track of which bulletin boards have been changed by keeping a list (Figure 11-4) that is updated periodically. The listing of a key word used on the bulletin board will alert you to a new one.

The Showcase Appearance

Some schools have a showcase usually located in the lobby. The display in the showcase should be rotated among the grades of the school, with each teacher of the grade contributing student products around a theme cooperatively decided upon. Suggestions for themes include:

School Is Fun

We Learn to Read

Grade Five Learns About ...

See How We Work

Assign the showcase on a monthly basis. It is the responsibility of the grade leader to coordinate the collection of material for the showcase and to provide for mounting and removing the display so that the showcase is never empty.

Months Assigned	Grades
June and September	K
October and November	6
December and January	5
February	4
March	3
April	2
May	1

The particular month(s) of responsibility should be changed each year with the exception of the kindergarten because the kindergarten will probably have more to display in June. That grade display can be retained in the showcase during the summer and September so that the showcase will not be empty when school opens.

HALL BULLETIN BOARDS

CLASS	SEPT.	OCT.	NOV.	DEC.	JAN.	FEB.	MAR.	APR.	MAY	JUNE

Figure 11-4

If more than one showcase is available, assign the responsibility for the other(s) to special program teachers, such as science, music, art, and bilingual education. That showcase can be rotated among the special program teachers on a two-month or three-month basis.

Classroom Appearance

Habits and attitudes of pride in the school's appearance and concern for its maintenance are developed by the classroom teachers, who should insist upon neat and orderly rooms. Students should be encouraged to:

- keep their desks clean both inside and out
- keep the floor free of books and book bags
- store materials that do not fit in their desks in cubbies or the wardrobe closet
- pick up any papers found on the floor near their desks
- replace materials to the correct bookcase or kit in order and neatly
- empty their desks before long vacation periods so that the custodial staff can clean them

Teachers should develop these habits and attitudes by:

- setting a good example of neatness and order
- assigning monitors to take the basket around the room twice a day
- assigning monitors to maintain bookcases and kits in good order
- insisting upon the rules and standards set

These efforts will not only be rewarded by an improved classroom appearance, but will also contribute to the life of instructional materials and the learning abilities of the students. Recent studies indicate that learning is an orderly process enhanced by both visual neatness and appearance as well as the development of good work and study habits. Hopefully, the habits and attitudes learned in the classroom will also be carried on in the halls, the lunchroom, and in the homes of the students. You will know these aims are being achieved when:

- the hall bulletin boards are unmarked and neat
- the halls of the school are free of litter
- the lunchroom has a minimum of food and litter on the floor
- the parents begin to comment about the neatness of their children at home

Involve the Students

The establishment of a Student Council, elected by their peers and directed by a staff member who is assigned by you, will assist beautifying efforts. This Student Council should meet to plan actions designed to solve school problems and to improve the current status. The Student Council's plan may include some of the following suggestions:

- Contests
  a. neatest classroom of the week
  b. most appealing bulletin board of the month
  c. cleanest lunchroom table of the day

The reward for each contest may include:
  a. a commendation card from you
  b. a class party
  c. an Honor List posted in the hall

- Campaigns
  a. cleaning the school yard
  b. working on the school garden
  c. cleaning the graffiti around the building
  d. painting a mural on an inside or outside wall
  e. picking up litter in the halls

- Responsibilities
  a. judging contests and selecting the winners
  b. determining the reward for each contest
  c. working on projects and campaigns
  d. making the student body aware of current work
  e. speaking to students in classrooms or at assemblies about the efforts of the Student Council
  f. working with the assigned staff member who will keep you informed of all actions

Monitor the Process

You should monitor the effectiveness of the beautification plans by visual inspection during tours of the building and classrooms. Modification of plans can then be made when necessary.

The Mysterious Offender

One of your most frustrating experiences as principal is the malicious work of an unknown offender. The actions of such an offender may include:

setting off the fire alarm

writing on the bathroom walls

throwing wet paper balls on the ceiling

writing on the stairways

urinating on the floor

There is an effective strategy that may help you catch the offender or stop him or her from these actions. The first step is to require each teacher to maintain an "out of the room" notebook, kept in a particular place in each classroom. Any student wanting to go to the bathroom or get a drink of water is required to sign his or her name and the time in the book. (Girls are usually asked to go to the bathroom in pairs.) The next step is to require the custodial staff to observe the bathrooms and hallways of the building every one to two hours each day. When a malicious action is observed, you are notified and then the plan can go into action.

● Announce over the public address system that there is a problem and ask each teacher to send a list of the students out of the room during the period of time in which the action must have occurred.

● Keep these lists of names with a notation of the date.

● When a second action occurs, request a similar list over the public address system. The students repeated on the second list are then interviewed.

● Call to your office those students whose names occur on both the first and second list. Speak to them first individually, and then as a group. Tell these students that they are being watched.

● The action usually will not occur a third time. If it does, the list of students whose names appear three times are then identified and questioned separately. Tell them of the possible actions that can be taken, such as notification of parents and suspension. Usually, the plan is effective.

● When the problem involves setting off the fire alarm, you can take another action. Ask the custodian to paint the alarm handles with a florescent paint. Publicizing that this has been done usually stops the student from a repeated offense.

UTILIZE SPACE

Either too much or not enough space in a school building can be a problem. Each problem requires a different approach to solve it.

Too Much Space

Having unoccupied rooms in a school building can cause two problems for you: (1) there is the ever-constant threat of closing schools; and (2) if the school is not closed, rooms or a floor of the building might be closed by the central office, causing a reduction in the allocation of staff and funds for the custodial force. Both of these possibilities can have a negative effect on the school. Your concern, then, is to find effective uses for the empty rooms.

Empty rooms can be put to many uses. The following represent some concrete suggestions.

A Television Viewing Room. Many educational programs are offered on a wide variety of subjects. You can usually become informed about these programs through the mail or by contacting the district or state education department. In addition, many state departments of education produce their own educational television series that are available to schools at a nominal cost or at no cost.

Some educational television series are also available on videotape and may be viewed by purchasing or securing these tapes, an investment that can be a tremendous asset to a school. The availability of these programs and a schedule of when they are available for viewing should be circulated among the teachers, who can then reserve the television viewing room on a regularly scheduled basis. The videotapes are an advantage when using a television viewing room because the time desired for use does not depend upon when the program is broadcast; it can be viewed at any time.

A Laboratory Room. This room would contain materials that are not available in the classroom. The materials might include such items as Madison Project Math Lab, Invictor Math Materials, creative measuring materials using string or other objects, Cuisinaire® Company materials, and selected metric activities. The laboratory might also contain materials in different areas of the curriculum, such as Fountain Valley reading materials and scientific equipment. Classes can be scheduled to use the room on a request basis or at your direction.

A Media Center. The development of a media center involves the availability of a variety of teaching machines that can be profitably used by students who require remediation, enrichment, or additional help in learning English as a second language. The most popular teaching devices used successfully in a media center include Systems 80, Bell and Howell Language Masters, microfiche and microfiche readers, filmstrips and tapes, film loops and tacho-flashers. Each of these teaching machines is designed to use programs that are written on a wide range of topics in all areas of the curriculum and designed for specific needs of individual students. Students may be scheduled to use a particular program in the media center on a regular basis. (If the scheduling of individual students is not practical, schedule classes to use the center with their teacher.) The scheduling of individuals to the media center requires personnel available in the center to direct and assist the students as well as to maintain records of their progress on the programs. When professional staff are not available for this, parent volunteers can be used most effectively after training. Although these machines are expensive and probably cannot be found through the regular school allocation, use of funds raised by the Parents Association can be very effective.

Special Programs. When possible, place each teacher offering a special program in an individual room. These programs may include those offered on a schoolwide basis, such as programs for the gifted, programs for the learning disabled, speech improvement, vocal and instrumental music, Chapter I reading or mathematics, and the performing arts.

A Teacher Center. The establishment of a teacher center is an excellent use of an empty room. Prepare the room with a wide variety of materials so that it will meet the needs of the teachers who use it. These materials should include:

- curriculum bulletins on all subject areas and levels
- special bulletins prepared by the state or national Office of Education
- sample copies of books and materials supplied by publishers
- one-of-a-kind teacher materials
- materials concerning instructional strategies and techniques included in books, magazines, pamphlets, and articles
- supplies for creating activity or task cards
- ditto stencils or mimeo stencils

A Parent's Room. This room should be reserved for the exclusive use of the Parents Association and the Executive Board for keeping their records and supplies, meetings with various people with whom they have business, distributing articles sold during fund raisers, and a gathering place for parents to relax, wait for youngsters, and speak with members of the board or other parents.

A School Museum. This room affords space to prepare and display exhibits on any topic in which the school may have an interest: items involved with the history of the school or the community, or items collected by a class or a grade on a particular subject. The museum may be used by teachers, classes of students, parents, or individual students. If individual students are permitted to visit the museum, someone should be assigned to the room.

A Meeting Room. This room may be used by any group wanting meeting space—teachers may meet here for their grade conference, a group of parents may meet here, or the student council may use the room for a meeting. To avoid confusion, there should be a posted schedule of when the room has been reserved.

Guidance Services. When guidance services are performed in the school, professionals who come to the school to evaluate particular youngsters require space for those evaluations. This is an excellent use of an available room and may contribute to speeding up the process.

Universities. If your school has student- or associate-teacher programs, use the room for storing their materials and equipment.

At times, universities require space to conduct field courses. The advantage of holding a field-based university course in a school is that it is immediately available to the school staff, and teachers within that building may be encouraged to participate in those courses.

Outside Educational Groups. School programs such as nursery or day-care groups outside of the school system require space for classes. Offer your school's services to the community by letting the groups meet in the room.

Special Education. Classes that are organized to meet the needs of certified special education students usually draw their population from a wide geographic area. These classes are usually housed within regular school buildings and represent an excellent use of available space. It is important for you to know who will be responsible for supervising these classes and what services and materials accompany them before agreeing to house such classes.

Not Enough Space

Of the two problems—too much or not enough—finding space is the larger problem. Some schools in overpopulated areas are often desperate to find space for all the students let alone special programs that are available. The following suggestions are offered for finding that space.

Sharing Room. Although sharing a room has many negative aspects, at times this may be the only solution. Rooms that are shared cannot be used by two large groups of students at the same time, but they can be used by one large group of students for different purposes at different times. For example, a television viewing room may also serve—at another time—as a laboratory setting. The parents' room may be used at other times for guidance services or by university faculty. When rooms are shared, it is important to clarify when the room will be available for each purpose. It is also important to specify what may be kept in the room and where it may be stored.

When the room is used for the instruction of small groups of students, it is possible to schedule the same room at the same time to two different small groups. This requires the cooperation of the two teachers who will be working simultaneously.

Floating Programs. Laboratories and the media center may be placed on rolling carts that are brought to particular classrooms when there is no room in which to house them. In this way, students or classes who may be involved in the programs can receive services in their own classroom rather than going to another room.

The Auditorium/Cafeteria/Gymnasium. When not used for other purposes and on a scheduled basis, these large group rooms may be used for instructional purposes such as for television or videotape viewing. One advantage of the larger setting is that more than one class may be seated at one time. It is necessary, however, that the teacher follow up the viewing with a class lesson since conducting a discussion in an auditorium with several classes is usually not effective.

Schools with extremely bad space problems sometimes use these facilities as regular classrooms. This is an extremely poor situation and should be avoided if possible.

The Auditorium Stage. Schools that are very pressed for space might consider using the auditorium stage for groups of students in special programs. When the curtain is closed and portable furniture is placed on the stage, a mini-classroom results. Since the furniture is portable, it can be moved backstage when the stage is required for assemblies.

Other Small Rooms. Most schools have small rooms that were intended for specific purposes:

    auditorium dressing rooms

    nurse's office

    assistant principal's office

    teacher's room

    locker room

It is important to note if these rooms have windows, and to know the heating and ventilating problems. Remember that these rooms may be the only alternatives for special small group programs. IMPORTANT: If the teacher's room is being considered for special programs, the union representative should be included in the discussion before the room is assigned. Be sure that there are adequate toilet facilities for teachers before using the teacher's room.

ENSURE BUILDING SECURITY

Good education begins with safety for students and staff, with nothing more important than this consideration. Once the safety and security of the school building is ensured, the educational process becomes effective. Thus, safety should be first on your list of priorities.

Safety Plan

Each school should have a cooperatively developed and written safety plan (Figure 11-5) that is communicated to teachers. It is the teacher's responsibility to be familiar with the safety plan and be ready to implement it if necessary.

SCHOOL SAFETY PLAN

A. SCHOOL SAFETY COMMITTEE

The School Safety Committee shall meet as often as it deems necessary. It shall receive reports on safety conditions in the school. The School Safety Committee will revise the School Safety Plan in accordance with the needs of our school.

The School Safety Committee consists of:

1. Principal
2. Parents Association President plus 2 other members
3. Union representative
4. Two teachers
5. Custodian

B. PRINCIPAL'S RESPONSIBILITY

The principal has the responsibility of maintaining security and safety in the school by implementing appropriate procedures, providing safe conditions, facilities, supervision of staff, and taking action against those who threaten the safety of the school.

C. GENERAL SECURITY

1. A special public address announcement of "School Alert" shall alert teachers that an intruder is in the building or that an emergency situation exists. The procedure to follow is to lock the classroom door and allow no children out of the room.
2. Strangers in the halls are to be reported to the Main Office the fastest possible way via telephones in the rooms.
3. The school public address system shall be maintained in repair. All personnel are to be made aware of this.
4. The police phone number shall be taped to the secretary's telephone. All personnel are to be made aware of this.
5. The principal shall designate a representative to be charged with maintaining safety when he or she is absent.

D. DOOR AND BUILDING SECURITY

1. All doors shall be maintained in good repair at all times. A regular periodic check shall be made to insure that the doors are locked. Defective or damaged doors must be reported to the custodian.

---

2. All doors shall be locked to the outside when not in use to admit or dismiss children with the exception of the Main Door. The Main Door shall be locked from 12 noon to 1 p.m.

3. Aides or parent volunteers are stationed at the desk near the Main Door at all times.

4. Morning and afternoon rounds to check the security of the building shall be made.

5. Teachers in end rooms, near the outer doors to the yard, shall check doors periodically during the day.

6. Bathrooms and lounges shall be checked periodically.

E. VISITORS

1. A sign at the Main Door entrance shall read, "All persons entering the school must report to the Main Office, sign the visitor's guest book, and obtain a pass."

2. All visitors in the building shall be required to have a visitor's pass. These will be issued at the Main Office.

3. All visitors are urged to make an appointment with the teacher so that instruction time will not be interfered with.

4. Each classroom shall display a card in the window stating that visitors are to obtain a pass at the Main Office.

5. Classroom teachers shall notify his or her neighbor(s) of difficulty or suspicion of intruder.

6. Visitors must sign out and leave building by the Main Door.

F. DEALING WITH INTRUDERS

1. The fastest possible way to report intruders in the building to the Main Office should be used.

2. The following actions will be taken when the safety of the school is threatened:
   a. Notify police
   b. Attempt to remove from school property all persons who threaten the safety of the school
   c. Press charges against any person who commits a crime on school property

G. SAFE SCHOOL ATMOSPHERE

1. Suggestions from staff members to make security more effective shall be encouraged.

2. When the special public address alert sounds, school aides, clusters, teachers on preparation periods, supervisors, and custodians shall check for children in halls, gym, bathrooms, yard and auditorium, and bring children to the closest classroom. A second announcement will give the "all clear" signal.

3. All employees shall leave the building within fifteen minutes of dismissal. If teachers plan to stay in school after dismissal, they shall notify the Main Office in writing.

4. No person, staff or children shall be permitted to be in isolated areas of the building alone.

5. Classroom doors shall be locked when the teacher and children leave the room.

6. Classes going to the yard shall lock the door behind them. They are to re-enter the school via the Main Door.

7. All children must have a pass when they leave the room. Girls are to go in pairs.

8. Teachers are to keep a "leave the room" book. Pupils are to sign the time of leaving and returning.

9. At dismissal, the classroom door shall be locked after children exit.

11. In the event of a break-in, teachers should inventory their rooms to report any and all missing materials.

11. Classroom precautions shall include:
   a. Never leave money in school. Children shall be asked to do the same.
   b. Do not give keys to children. They can be easily lost and then used by intruders.
   c. Keep record cards, audiovisual equipment and other valuable items locked in the teacher's coat closet.
   d. Teachers are not to leave their pocketbooks, wallets, and other personal items on their desks. These should be locked in their closets.

12. All substitutes shall be acquainted with regular and emergency safety procedures.

13. All students shall become acquainted with safety program information.

14. All alarm systems are to be tested daily by the custodian.

Figure 11-5

Emergency Plan

In addition to a written school safety plan, a written plan to deal with emergency situations (Figure 11-6) should also be developed and communicated to the staff. Teachers and all other school personnel should be familiar with the plan and ready to implement it if necessary.

SCHOOL PLAN FOR NEIGHBORHOOD DISASTER

GENERAL INSTRUCTIONS

A. Fire and Shelter Drill intructions, signals and responses REMAIN UNCHANGED and must be observed.

B. For Neighborhood Disaster Emergency Conditions:

1. Teachers who are supervising classes—in classrooms, gymnasium, auditorium—are to REMAIN with the pupils, wherever they are, while awaiting specific instructions. In the meantime, do the following:

   a. Secure immediate attention and order.

   b. By remaining calm, self-assured, and good humored, reassure pupils that matters are under control.

   c. Start a game or song that will engage the children's interest and take their minds off the situation.

   d. Do NOT send pupils out of the room to the Main Office or elsewhere for ANY reason. Keep pupils with you and wait for further instructions.

2. Teachers who are on yard duty or class outdoor period are to bring pupils into line-up area AT ONCE and bring the students to the closest shelter areas within the school.

3. If disaster emergency occurs while teacher and class are in transit between classroom and some other part of the school building, go with pupils to official room if possible, or to assigned room Shelter Area.

4. During such an emergency situation, adults may rush into the school to pick up children in order to take them home. Pupils may be released ONLY if you KNOW the adult is the parent or guardian of the child in question. A child may NOT be released to an adult who is not the child's parent or guardian unless release is authorized IN WRITING by the Main Office. Make a record, by name, of all pupils whom you have released.

5. If emergency occurs during time when pupils are arriving for the beginning of the session, the teachers will report to their classes in the area where the students are assembled.

6. HANDICAPPED CHILDREN—Make sure that all handicapped children are accounted for and that special provisions are made for them.

DIRECTIONS FOR IMPLEMENTING SHELTER-DISPERSAL DRILL PLAN

I. FOR TEACHERS OF GRADES 4, 5, and 6

A. *At the first signal (2 bells)*
  1. All children will get clothing, open at least one window, lower shades.

B. *At the second signal (5 bells)*
  1. Children in Grades 4, 5, and 6 who are to take younger children home are to leave and call for designated children. They are to leave through the MAIN DOOR.

  An aide will be in charge at the Main Door.

  2. Bus children will go to the auditorium (supervised by aides).

  3. All teachers are to keep their doors open and assist in the supervision of children who are passing through the halls. NO TALKING IS PERMITTED.

C. *At the third signal (5 bells—3 times)*
  1. Conduct your class down. Children who are to remain in school are to be at the head of the line. They are to drop off the line before your class leaves the school building. They will go to the gymnasium and will be lined up by aides.

  2. After teachers have dismissed students going home, they will return to the gym, pick up the remaining children of the class and take them to the regular shelter area position.

D. *At the fourth signal (1 bell)*
  1. Dismiss as usual.

II. FOR TEACHERS OF GRADES K, 1, 2, AND 3

A. *At the first signal (2 bells)*
  1. All children will get clothing, open at least one window, lower shades.

B. *At the second signal (5 bells)*
  1. Release the designated children to the custody of an older brother or sister.

  2. Same as B.2 above.

  3. Same as B.3 above.

C. *At the third signal (5 bells—3 times)*
  1. Take the remainder of the class to the Shelter-Area position.

D. *At the fourth signal (1 bell)*
  1. Dismiss as usual.

NOTE: An aide will be stationed at the corner of the school. He or she will insist that all children go home at once.

STAFF ASSIGNMENTS DURING ALL EMERGENCY SITUATIONS

A. PRINCIPAL—Take post in hallway outside of Main Office door to give directions, etc.

B. ENRICHMENT & REMEDIATION TEACHER—Take post at main entrance of occupied floor above OR below on which PRINCIPAL is stationed, depending on conditions. Supervise your floor, take any IMMEDIATE action that may be necessary on the floor, and stand by for orders from the PRINCIPAL. AS SOON AS POSSIBLE, report conditions to the Principal via adult messenger. Take command of the school if the Principal is absent or incapacitated.

C. SECRETARIES—Take post in the Main Office, unless ordered otherwise by person in charge of school, to monitor telephone and radio broadcasts. Transmit messages to and from person in charge of school. Make office supply of First Aid materials available as ordered. Refer to the person in charge of the school all requests from adults to take students home. See to it that nobody uses the telephone for outgoing calls without authorization from the person in charge of the school. PHONES MUST BE KEPT OPEN.

D. OTHER TEACHERS—If not on assignment with pupils when emergency occurs, report to person in charge of school for special assignments.

E. SCHOOL NURSE—Take post in Medical Office or room designated previously by principal.

F. SCHOOL AIDES AND PARA-PROFESSIONALS (Lunchroom, Audiovisual, Educational Assistants, Teacher Aides, Family Workers and Family Assistants)—Report to person in charge of school for assignments. This procedure also applies to SCHOOL SECURITY GUARDS.

G. CUSTODIAL STAFF.
   1. Custodian and Assistants
      FIRST—Secure operational plant factors for safety, i.e., water lines, gas lines, electric lines, furnace fires, etc.
      SECOND—Check all possible building damage factors.
      THIRD—Report plant conditions to person in charge of school *as soon as possible.*
      FOURTH—"Stand by" for orders from person in charge of school.
   2. Matron—Report *at once* to the person in charge of the school for duty assignments.

III. CHANGE OF COMMAND SUCCESSION

Three teachers have been designated to take charge of the school in the event that ALL supervisors are absent and/or incapacitated. These teachers have been assigned a "priority number" from 1 to 3 and will take charge of the school, as conditions require it, in the order of their priority starting with number 1. These three teachers are designated by name on the notice that is posted in the Main Office on the school bell signal system board.

IV. TELEPHONE COMMUNICATION

A. The school telephone may NOT be used by ANY person for outgoing calls of any kind during an emergency, except when authorized by the principal.

B. The person in charge of the school will find cards posted above the principal's telephone and on the Main Office bell signal board listing telephone numbers to be called for various purposes during an emergency.

Figure 11-6

A Door Check

Exit doors should be checked throughout the day. A specific person should be assigned to monitor the doors to ensure that they are closed, locked from the outside, and free from any objects that might keep them ajar. The individual assigned to the inspection should initial the inspection sheet (Figure 11-7) posted in the office to indicate that the doors have been checked during the morning and afternoon hours.

**EXIT DOOR INSPECTION
FOR THE 19XX-XX SCHOOL YEAR**

SEPTEMBER

(date)																														
A.M.																														
P.M.																														

OCTOBER

(date)																														
A.M.																														
P.M.																														

NOVEMBER

(date)
A.M.
P.M.

DECEMBER

(date)
A.M.
P.M.

JANUARY

(date)
A.M.
P.M.

FEBRUARY

(date)
A.M.
P.M.

MARCH

(date)
A.M.
P.M.

APRIL

(date)
A.M.
P.M.

MAY

(date)
A.M.
P.M.

JUNE

(date)
A.M.
P.M.

Figure 11-7

12

FROM STUDENT PROFILES TO FIRE DRILLS: HOW TO FORMULATE SCHOOL POLICY

Administering an elementary school involves attention to a seemingly endless number of details, each important because it involves large numbers of students and staff who may be affected by poor management. At times, forgetting to consider the consequences of one action or inaction may lead to utter chaos. Since so many details are unanticipated or usually not considered, the formation of a school policy for those details that can be anticipated and are considered will help make the school a smoothly operating organization.

PREPLAN FOR A SMOOTH FIRST DAY

The first day of a new term is important to students and staff because it sets the tone for the entire year. Parents are just as anxious about their children's new class and teacher as the children themselves, and school personnel are anxious to start off on the right foot by creating an impression of the serious nature of school. You can contribute to setting this proper tone of order and reassurance for all the populations involved by preplanning the details.

The procedure for the first day of school should be clearly explained at the opening faculty conference. Some of the details involved with minimizing first-day problems include the following.

Yard Line-Up Positions

Give a listing of class yard line-up positions to the teachers. These positions should be painted in large white numerals (the room numbers) on the surface of the school yard. (See the sample.)

YELLOWBIRD LANE						
1		102		201		
2		101		203		
3	GRADE	103	GRADES	202	GRADES	
5	1	104	2 and 3	204	4, 5, and 6	
7		106		206		
		105		205		
		108		208		
		120		207		
				209		
				210		
BUILDING ENTRANCE (EXIT)						

The room numbers are listed in sequence as they are in the school halls. The numbers, however, are listed so that the room most distant from the yard entrance enters the building first. This will relieve congestion in the halls as classes arrive at their doors and enter their rooms.

Kindergarten classes that have a separate entrance should use that entrance and not line up in the school yard. In schools where there is no separate entrance for kindergarten classes, another section of the yard should be designated for their use.

Schools without yards should establish class line-up positions using whatever landmarks are available. Schools with grassy line-up areas might consider using rocks or digging low posts as designations for line-up positions.

Facilitate First Day Line-Up

Each student should have the new class and room listed on his or her report card, which is distributed the last day of school. New admissions, registered before school opens, should have also been given this class and room information. The name of the teacher may be omitted from this information since staff assignment sometimes changes during the summer. It is more difficult to explain that a teacher has been changed than to ask students to wait until school opens to find out the name of their teachers.

On the first day of school, instruct each teacher to prepare a sign that designates the class and room number corresponding to the report card listing. Teachers are to hold these signs in the school yard to assist parents and students in finding their correct lines.

Inclement Weather Line-Up Positions

You must also provide for inclement weather line-up positions, the designation of which depends upon your school's facilities. In schools where both a cafeteria and a gymnasium are available, line-up positions may be separated for lower grades (1, 2) from upper grades (3, 4, 5, 6). In schools where the cafeteria and the gymnasium may be a miltipurpose room, another area, such as the auditorium or a corridor, may be used.

The inclement weather positions should be clearly set in the minds of the students on the first day of school. Teachers should be asked to follow directions on the first day, to conduct their classes to inclement weather positions after leaving the yard, and before going to the classrooms. You and a teacher (or assistant principal) without a class responsibility should be assigned to each inclement weather line-up area to assist teachers and students in finding their assigned spots.

Reinforce School Line-Up Policy

In general, ask teachers to continue to pick up their classes for the first week of school to ensure that the students know, understand, and observe (1) the class line-up positions in good and inclement weather, and (2) correct order and behavior in entering the school building.

You should monitor this morning line-up to discontinue the teachers' attendance as soon as possible; the teachers' morning time is better spent in the classroom preparing for the students' arrival than in the school yard. Once proper procedure has been established, the teacher on morning line or yard duty or the school aide assigned to this duty should be left in charge of morning line-up. At any time during the school year when morning line-up does not continue in good order, teachers should be asked to pick up their classes from the yard and continue this practice until good order has once again been established. Since most teachers would rather not go to the yard to pick up their classes, they will usually be cooperative in discussing correct line-up behavior with their classes. When only particular classes cause yard line-up problems, only those teachers should be asked to pick up their classes.

PREPARE FOR SCHOOL DRILLS

Both fire drills and shelter drills are usually mandated by state law. They contribute to the safety of a school building and should be observed by everyone within the school. You are responsible for both designing the process for these drills and for implementing them periodically throughout the year.

General Instructions

1. Every room within the school building should have both a Fire Drill Chart and a Shelter Drill Chart posted on the wall next to the door. Never remove these charts; they should remain posted even at the end of the school year. If the charts become torn or unreadable, teachers should request new charts from the general office.

2. Each teacher is responsible for seeing that no child is left behind in the building. Students attending special programs when a drill occurs should return immediately to the classroom to get clothing. The teacher in charge of the special program should accompany the children to ensure that the class has not left the building. In circumstances when the class

is no longer in the room, the special teacher will take those students with him or her when evacuating the building. In extreme emergencies, students shall be escorted outside of the building without coats.

3. All drills should be conducted in silence. Teachers are responsible for the behavior and order of their classes.

4. No class should wait for another class. Each class, led by the teacher, proceeds when ready.

5. Each class moves as a unit, two by two.

6. Walk briskly but do not run. The order and safety of the students are paramount. Chaos that may result from running in disorder may be less effective than the speed it might accomplish.

7. Become familiar with the instructions posted on the drill charts in the classrooms and follow their instructions.

8. Ask the last student out of the room to close the classroom door.

Fire Drills

1. Post a Fire Drill Chart (Figure 12-1) in each classroom.

FIRE DRILL CHART

Room _____

Signal: Two short bells followed by a continuous bell signal lasting one
    minute.

Instructions: Students are to be immediately asked for silence. They are
    then instructed to get clothing in good order. They are to line up and
    be conducted out of the building as quickly as possible.

Exit: This classroom will use Exit _____to get out of the building.
    Follow _____to _____.
    Wait there with the class until the "all clear" signal is given.

Figure 12-1

2. Exits may be impassable during drills or because of actual fire. When this occurs, the nearest passable exit should be used. Silent fire drills should be periodically conducted to simulate the possible circumstance when the bell system not working. When a silent fire drill is in progress, a monitor appears at the door with a sign stating SILENT FIRE DRILL. The monitor should remain until the teacher sees the sign. The procedures to follow are the same as during a regular fire drill.

3. Be sure all teachers and students know their fire drill positions. Here is a sample of one posted map.

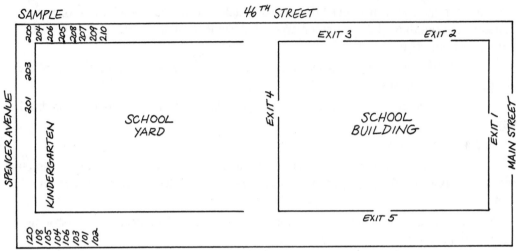

Shelter Drills

1. Post a Shelter Drill Chart (Figure 12-2) in each classroom.

SHELTER DRILL CHART

Room _____

Preliminary Signal: At two bells, all the children are to get their clothing, open the door and at least one window, and lower the shades.

Second Signal: At five gongs, everyone is to proceed to the shelter drill position.

Third Signal: At one gong, everyone can return to the classroom.

ROOM DRILL POSITION: Use Exit _____and proceed to _____
_____.

Figure 12-2

---

2. Exits may be impassable during drills or because of actual glass or fallen debris. When this occurs, the nearest passable exit should be used. Silent shelter drills should be periodically conducted to simulate the possibility of the bell system not working. When a silent shelter drill is in progress, a monitor appears at the door with a sign stating SILENT SHELTER DRILL. The monitor should remain until the teacher sees the sign. The procedures to follow are the same as during a regular shelter drill.

3. Be sure all teachers and students know their shelter drill positions. Here is a sample.

SAMPLE

	122	120	106	108	104/102
105		120	106	108	104
107	117	103	101	102	204
	117	LIBRARY	107	105/103	101

AUDITORIUM

				8	4	
205	203	207	8		4	2
206	201	7	5	3	3	1
17	11	7	5	3		1

Bus Safety Drill

1. At least three bus safety drills should be conducted during the school year. The first drill should occur within the first week of the new school year. The second drill should occur between November and December, and the third between March and April.

2. The following information should be covered in the drills: correct boarding and unboarding procedures, attention to the driver, emergency procedures, and location of emergency exits.

3. All students should participate in the bus safety drills. If the majority of students in the school use bus transportation, the drills might take place when the students arrive in the morning or before they leave in the afternoon. The drill may also be conducted at any time during the day that the students can easily be released from classes. If the majority of students do not use the school bus, a different strategy might be more practical. Those students who take the bus can be involved in a bus drill when they are on the bus. The other students can participate in a bus drill during the first class trip. This procedure will eliminate the problem of taking large groups of students out of class during the day.

4. You should send a statement to the district office about having conducted a bus drill or having initiated the drill.

ESTABLISH A TRIP PROCEDURE

Trips can greatly add to the education of the students. In addition to the content of the trip, youngsters are provided opportunities to learn how to conduct themselves in a public vehicle, as an audience, and as part of the group. Whenever a group of students leave the building, however, their security and safety must be secured. Since the students are your responsibility during school hours regardless of whether or not they are *physically* within the school building, a specific trip procedure and policy are important.

Checklist for Class Trips

1. Post and update appropriate trip sites on the office bulletin board. Those that are removed and still current can be found in a box labeled TRIPS in the library. When considering a trip, be sure to examine if: (1) the trip is appropriate to the grade's curriculum; (2) the trip is appropriate to the level of maturity of the students; and (3) the trip is within a reasonable distance from the school.

2. Contact those persons who are in charge of the trip site. Determine the length of time required for the visit, ask about facilities for eating lunch, ask about toilet facilities, and ask about having a guide to escort the class. Remember, too, to select an appropriate date when a bus is available.

3. Teachers planning a trip should complete and submit a School Trip Permission Form (Figure 12-3) about one month before the trip is planned.

SCHOOL TRIP PERMISSION FORM

Teacher's name _____ Class _____
Request date _____ Trip date _____
Provision made for bus _____
Site to be visited _____
Educational value _____

Procedures completed for: parent consent _____, parents to accompany _____, lunchroom notification _____, lunch on trip day _____.

Figure 12-3

4. A Parent Trip Consent (Figure 12-4) should be sent home at least one month before the trip. These forms should be signed by the parent and returned to school to be filed for the remainder of the school year.

No student should be permitted to go on the trip without the return of a signed consent form. Each class going on a trip should be accompanied by one adult for every ten students in the upper grades, and one adult for every five students in the lower grades.

PARENT TRIP CONSENT FORM

Date _____

Dear Parents,

Your child _____ of class _____
is invited to participate in a class trip to _____
_____
on _____. The class will leave at _____
and return at _____. Lunch that day will _____
_____. Therefore please send _____
with your child. The costs of the trip include _____
_____. The money will be collected from _____
to _____. Your child may bring some spending money for the trip. Please do not
give your child more than _____ to spend.

We are interested in having some parents with us on the trip to help supervise the students. If
you are able to accompany the class on _____, please check the box below.

Whether or not you will accompany us, please sign the tear-off slip below to give your child
permission to go on the trip. Keep this top half to remind yourself of the date and the site of the
trip.

Sincerely,

_____
Teacher

(tear off and return)

I give my child _____ of class _____
permission to attend the class trip on _____.

I will be able to accompany the class. ☐

I will not be able to accompany the class. ☐

_____
Parent's signature

Figure 12-4

SIGN-OUT BOOK

Class _____

NAME	DATE	TIME OUT	TIME IN

Figure 12-5

ORGANIZE AN OUT-OF-THE-ROOM PROCEDURE

Each teacher should be required to maintain a special notebook (Figure 12-5) for recording the names of the students who leave the room without supervision and the time they leave. This record has several useful purposes:

- parents may be interested in noting how frequently their children are out of the classroom

- when incidents occur, you can use this list in an attempt to determine which students were out of their classrooms and possibly involved in the incident

- the teachers will be able to keep track of those students who are out of the room more often than necessary and those students who are out of the room for protracted periods of time

No student in grades 2 through 6 should be permitted to leave the room without signing his or her name and the time in the sign-out book. First graders and those second graders who are considered too young to use the sign-out book should be taken to the toilets in groups in the morning and the afternoon under the supervision of an adult. Girls should always be required to leave the classroom in pairs.

At times, children play or fight in the toilets when they are unsupervised. If this becomes a problem, it might be wise to remove and store the hall doors to the toilets. When the doors are removed, the students who are spending time inappropriately may be observed by an adult passing by.

DEAL WITH BROKEN EQUIPMENT

Machines often become unuseable. At times, the repair may be of a minor nature, such as the replacement of a bulb; at other times, the repair can be major. Machines that cannot be used detract from the educational program because the machines may provide vital services to particular students whose educational sequence is interrupted when they are not in use.

A procedure for dealing with broken machines will help to repair them and send them back to the classroom as quickly as possible. Teachers should be made aware of exactly what to do when a machine does not function properly.

1. Complete the Machine Repair Request (Figure 12-6) and attach it to the malfunctioning machine.

2. Prepare the Receipt (Figure 12-7) and give it to the monitor who will transport the broken machine.

MACHINE REPAIR REQUEST

Teacher _____ Class _____ Date _____
Machine needing repair _____
Problem _____

Figure 12-6

RECEIPT

A _____ machine has been received for repair
by _____
on _____. This machine is assigned to

_____. _____.
         (teacher's name)   (class)

Figure 12-7

3. Send the broken machine to the media center to the attention of the media aide.

4. Hold the signed receipt until the repaired machine is returned.

5. If the teacher must have a replacement machine while the broken machine is in repair, the teacher should prepare the Machine Replacement Request (Figure 12-8) and sent it to the Media Request Box in the central office.

MACHINE REPLACEMENT REQUEST

Teacher _____ Class _____ Date _____
Please provide a _____
to temporarily replace the machine in repair.

Figure 12-8

The school should train at least one person to work with machines that are not functioning. The time and money saved by the school in minor repair done by this person will more than pay for the course that was taken. Generally, a school aide can be sent to take a media course.

If the school has available machines to temporarily replace one that is in repair, it may be easy to fill the teacher's request. At times, old machines that may function are kept for this purpose when newer machines have been purchased. If no other machine is available to replace the machine in repair, the teacher may have to share a machine with another class.

MONITOR ATTENDANCE RECORDS

Attendance procedures vary from district to district and county to county; however, they are all official documents that must be kept with accuracy and care. The teacher is responsible for correctly completing the requested information, which you should monitor at least once each term. To prepare teachers for the inspection and to assist them in properly completing the attendance requirements, a Self-Evaluation Guide (Figure 12-9) should be prepared and distributed along with the attendance documents to the teachers at the beginning of the school year. Remember that the contents of the Self-Evaluation guide will vary with the requirements of attendance documents in each particular school district.

SELF-EVALUATION GUIDE

Teacher _____ Class _____ Room _____ Year _____

A. Initial Entries

1. *Class Register Summary Card* (list boys/girls separately)
   a. School year
   b. Class
   c. School
   d. Date (school began)
   e. Teacher
   f. Pupils' Names (Last/First)
   g. Date of Birth
   h. Admitted from:
   i. Discharged to:

2. *Individual Student Cards*
   Top
   a. School year
   b. School
   c. Boro
   d. Current New Class
   e. Class as of 6/XX
   f. Pupil's Name
   g. Fall/Spring
   h. Total Abs. last year
   i. Circle M/F
   j. Birth Date
   k. Parent/Guardian
   l. Home Phone
   m. Business Phone
   n. Address
   o. 19XX (two places)
   p. Teacher
   Bottom
   p. Omit I.D.#
   q. Pupil's Name
   r. Mark "H" holidays

Other side—Additional Information
   s. School year 19XX
   t. Month and Day
      1. postcard sent
      2. reason for absence

B. Ongoing Entries

1. *Attendance* (Individual Cards)
   a. present in school—no mark
   b. absent all day A
   c. absent a.m. [a diagonal box]
   c. absent p.m. [a diagonal box]
   e. admission)
   f. discharge) student card
      and
   g. interclass) class summary
   h. ½ day school (last card)
      date, hours, reason

C. Monthly Entries

1. No. of Days
   a. Max. school days
   b. Attendance
   c. Absence
   d. Late
2. Mid-year totals (a–d above)
3. Second-half totals (a–d above)
4. End-year totals (a–d above)

D. Miscellaneous

1. All entries in blue ink
2. Corrections in red ink
3. Attendance books collected—15th of month

Figure 12-9

The Self-Evaluation Guide shown here is appropriate for an attendance system that uses individual attendance cards for each student. This guide may be similar to data processing cards that are also prepared for each student at the beginning of the year when a computer system is used.

COPE WITH HEALTH PROBLEMS

Each school has students who have health problems that can range from temporary ones, such as a broken arm, to chronic ones, such as petit mal or asthma. When a student with a health problem is discovered, several actions should be taken.

1. The nurse should be notified in order to keep a list of students who have health problems. This list should be updated each school year. If the health case is not a new one, the nurse should make the teacher aware of the child's condition.

2. The teacher should meet with the nurse to become more informed about the specific health requirements of the children in the class.

3. The nurse should send a letter home to each student who is listed in the file as a health problem. The parent is requested to state the current condition of the child and to supply a doctor's note detailing the physical limitations of the youngster.

Teachers should be made aware of the restrictions that they face concerning possible requests from parents. Teachers may not administer medication to youngsters; a child who requires any during the day should be encouraged to go home for lunch to take it. If this is not possible, the teacher may keep the medication in his or her desk, but the student must take it him- or herself. Most states have specific legislation concerning these actions.

In certain cases, the physical limitations of the student may prevent the youngster from particular activities, such as gym, and certain class requirements, such as fire drills. When a teacher has such a child in the class, you should be notified so that special provisions for entering and exiting the school building as well as safety during school drills may be provided.

Children who are wearing casts of any type create a potential hazard for themselves and the school. Such students should not be permitted to attend school while wearing a plaster cast or other orthopedic device without a release (Figure 12-10) signed by the parent.

ESTABLISH A HOMEWORK POLICY

A parent's one daily touch with the school is through the student's homework. When parents become troubled or concerned about their children's homework, more harm to the school's image is achieved than by any other means. Therefore, you should prepare a homework policy and effectively communicate this policy to teachers, who, in turn, can explain to parents early in the school year the type of homework to expect. This may be accomplished through a Curriculum Information Day Conference for parents that is held after school during September.

Certain general guidelines concerning homework, regardless of grade or age level, should also be communicated to parents through school publications. This communication

---

RELEASE FORM

Date _____

I hereby release _____ of any
                           (school's name)
responsibility for accidents or harm that may happen to my child while he or
she is attending school wearing an orthopedic device.

Child's name _____ Class _____

_____
               Parent's signature

Figure 12-10

(Figure 12-11) may be sent home as an open letter from you or as a part of your message in the school bulletin or newsletter published by the school or the Parents Association.

Teachers should also be provided with guidelines about homework. They should be given a set of criteria to evaluate their homework assignments.

1. Homework should serve a sound educational purpose. It is not intended as punishment or busy work.

2. Homework must be within the capabilities of the individual student. Homework that cannot be independently completed by students has no value.

3. Students should be motivated to correctly and carefully complete the homework assignment.

4. The homework assignment should grow out of a school experience. Only homework that has a creative objective should be given without previous preparation. Even in this case, the form and procedure should be thoroughly explained.

5. Whenever possible, homework should be related to students' interests.

6. Homework should be intended to enlarge or extend the children's knowledge and understanding of the concept.

7. Homework must be suited to individual student's needs and capabilities.

8. Students must be completely clear about what they are to do and how they are to accomplish their homework.

9. Students should be able to complete homework by themselves without the help of their friends or parents.

10. Homework should be in a form that discourages copying from any source.

11. Homework should be given within a reasonable time frame for completion. Students in the lower grades should not be asked to do homework for more than

HOMEWORK GUIDELINES

**The Elementary School
Office of the Principal**

Dear Parents,

Homework serves an important purpose in your child's school life. It is a means of reviewing and reinforcing the lessons taught in school. Homework is also a way to help your child to develop work and study habits that will assist him or her throughout the years spent in school.

You can help your child develop some routines that will be of assistance in successfully completing homework assignments. The following suggestions are offered for this purpose.

1. Ask your child if he or she has homework that day. Be aware that homework is generally assigned every day except Friday or the day before a holiday. By asking your child about homework, you are helping him or her to remember that there is an assignment to be completed.

2. Become interested in your child's homework. Ask him or her to show the homework to you and to explain what the work completed was about. Sharing your child's work with him or her reinforces the importance of homework and helps the child to understand that you are interested in his or her progress. Looking at your child's homework also keeps you informed about the progress of the child and the way in which your child is able to complete the work assigned.

3. Remember that homework is your child's work—not yours. You should not do the work for the child; rather, you should be concerned with whether or not your child did the work. If your child has trouble with a homework assignment and cannot complete it, write a note telling the teacher about the problem. It is the teacher's responsibility to make the homework assignment clearly understood by each student.

4. Help your child set a regular homework time each day and remain with that commitment. Free your child of other responsibilities at that time.

5. Provide your child with a quiet place to work and study where he or she is not disturbed by younger children or pets.

Homework will help your youngster grow and develop.

Sincerely,

_____

Principal

Figure 12-11

twenty to thirty minutes. In the upper grades, homework time should be between forty-five minutes to an hour.

12. Homework should serve a useful purpose within the classroom and be related to the total class program. It must always be checked and corrected the next day. Homework that will not be checked and corrected should not be given.

13. Consideration for the particular circumstances of an individual student should be made when homework is assigned.

You might also provide teachers with a set of examples of appropriate homework assignments.

- Assemble materials for a notebook, scrapbook, or set of samples.
- Create charts, maps, and pictures to demonstrate an understanding of a concept that has been taught.
- Review and reinforce needed skills in mathematics, reading, and/or grammar.
- Make notes or prepare an outline for an oral or written report.
- Write stories, themes, or poems on topics that have been discussed in class.
- Complete an assignment that was begun in a small group lesson.
- Complete an individual assignment that represents the need of an individual student.
- Write about an experiment or laboratory activity that was conducted during the day and for which the student has taken some notes.
- Read a passage or selection for a specific aim that will be discussed in a lesson the following day.
- Review for a test.
- Define and use vocabulary words found in independent reading books.
- Ongoing homework assignments: a collection of news articles on a specific topic; a chart of personal eating and sleeping habits; interviews of particular persons whose work is a topic of study; observations of the change of seasons or weather.

DISTRIBUTE NOTICES TO PARENTS

Ensuring that school notices are distributed is a vital concern of yours. Important pieces of information are often distributed in notices or flyers that should be given to students on the day teachers receive them. Teachers should be reminded about the notices-to-parents procedures used in the school and should be asked to encourage students to hand the notice to a parent when they arrive home.

Whenever possible, notices should be prepared at least two weeks before the date of the information contained in the notice; of course, information of an emergency nature will be prepared and distributed as quickly as possible. But information concerned with certain yearly school events, such as teacher conference days or the science fair, can be anticipated and prepared in advance.

After the notices or flyers have been prepared and reproduced, they should be counted out by office staff or aides in the correct quantity for each class. The notices are then placed in each teacher's letterbox. Notices of an emergency nature should be hand delivered to the classrooms so that they can be distributed before the students leave that day.

When teachers receive notices in their letterbox, they should be made aware that the notice is to be distributed *that same day*. All students should carry the notice home on the same day rather than on different days, avoiding the possibility of parents calling to say that a friend's child brought home a notice that they did not receive. To accomplish this uniform distribution on the same day, notices should be placed in teacher's letterboxes after the lunch hour. In this way, teachers will receive the notices when they go to their letterboxes the next morning. Hopefully, then, each child will receive the notice that same afternoon. Notices announcing a school event should be distributed a week in advance of that event to permit parents the time to adjust their schedules or hire sitters so that they can attend.

If problems with the distribution of notices occur in your school, you may want to modify the procedure. One way of reminding teachers about distributing notices is to post a school organization sheet. When teachers read the office bulletin board, the organization sheet will inform them that a notice is to be found in their letterbox and must be distributed to students before dismissal that day. Ask the teachers to initial the sheet so that you know they have read the posted message; some teachers require this constant reminder.

HANDLE ACCIDENTS

Despite efforts to make the school building safe for students and staff, accidents do occur. These accidents take many different forms and require different types of actions. No accident should go unnoticed, so a parent should be informed about the accident that his or her child has had. The way in which the parent is informed depends upon the type of accident that has occurred.

Accidents of a minor nature usually include a scrape or a bruise that appears to be superficial. When the accident is discovered by the teacher, the child should be sent to the office. The secretary or the school nurse can then make the decision about how serious the wound appears to be. If the wound is not considered serious, it may be washed and bandaged. An Incident Report (Figure 12-12) should then be completed.

The person who attended to the youngster should fill in his or her name as the contact person for the parent.

Other accidents appear to be more serious in nature, and may include a deep wound that is bleeding, a lump that is raised or discolored, a youngster who is in pain or discomfort, or a cut that is extensive and requires stitches. When in doubt about the nature of the wound, it is best to treat it as an accident of a serious nature. It is a mistake to make major judgments that really should be reserved for a physician.

When the wound appears to be serious, take the following actions:

1. Calm the child.
2. Make the child as comfortable as possible.
3. Attempt to stop the bleeding if possible.

INCIDENT REPORT

Date _____

Dear Parent,

Today your child _____ sustained the following:

_____

_____

_____

We took the following action:

_____ we attempted to call you but you could not be reached by telephone.

_____ we did not call you because we judged the bruise to be minor.

Your child was given first aid and returned to class with this note. If you want further information about the incident, please call the school and ask to speak with _____.

Thank you.

_____
Principal

Figure 12-12

4. Cover the wound with a sterile bandage or gauze pad.

5. Wash the blood off the child's hands and face and clothing. This will help calm both the child and the parent.

6. Do not give the child candy or cookies. If the wound requires surgery, the child should have nothing to eat.

7. IMPORTANT: Notify the parent of the accident and ask the parent to come to school to take the child to a doctor.

If the parent cannot be reached, a friend or relative of the child should be contacted. It is important that a responsible adult who knows the child take charge of his or her care. In those rare circumstances when no home contact can be made and the child appears to be seriously injured, you may decide to call for an ambulance and send the child to the hospital. An action such as this is the safest route when there is doubt about what to do for the youngster.

An official Accident Report (Figure 12-13) should be prepared. If possible, ask the injured child about the accident while waiting for the parent. The description will be far more accurate at this moment than several days later when the child returns to school. The child may be assisted in recording his or her explanation.

Since you, as principal, are legally responsible for the health and safety of the entire school population while classes are in session, the preparation of the Accident Report is very important. Thus, as much information as possible should be gathered. In many cases, the

---

ACCIDENT REPORT

Name of injured student _____

Class _____ Teacher _____

Date of the accident _____ Time of the accident _____

Activity in progress when the accident occurred. _____
_____

Place where the accident occurred. _____
_____

Teacher in charge of the activity. _____

Nature of the accident. _____
_____
_____

Structural and/or physical defects at the accident site. _____
_____

Statement of the teacher in charge.* _____
_____

Statement of witness #1* _____
_____

Statement of witness #2.* _____
_____

Statement of the injured student.* _____
_____

Actions taken after the accident. _____
_____
_____

The custodian was notified about the accident. _____
                                                    (signature)
The principal was notified about the accident. _____
                                                    (signature)
The site of the accident was inspected by the principal. ____yes ____ no

                                        _____
*add extra pages if necessary   Principal's signature

Figure 12-13

parent will attempt to sue the school, so you should personally inspect the site of the accident and ensure that no physical or structural defects may have contributed to the accident. The documentation will then be of great importance.

As soon as possible after the accident, a copy of the Accident Report should be sent to the appropriate person at the district office. Other copies should be retained by you and the custodian.

In cases where a physical or structural defect was observed, it is important to be able to document that the defect was reported by you and the custodian in the Plant Status Report and that a request for repair was made. (See Chapter 11.)

PROVIDE AN EMERGENCY CONTACT WITH PARENTS

An emergency contact system with parents is a necessary communication link used whenever a child has been injured or is ill and the parent has to be contacted to take the child home. Once the parent has been contacted, he or she makes the decision about picking up the child. The parent who requests that the child remain in school then takes responsibility for that youngster's health and welfare.

The Emergency Contact Card (Figure 12-14) should be kept in the office and filed alphabetically by class, with care taken to verify the accuracy of the information. Parents should be asked at the end of each school year to update their cards and certainly whenever they change jobs, telephone numbers, or addresses. Each teacher should check the records of the students who will be in the class the next term to ensure that a new Emergency Contact Card has been received for each youngster.

EMERGENCY CONTACT CARD

School Year _____

Student _____ Class _____ Room _____
    (last)   (first)   (initial)

Mother/Guardian _____

Home address _____ Telephone _____

Business address _____ Telephone _____

Father/Guardian _____

Home address _____ Telephone _____

Business address _____ Telephone _____

If there is no home phone, at what number can parent be reached?

_____

If parent cannot be reached, who should be called in an emergency?

Name _____ Telephone _____

Family Doctor: Name _____ Telephone _____

If none of the above can be reached by phone, WHAT SHOULD THE SCHOOL DO if the child is sick or injured? _____

The final decision for action taken will be the judgment of school authorities. If any of the above is changed, contact the principal in writing as soon as possible.

_____
Signature of parent or guardian

Figure 12-14

DISCOURAGE TRUANCY AND LATENESS

Truancy is, of course, a serious matter because students cannot receive instruction if they do not attend school. Teachers may be suspicious about the absence of certain students if:

- absence is frequent
- students do not bring a note of explanation when they return
- the absent student is observed in the streets during school hours

The teacher should bring a suspected case of truancy to your attention; it is then your responsibility to take action. The first step to discourage truancy is to discuss the student with the teacher.

The teacher should be asked about the academic and social record of the particular student. Information concerning the student's home conditions, as well as a record of the days of absence prepared by the teacher, should also be taken into consideration. After you have this information, the second step should be taken.

In cases where the truancy is a first offense (that has never been done before) by the youngster, a letter of notification (Figure 12-15) may be sent to the parent. Parents are usually unaware of the action by their youngster and are extremely cooperative.

TRUANCY LETTER

The Elementary School
Office of the Principal

_____
date

_____
_____
_____

Dear _____,

We have reason to believe that your child was absent from school without permission on _____.
Since your child did not come to school that day, the child has been marked truant.

Continuous attendance at school is essential for the academic and social development of your child. It is the parent's responsibility to ensure that the youngster is in daily attendance.

I am bringing this matter to your attention so that you can impress your child with the importance of school and the obligation to attend school each day that the child is able to do so.

Sincerely,

_____
Principal

Figure 12-15

In cases where the letter has previously been sent or where truancy is a repeated action that has only recently been discovered, your second step may be a telephone call to the parent to ask him or her to come to school for a conference. If the parent cannot be reached, a letter similar to Figure 12-15 may be sent with an additional request for a conference date.

The teacher should join the parent and you at the conference. Every effort should be made to discover the reason for the truancy and to formulate plans to correct or modify the existing situation so that the child is in daily attendance at school. The parent should also be told that excessive absence from school is a cause for retention. You might want to include the youngster in the conference and encourage the child to discuss the reasons for his or her absence.

If the truancy pattern continues or if the information discussed at the conference appears to warrent it, guidance services may be suggested as a means of helping the student and the family.

LATENESS LETTER

The Elementary School
Office of the Principal

_____
date

_____
_____
_____

Dear _____,

Your child's teacher, _____, has informed me about the frequent lateness of your child. Repeated lateness is of harm both to your child's educational progress and to the class which is disturbed.

I am most anxious to meet with you to discuss this problem and arrive at a satisfactory solution. Please come to my office on _____ at _____. Your child's teacher will also attend this meeting.

If the date and/or time are not convenient for you, call this office to make another appointment.

Sincerely,

_____
Principal

Figure 12-16

You should ask the teacher to keep you informed about the youngster. Once the truancy has been discovered and action has been taken, the problem should end.

Lateness is a problem similar to truancy. A student who is consistently late disrupts the class with his or her late entrance and is missing valuable instructional time. Students should be asked by the teacher about why they are late. The reasons for lateness vary greatly and may or may not be true. Some reasons generally stated by youngsters include:

- "My mother overslept and did not wake me."
- "My mother goes to work before I wake up and I overslept."
- "Dad asked me to do some chores before school."
- "I was not feeling well this morning."
- "I fell on the way to school and had to go back home."

The teacher then must make a decision about the truth of the child's statement. A first lateness is generally overlooked by the teacher, but recorded in attendance records and noted on the report card. Repeated latenesses must be acted upon.

The first step to take when a student is repeatedly late is for the teacher to ask the parent to come to school for a conference. At that time, the teacher discusses the frequent latenesses with the parent and documents the dates and times of arrival at school. The parent is asked to cooperate with the school in helping the student arrive on time. Sometimes the lateness is the fault of the parent who must be made to understand that prompt arrival is important for the youngster. At other times, the lateness may be the fault of the student who is sent out of the house on time, but arrives late. In any case, the first resource is the parent's assistance.

If the lateness continues or if the parent does not respond to the teacher's request for a meeting, you should send a letter to the parent. This letter (Figure 12-16) will set the day and time for a conference among the parent, the teacher and you.

As with truancy, if the problem persists or if the discussion at the conference appears to warrent it, guidance services may be involved with the case.

SELECT MONITORS

Monitors are an important part of the smooth operation of the school. They assist with the entrance and exit of the students as well as conducting younger students to and from classes. Monitors also serve as safety helpers in assisting youngsters to cross the streets to and from school. The selection of monitors should be taken very seriously, since the proper performance of their duties can assist teachers, while a poor performance of their duties can bring parents with complaints.

The monitors' positions should be reserved for the oldest students in the school, usually the sixth graders. Students who want to become monitors and offer service to the school should apply (Figures 12-17 and Figure 12-18) for the position and have a serious attitude about wanting to perform these duties.

Having received the letter, the students' next step is to complete the application forms. The fifth grade teachers are requested to recommend each student who applies on a scale that ranges from "with enthusiasm" to "disapproved." The selection process is then made based

---

SCHOOL SERVICES LETTER

The Elementary School
Office of the Principal

_____
date

Dear Fifth Graders,

In September you will be a member of the senior class and, as such, you may want to serve your school community. If you are interested in participating in school service, please complete the attached application. Then take the application home and have your parents sign it to indicate that they approve of your participation.

This application must be submitted to your teacher on or before June 1.

Sincerely,

_____
Principal

Figure 12-17

upon the students' statements and the teachers' recommendations. Special consideration should be given to potential antisocial students who hold leadership positions with their peers.

Once the selection of monitors is made, sixth grade students who will be leaving the school should train the fifth graders who will be taking their positions in September. Conduct this buddy training system during the last two weeks of the school year.

WRITE A SCHOOL HANDBOOK

Each school should have a handbook that is suited to its particular needs. Since no two schools are exactly alike, no two school handbooks can be identical; what is important, however, is that the handbook serve the purpose for which it is designed.

The Purpose of a School Handbook

A school handbook is intended to bring together under one cover all the procedures, policies, schedules, and responsibilities of the school and the staff, and to make the retrieval of this information easy. The handbook should be distributed to each member of the staff at the initial faculty conference and then collected at the end of the school year so that it can be updated.

SCHOOL SERVICE APPLICATION

School Year _____

Student _____ Class _____

I want to participate in the following school/community services. I have marked them in order of my preferences:

_____ School Safety Squad
_____ Class Line Monitor
_____ Audiovisual Squad

In brief paragraph form, explain why you want to participate in the service you selected as #1:

_____
_____
_____
_____
_____
_____

(You may use the back of this sheet to write additional comments, if necessary.)

TEACHER RECOMMENDATION:

__ with enthusiam   __ approved   __ with reservation   __ disapproved

_____

The selection will be made based upon the student's comments and the teacher's recommendation.

_____

_____
                                                        date

I give my child _____ of class _____
permission to participate in the above choices of school/community
service during the school year September _____to June _____.

_____
                                        Parent's signature

Figure 12-18

Sample Contents

Here is a sample listing of contents for a school handbook.

How to Use the Handbook

The handbook is intended to clarify or explain school policies, procedures, and schedules. Thus, it serves a useful purpose for everyone throughout the school year. A teacher, for example, may refer to the handbook to recall when composition samples are to be collected. You might refer to the handbook to find out which class is assigned to a particular bulletin board.

The handbook also becomes important as a means of communication between you and your staff. Therefore, you have the right to expect that teachers will follow written policies and procedures without being reminded. When a reminder is necessary, it is far easier to ask a teacher to refer to a particular handbook page than to write an explanation to that teacher.

The handbook statements also serve as a clarification and verification of policy and procedures to help prevent abuses. Anyone can refer to the handbook at any time, rather than interpret for him- or herself.

Give a copy of the school handbook to the Parents Association president and the district office, too, so that all parties concerned with the well-being of the school are aware of the procedures in use.

CREATE A NEW TERM CHECKLIST

The new September term is filled with chores and paperwork, so it is easy to forget some of the requirements and structure for the new class. Help teachers remember all of the items to be introduced or established by giving them a checklist (Figure 12-19). The checklist also lets you know if teachers are aware of the particular details required by the school. Actual implimentation of the details and the quality of the procedures can be checked by you during class visits.

NEW TERM CHECKLIST

__ 1. Room arrangement established.
__ 2. Materials arranged in suitable areas.
__ 3. Materials arranged in an organized way.
__ 4. Access to materials is free.
5. Materials have been selected to suit:
   __ diagnosed reading needs
   __ diagnosed mathematics needs
   __ ability levels
   __ learning styles
   __ student interest
   __ curriculum mandates
6. Curriculum programs have been initiated for:
   __ Individualized reading
      a. Teacher-directed skill instruction in __ reading, __ math
      b. Self-directed prescriptions in __ reading, __ math
      c. Language arts in __ spelling, __ handwriting,
         __ creative writing

___ Social Studies contract
___ Homework requirements
7. A classroom structure is understood and used by students for:
___ material selection and return
___ time and place to use materials
___ how and with whom to work
___ how and from whom to get help
___ how to request permission to leave the room
___ where to store possessions
___ how, when and what work is to be handed in and checked
___ control of noise level
___ care and maintenance of hardware
8. A written structure is understood and used by:
Students for ___ planning, ___ recordkeeping
Teacher for ___ planning, ___ recordkeeping
9. Housekeeping:
___ fire drill chart is posted on wall next to classroom door
___ shelter drill chart is posted on wall next to classroom door
___ teacher and students know the day and time of the fixed
scheduled periods
*___ Reading Survey and duplicate copy including pretest mean
returned to office
*___ Reading Prescription returned to office
*___ Mathematics Prescription returned to office
___ time schedules signed by a parent are pasted in students'
notebooks
___ new attendance cards completed
___ out-of-the-room notebook established
___ supplies received
___ register sheet checked with the office
___ materials preservation sheets signed by students and parents, and
filed

*Indicates items to be returned to office no later than October 1.

_____ _____
Teacher   Class

Figure 12-19

PREVENT JUNE HEADACHES

June is a very busy time of year, a time when you will find yourself overwhelmed with a myriad of details revolving around the closing of records of academic achievement and attendance. But June also begins the new school year since every student must be placed into a new class for the fall term. In addition, materials and equipment must be collected and inventoried, and classrooms prepared for summer cleaning. These details are best handled through a preplanned system.

How to Relieve the Pains of Reorganization

Moving every child in the school from a current class to a new placement for the fall term can be very difficult. The most advantageous placement for each child and each teacher depends upon a review of all available information for each student. This information can easily be gathered and immediately available through the use of a Pupil Profile card (Figure 12-20).

PUPIL PROFILE

June _____

_____

New Class _____   [H] [G] [M]

Last Name First Name	TEST DATA
Class _____	Read Score _____ E _____ Abs _____ New Admit _____
	Math Score _____ LA Score _____
COMMENTS	TEACHER ASSESSMENT
	Read level _____
	Math level _____
	Works Independently _____
	TEACHER DIRECTED SERIES AND LEVEL COMPLETED
SPECIAL DATA	Lipp _____ Mac _____ SFRS _____
Language: _____ M S	Sull _____ Hou/Miff _____ Discoveries _____
Holdover (grade) _____	Other _____
Twin/sibling _____ (class __)	SPECIAL PROGRAMS ABILITIES
Poor Attend. _____	PSEN R __ M __ ESL __ Art _____
Discipline: mod __ severe __	Bilingual _____ Music _____
Guidance _____/Agency _____	Resource Room (hrs) _____ Science _____
Separate from _____	Media Center _____ Writing _____
_____	Ch IMA _____ Leadership _____
Medical _____ Sight _____	Other _____
Hearing _____ Other _____	
Bus _____	

Figure 12-20

A Pupil Profile card is completed for each student in the school, detailing all available information about the student. The teacher, however, may have information that might not be included on the card. That is why the classroom teacher's judgment, in addition to the Profile, is so important when considering class placement for each youngster.

Reorganization is best accomplished by considering one grade at a time. The teachers of the classes of the grade being reorganized should meet with you and the teachers of the next grade who will receive the students. First consider the school policy for organization of classes. These policies may include:

- heterogeneous grouping
- homogeneous grouping

- one advanced class on a grade—the other classes heterogeneous
- ten percent of the students of the grade identified as superior and grouped together

Each student is then considered for class placement according to the school's organization policy. Consider separating students from others with whom there seems to be a problem. Also try to separate siblings. Whenever possible, consider teacher personality and teaching style when placing students.

As the students are placed in new classes, their Profile cards are marked with the new class and passed to that teacher. The teachers of the new classes can then review the Profile cards and examine the data. Equity concerned with size of the register of each new class, boy/girl ratio, number of potential discipline problems, and ability range should be determined.

At the end of the reorganization session, put the cards together in new class sets and keep them until all of the students have been assigned to a new class. Then sort the cards into the old classes and return them to the current teacher with the notation of the new class placement. The teachers can then complete the records for each child by recording the new class on the record cards and report cards.

The students' records are then passed in new class sets to the next teacher. Since it is generally considered advisable not to promote classes as a whole, the new teacher will most probably receive a set of records for new students from each teacher of the grade below. The Pupil Profile cards for the new students are passed to the new teacher with the records. These Profiles now serve a second purpose: they are the students' first introduction to the teacher. Using the Profile cards the teacher may:

- make a new class list
- determine the ability groups in the new class
- list the reading materials used the previous year
- note specific needs and abilities of the new students

The Profile cards contain a wealth of information and become a valuable reference source for the new teachers. When the teachers no longer need the Profile cards, they should be returned to you to be kept as a source of information.

The Pupil Profile cards are valuable if correctly completed by the teachers. Since limited space on the card does not permit a full explanation of terms, an instruction sheet (Figure 12-21) is helpful.

You must also maintain an accounting of the disbursement of students from one grade to the next. This accounting will enable you to solve problems that occur, prepare opening registers for September, and place students who are new to the school. The disbursement may easily be kept on graph paper as shown in the sample on page 247. The list on the left itemizes the number of students currently in each class on the grade. The new classes for the grade above are listed across the top of the sheet. The number of students from each old class placed into each new class is then recorded. The students are counted as boys + girls to maintain a balance in the new classes. At the end of the organization, the total number of students placed in new classes, minus the number of students who are not promoted, must equal the number of students currently in the grade.

INSTRUCTIONS FOR COMPLETION
OF PUPIL PROFILE

1. Circle H = Current Holdover
          G = Recommended Gifted
          M = Moving

2. Last name, First name
   Present class

3. COMMENTS
   Any remarks that will assist this
   evaluation.

4. SPECIAL DATA
   Language (Name)
      Students for whom English is a
      second language.
   M = Moderate language problem
   S = Severe
   Holdover (grade held over)
   Twin/sibling: name, class
   Poor Attendance (20 days or more)
   Discipline: moderate, severe
   Guidance: if a formal referral was
      made or Agency currently involved
      (name if known)
   Separate from: Those students who
      do not get along.
   Medical (or name health disability)
   Sight (state needs or wears glasses)
   Hearing (if you know or suspect a
      problem)
   Other (or state if there is any other
      problem (death, divorce, etc.)
   Bus (grades K and 1)

5. TEST DATA
   Reading Score (most recent test)
      E = Excused   Abs = Absent
      New A = New Admission
   Math Score (most recent standardized
      score)
   LA Score (most recent)

6. TEACHER ASSESSMENT (of work-
   ing level as Grade Equivalent)
   Reading level (functioning)
   Math level (functioning)
   Works Independently (always, some-
      times, never)

7. TEACHER DIRECTED SERIES
   AND LEVEL COMPLETED
   (write series level next to the name of
   the series used or state name and
   level of other major teacher-directed
   material used) Lippincott, Macmillan,
   Scott Foresman Reading Systems,
   Sullivan Program, Houghton Mifflin,
   Discoveries

8.

SPECIAL PROGRAMS (student officially participated)	ABILITIES (x or use a descriptive word)
PSEN (Winston/ Joshua)	Art
Reading	Music (organ group)
Math	Science
Bilingual	Writing
ESL	Leadership (may be positive or
Resource Room (hours)—1 or 2 per day	negative)
Media Center (had a pass)	Other
ChIMA	

Figure 12-21

SAMPLE DISBURSEMENT OF STUDENTS

Using the disbursement graph, you can now provide each teacher with a Composition of New Class sheet (see the sample below). This sheet outlines the number of records each teacher should receive from each sending teacher. By using the Composition sheet, the receiving teacher can check to determine that a complete set of records have been received, from each sending teacher, for each new student assigned to the class.

DISBURSEMENT OF STUDENTS

From		To		minus		Moving	
B+G=Tot	5-209	5-205	5-206	Holdover 4th		5-209 = 1	
4-201						5-205 - 0	
17+16=33	5+6=11	4+3=7	7+7=14	1+0=1		5-206=1	
4-207							
17+13=30	6+3=9	8+6=14	2+4=6	1+0=1			
4-203							
13+12=25	4+5=9	3+3=6	5+3=8	1+1=2			
47+41=88	15+14=29	15+12=27	14+14=28	3+1=4 = 47+41=88			
plus Holdover 5th							
5-209							
0+1=1		0+1=1					
5-205				HO 4th	HO 5th		
0+1=1		0+1=1					
0+2=2	15+14=29	15+13=28	14+15=29	88 - 4 + 2 = 84 total grade 5			

How to Detail End-Term Chores

The many tasks and details involved in end-term procedures can be more effectively handled by listing them, with date, in an end-term calendar (see sample below) that can be followed by teachers and monitored by you.

How to Provide a Checking System

You can help in monitoring and checking end-term procedures by using an End-Term Checklist (Figure 12-22) checked by specified personnel.

SAMPLE COMPOSITION OF NEW CLASS

June _____ 1985 _____

New Class _____ 5-205 _____   Teacher _____ Mrs. Rice _____

From	boys		girls	total
4-201	4	+	3	7
4-207	8	+	6	14
4-203	3	+	3	6
5-209 (holdover)	0	+	1	1
	15		13	28

SAMPLE END-TERM PROCEDURE

Dear Teachers:

This schedule has been prepared to provide a guide for the coordinated completion of all end-term records and exchanges. Please read it now and make all necessary entries on your desk calendar.

Your cooperation in adhering strictly to this schedule will make it possible for all of us to complete the necessary routines promptly and accurately.

Thank you for your cooperation.

_____
                                    Principal

APRIL   Distribution of:

1. Blank Pupil Profile cards and instruction sheets to all teachers. See Grade Leaders for clarification.
2. Dental control sheets and notes to the office.

MAY 29   Return of:

1. Completed Pupil Profile cards to office. NOTE: Each grade will meet with the sending grade and the receiving grade to reorganize the classes. Please make yourself available for such meetings. Plan to spend two lunch hours in reorganization.

SAMPLE END-TERM PROCEDURE (continued)

JUNE 1

1. Send Teacher's Handbook to the office to be updated.

Distribution of:

1. Sixth grade office cards to sixth grade teachers.
2. Sixth grade nurse's health cards to sixth grade teachers.
3. K-5 new emergency contact cards to teachers.

Library Closed—book circulation ends. Return library books borrowed for class use. Inventory begins.

Media Collection Begins.

JUNE 5   Books:

1. Have pupils mend torn books and erase as many markings as possible.
2. All books should be repaired.
3. Lost book money ($2.50 charge) to the office by this date.
4. Prepare a Book Report on Lost Books on 8½" x 11" paper.

CLASS _____ TEACHER _____ DATE _____

Name of Pupil   Title of Book Lost or Damaged

_____   _____

_____   _____

5. Send lost-book report to the office.
6. Each teacher is to submit a report. If no books are lost or damaged, write the word NONE.

NOTE: Be sure that teaching continues through the last day of the term. No comic books are to be brought to school!

JUNE 11   Clerical Half-day

1. Special procedures for recording pupil attendance on this half-day.
   The following procedures should be used on the attendance card:

   No entry for pupil present   ____
   Pupil absent in the morning   _A_
   Make no entry for afternoon.
2. Explanation to be written in attendance book (last card).
   Mark date, hours, reason (released time for clerical work).

SAMPLE END-TERM PROCEDURE (continued)

Kindergarten teachers should indicate the time of sessions for their classes on this day.

3. <u>Totals on attendance sheet, attendance cards and record cards</u>.

These entries will not change your totals on the attendance sheet, in your attendance book, or on your record cards. With respect to ALL TOTALS, absence or presence in the morning is to be counted as absence or presence for the ENTIRE day.

4. <u>Time of attendance for Kindergarten and Grades 1-6</u>.

The morning Kindergarten will attend from 8:40 to 10:15, and the afternoon Kindergarten from 10:25 to 12 noon. The 1-6 grades will attend from 8:40 to 12 noon. The all-day Kindergarten will attend from 8:30 to 12 noon.

Record Card Entries

In completing the record cards, please follow these instructions:

1. All classes use only symbols E, G, F, U, I and S. (See section 5.2)

2. Enter the official designation of the class, e.g., 3-F, 4-F, etc.

3. If a child has been assigned to a class as a holdover, indicate by placing HO in parenthesis in the same box as the class designation, e.g., 3-F (HO).

4. Print or stamp the last name of the class teacher. Include the first name if space permits (no initial).

5. The entries on the cumulative record card MUST BE IDENTICAL with the final report card marks. (See 5.2)

    5.1 Social Behavior: Mark S, I, or U.
        Work and Study Habits: Mark S, I, or U.
        Reading: Mark E, G, F, or U, plus the ESTIMATED GRADE
                LEVEL in half years, e.g., 2.0, 2.5, 3.0, 3.5, etc.
        Oral Expression: Mark E, G, F, or U.
        Written Expression: Mark E, G, F, or U.
        Spelling: Mark E, G, F, or U.
        Handwriting: Mark E, G, F, or U.
        Social Studies: Mark E, G, F, or U.
        Mathematics: Mark E, G, F, or U.
        Science: Mark E, G, F, I, or U.
        Health: Mark S, I, or U.
        Art: Mark S, I, or U.

        Print the word "homework" in the space <u>under</u> "Industrial Arts Grade 7-8" and mark S, I, or U.

NOTE: The reverse side of the cumulative record card is to be filled out. Under Personal Social Behavior are columns in each category for "Satisfactory" and "Unsatisfactory." Please put a cross (X) in either one of these two columns OR put a cross on

SAMPLE END-TERM PROCEDURE (continued)

the vertical line between the two columns to indicate "Doubt." Such a "Doubt" would qualify for an "I" rating on the report card.

5.2 Relationship to Report Card

E	(Excellent)	E
G	(Good)	G
S	(Satisfactory)	G
L	(Less than satisfactory)	F or I (Improving)
U	(Unsatisfactory)	U

6. The total number of days in the school year is 184.

Period 1 (Sept.) 15 days	Period	6 (Feb.) 18 days
2 (Oct.) 22 days		7 (Mar.) 22 days
3 (Nov.) 16 days		8 (Apr.) 16 days
4 (Dec.) 17 days		9 (May) 20 days
5 (Jan.) 19 days		10 (June) 19 days

7. Closing entry for present class is to read:
   To: (indicate new class)
   Date:
   Reason: (leave blank)
   7.1 Entry date for new class 9/10.
   7.2 Be sure to consider carefully and fill in all items on the reverse side of the card relating to personality traits. Personality ratings should be consistent with report card ratings.

8. Health Cards (pink)

   8.1 Health records are to be completed.
   8.2 Follow code on card.
   8.3 The new class should be indicated.
   8.4 Enter the summary of absences due to illnesses.
   8.5 Enter the accidents, operations, childhood diseases and chronic illnesses.
   8.6 If no symptoms are noted, write "NSN."
   8.7 Enter completion date of dental work, if needed.
   8.8 Be sure that Audiometer Test results have been entered.

9. Test Record Cards

   All test results are to be entered in the proper space on the test cards.

10. Be sure Special Programs are listed under "Special Abilities or Disabilities" on the yellow record card.

SAMPLE END-TERM PROCEDURE (continued)

5. Distribution of
    1. Tentative Organization Sheet for September.
    2. Composition of New Class for September.

6. Report Cards
    Attendance period 3/23-6/26.
    Note comments under Record Cards.
    Date of new term: 9/14.
    New Class _____ Room _____

JUNE 8-12   Collection of:

Overhead projectors
Software
Made by notification. Please be ready to respond immediately.
STORE AND LOCK in the teacher's closet: tape recorders, television sets, projectors (Large and Small), headsets.

Closing of:

1. Attendance on attendance sheet. (NOTE: The attendance book record must show the actual attendance through the last day of school.)
2. The completed Attendance Sheets will be collected on 6/12 by the office.

JUNE 10   Return of:

1. All records and List Notices to office (grade 6)
2. Nurse's health cards to office (grade 6)

JUNE 11   Clerical Half-day

Distribution of:

1. Office Record Cards
2. Name Cards
3. Address Cards   By office for entry of new class data
4. Nurse's Health Cards

JUNE 12   List Notices due at Junior High School.

Closing of Registers—No further admissions or discharges after today.

SAMPLE END-TERM PROCEDURE (continued)

JUNE 17   Clerical Half-day (See attendance procedures for June 11.)

Collection of:

1. Anecdotal reports plus pupil's New Class card.

Exchange of:

1. Pupil Promotion Cards
2. Nurse's Medical Records*
3. Office Record Cards*
4. Name Cards*
5. Address Cards*
6. Cumulative Class Record Cards*
7. Completed Health (pink) and Test records to "new" teacher

*To be sent by present teacher to new teacher in sealed envelope.

NOTE: Be sure that all data have been recorded. It is the responsibility of the teachers receiving records to see that all entries have been correctly made. Incomplete records must be returned for completion at once.

Distribution of:

New attendance cards. Keep red binders.

JUNE 22   Media Center Closed—Return all filmstrips.

Return of: (by "new" teachers to office)

1. Office Record Cards. Arrange alphabetically. Do not separate by sex.
2. Address cards. Separate by street.
3. Name Cards. Arrange alphabetically. Do not separate by sex.
4. Present course certificates of required courses taken for salary increments to the secretary.

Distribution of:

1. Old Emergency Contact Cards—by office. Enter new class designation only on cards where children have not returned "new" updated card. Destroy old cards that have been replaced.

JUNE 22   Return of:

Metal file cases containing Class Record (with Health and Test Cards inserted) to _____at 2:15 p.m.

SAMPLE END-TERM PROCEDURE (continued)

JUNE 23   Send emergency contact cards to "new" teacher.

JUNE 24   Return of:

1. Emergency Contact Cards to office. Alphabetized only.
2. Pupil Profile Cards (pink and blue to office).
3. Class Summary Cards for new class to office.

Send:

1. "New" attendance cards in red binders to office at 2:15 p.m.

JUNE 26   In Morning: Collection of:

1. "Old" attendance cards—picked up by _____ before 12 noon. Complete End of Year Affidavit. Have _____ sign. Place attendance cards in report card envelope with name, class, room number and school year indicated. Do not seal envelope.
2. Report Cards of absentees who left no self-addressed envelopes are to be placed into individual envelopes ADDRESSED TO THE PARENT. DO NOT STAMP OR PUT A RETURN ADDRESS. Place envelopes of absentees in principal's letterbox.
3. Report Cards of absentees in self-addressed, stamped envelopes are to be placed in principal's letterbox.

Distribution of Report Cards or Promotion Slips:

Include new class and room. Do not distribute before 15 minutes prior to the close of school.

JUNE 26   In Afternoon:

Completed End Term Checklist reviewed and signed.
Distribution of payroll.

How to Monitor Records

It is the receiving teacher's responsibility to examine the records of the new students assigned to the fall class and return to or question the sending teacher concerning those records. The receiving teacher is held responsible for the accuracy and completeness of the records received.

END-TERM CHECKLIST

(Submit before receiving your check.)

_____ submitted the following:
Teacher's signature

Initialed By

1. Metal file containing new class: record cards, test cards, health cards _____

2. Pupil Profile cards _____

3. Class Summary Card _____

4. Attendance Cards _____

5. Emergency Contact Cards _____

6. Office record cards _____

7. Address cards _____

8. Name cards _____

9. Attendance Sheet _____

10. Teacher's course card _____

11. Nurse's medical cards (Nurse) _____

12. Old Attendance Cards _____

13. Keys (hung on hook) _____

14. Signed time card _____

15. Absentee Report Cards—enveloped addressed and placed in outgoing mail box _____

16. Resources returned _____

17. Room prepared for summer (Custodian) _____

18. Book Report _____

Date completed _____

Approved _____
Principal's signature

Figure 12-22

MAKE SCHEDULES WORK

Schedules can create a multitude of problems if they are not properly read and followed. It is the classroom teachers' responsibility to review the distributed schedules and identify the problems or conflicts that the schedules may create.

A Time Schedule

Publish a school time schedule (see sample) and require that each student take the schedule home to have it signed. This may help eliminate problems concerned with the entrance and exit of youngsters.

SAMPLE TIME SCHEDULE

GOOD WEATHER

Morning at 8:40 a.m.—Grades 1-6—YARD LINE UP

Lunch: 11:20-12:20—Grades 4-6—YARD LINE UP

11:55-12:55—Grades 1-3—YARD LINE UP

BAD WEATHER

Morning at 8:40 a.m.—Grades 1 and 2—CAFETERIA LINE UP

Grades 3-6—GYM LINE UP

Lunch: 11:20-12:20—Grades 4-6—USE GYM DOOR TO GO TO AUDITORIUM

11:55-12:55—Grades 1-3—USE GYM DOOR TO GO TO CAFETERIA

STUDENTS ARRIVING BEFORE THE SCHEDULED TIME WILL NOT BE ADMITTED TO BUILDING.

KINDERGARTEN SCHEDULE—ALL WEATHER

Go directly to the outside Kindergarten doors to the classrooms. Use the outside corridor next to the playground.

Morning: 8:40-11:15—BUS DISMISSAL AT 11:15. PLEASE BE PROMPT.

Afternoon: 12:20-2:55—BUS DISMISSAL AT 2:55. PLEASE BE PROMPT.

THIS NOTICE IS TO BE SIGNED BY PARENT AND PASTED IN STUDENT'S NOTEBOOK.

_____

Parent's signature

A Dismissal Schedule

The dismissal of primary youngsters who do not walk home themselves can become a problem, especially in neighborhoods where both parents work and various people assume the responsibility for picking up the children. A formal procedure will help to make parents responsible for pinpointing the individual who will pick up their youngsters. The pick-up procedure (Figure 12-23) alerts the teacher to the individual to whom the parent wants the child released at the close of the school day.

PICK-UP PROCEDURE

My child, _____, of
class _____ will be picked up at noon and/or
in the afternoon by:

(Please check appropriate one)

_____ 1. the parent

_____ 2. an older child* (Class ____ Name _____)

_____ 3. a neighbor (Name _____ Phone _____)

_____ 4. a baby sitter (Name _____ Phone _____)

_____ 5. other (Name _____ Phone _____)

_____ 6. may walk home him- or herself

*If an older child picks up your youngster, be aware of days when the older
 child is ill or goes home from school ill. Older students who pick up
 primary youngsters will <u>come to the classroom.</u>

_____
Parent's signature

Figure 12-23

Primary Grade Dismissal

1. Check pick-up person for each child. A Pick-Up Procedure form must be on file for each child.

2. Information obtained from the Pick-Up Procedure form should be itemized on a class list and placed in the substitute folder in the center drawer of the teacher's desk.

3. Good weather:
   a. dismiss one class at a time.
   b. take children outside to the top of the steps (noon and afternoon) to wait for individual pick up.

4. Bad weather:
   a. classes line up against wall
   b. parents will be admitted to the gym lobby area
   c. each class will dismiss individual students to pick-up person

An Assembly Schedule

During the school year, each class should have an opportunity to perform in the assembly. During the month of June, a schedule of assembly dates for the forthcoming year should be circulated among the teachers. The schedule (see sample) blocks off the dates of particular schoolwide performances, such as Pan American Day, Music Festival, and awards.

SAMPLE ASSEMBLY SCHEDULE

GRADES 3 and 4		GRADES 5 and 6	
Sept. 24	Organization	Sept. 25	Organization
Oct. 1		Oct. 2	
8		9	
15		16	
22		23	
29		30	
Nov. 5		Nov. 6	
12		13	
19	Class 3L	20	
Dec. 3		Dec. 4	
10		11	Class 5C
17		18	
Jan. 7		Jan. 8	
14		15	
21		22	
28		29	Class 6M
Feb. 4		Feb. 5	
11		12	
18	Class 4R	19	
25		26	
Mar. 4	Class 3R	Mar. 5	
11		12	
18	Class 3C	19	
25		26	Class 5R
Apr. 1		Apr. 2	Class 5S
22	Pan American Day	23	Pan American Day
29		30	
May 6	Class 4B	May 7	Class 6S
13		14	Class 6A
20	Music Festival	21	Music Festival
		28	Awards

The teachers should then be asked to select any other date for their class performance. Dates that are not occupied by class performances can be filled with films, speakers and music assemblies.

A Monitor Schedule

Using monitors effectively contributes to the smooth operation of the school. Specific assignments should be given to the monitor squad, so prepare a schedule in writing by the teacher/coordinator. You should keep a copy of the squad schedules.

SAMPLE SAFETY PATROL SQUAD POSTS

Exit 1
8:00-9:00   Penny C. 6-206, Edward D. 6-206, Larissa M. 6-206
2:50-3:00   Jason R. 6-206, Chris L. 6-206

Exit 2
8:30-9:00   Michael G. 6-206, Alexandria C. 6-208
2:50-3:00   Michele D. 6-208, Richard S. 6-204

Exit 3
8:30-9:00   Theresa R. 6-206, Dalia S. 6-208
2:50-3:00   Daniel H. 6-204, Eleana N. 6-204

Exit 4
8:30-9:00   Stephen B. 6-208, Cathy D. 6-208
2:50-3:00   Chuck P. 6-208, Valerie N. 6-204

Bad Weather:
Exit 7   Stephen B. 6-208, Cathy D. 6-208, Chuck P. 6-208
Auditorium Steps   Terry U. 6-204, Dalia S. 6-208, Alexandria C. 6-208

Outdoor Posts:
School Corner   Albert H. 6-208, Karen M. 6-208
Mailbox   Sven K. 6-204
Across Street   Derrick W. 6-204
Far school corner   Kenneth G. 6-208, Robin S. 6-204

Class Line Monitors:
Kindergarten   Paul C. 6-208, Dina C. 6-208
1 - room 7   Jeana K. 6-204, Karen C. 6-204
1 - room 3   Pascale C. 6-204, Kia J. 6-208
1 - room 5   Clarisse S. 6-208, Suzie S. 6-204
1 - room 106   Lisa D. 6-206, Evan M. 6-208
2 - room 104   Christine M. 6-206, Ruth B. 6-204
2 - room 102   Ingrid T. 6-204, Stephanie P. 6-206

Changes in Schedules

At times, even the most perfectly prepared schedules must be changed to meet a particular situation that arises. When this need occurs, there should be a specific manner in which a teacher can request this change (Figure 12-24) and submit it to you for approval. The approved change must then be transmitted to all concerned parties, including the secretary who must monitor absence of teachers on the specific day. These requests for change in schedule must be submitted in advance of the requested date.

TEMPORARY CHANGE OF SCHEDULE REQUEST

Requesting Teacher _____

Class _____ Date of Request _____

Reason: _____

_____

_____

Change Requested*   Preparation _____   Duty _____

Indicate the exchange:

Teacher 1 _____ Teacher 2 _____
                      name   name

From: Date _____ From: Date _____

Day _____   Day _____

Time _____   Time _____

Subject _____   Subject _____

To: Date _____ To: Date _____

Day _____   Day _____

Time _____   Time _____

Subject _____   Subject _____

- -

*submit to the principal   Teachers involved (initial and return)

_____

_____

_____

Approved: _____
                Principal's signature

Figure 12-24

Reasons for a requested change include conflict between lunch duty and a preparation period, class trip, or special testing programs.

BROADCAST A POSITIVE SCHOOL IMAGE

The single most effective means for a school to promote its public image is through a well-developed public relations programs. Each parent in the school and each member of the community views the school in terms of individual experiences with students, teachers, and you. Very often, these private experiences are the result of a personal concern which, in many cases, may not project the true image of that school. For example, if a member of the community calls you to say that some children destroyed a bush on his or her property on the way to school, your school is placed in a poor light. The incident is all that the community member knows about the school, thus resulting in a negative point of view.

This is why an effective public relations program is vital to the well-being of the school. The true story about the efforts and successes of the school must be told to the parents and community members so that they will support your school.

Identify the Story to Be Told

Every story about a school success or event is important to tell. Celebrate certain school and cultural events on an annual basis and invite parents and community members to view them. The wider the audience for school events, the better the opportunity for the school to display its sincere efforts and accomplishments.

Make School Events Visible

One means of communication open to the school is the flyer that can be sent home and placed in shop or store windows in the community. These flyers announce an event and invite everyone to come to school to participate. Even though community members who do not have students in the school will rarely come to view the event, the publicity helps to place the school in a favorable light. The flyers should be as appealing as possible and give the message as clearly as possible.

13

HOW TO MAKE PARENTS
YOUR GREATEST ASSET

The single most important aspect of good parent/school/community relationships is communication. Keeping these communication lines open helps to encourage: (1) a trust relationship; (2) an exchange of ideas; and (3) dialogue before problems develop.

FACILITATE CONFERENCES BETWEEN PARENTS AND TEACHERS

The first concern of every parent is communicating with the class teacher, so many opportunities for conference time between the teacher and the parent should be made available. These conferences should be scheduled at the request of the parent or the teacher, with time after school or before school as well as during the teacher's preparation period used for this purpose. The office personnel can assist by taking messages from parents during the day and scheduling conferences with the teacher.

Official conference time, usually scheduled twice during the school year, also' contributes to encouraging communication between the parent and the teacher. Every parent should be encouraged to come to school during these conference times to speak with the class teacher about the progress of the individual student.

The preparation of the teacher for these conferences by reviewing and making available to the parent particular information about the student and documentation of work completed has been previously discussed. What is important to keep in mind is to consider the parent's point of view. The parent is aware of the attitudes and reactions of the child when he or she arrives home from school, so the parent naturally has a point of view that is (usually) in defense of the youngster; the parent rarely has the teacher's point of view. The reasons why a report was not acceptable or the student did not satisfactorily complete the assignment are not always available to the parent until the face-to-face conference with the teacher. It is at this time that former issues become clear and the parent is made aware of the *actual* performance of the student in class.

You can assist the successful completion of parent conference time in several ways. Of prime importance is to assist the teacher in making appointments for the scheduled conferences. An information flyer (Figure 13-1) with a request for response is the first step.

PARENT/TEACHER CONFERENCES

Dear Parents,

This is a notice of the forthcoming days of parent/teacher conferences during which you will be able to participate in the discussion of your child's progress.

_____ from 1:00 to 3:00 P.M.

_____ from 6:30 to 9:00 P.M.

On the first day of conferences, the children will be dismissed at noon and will eat lunch at home. They are not to return for the afternoon session. Bus children will be dismissed at approximately 11:30 A.M. The classrooms will be open from 1:00 to 3:00 for parent/teacher conferences.

On the second day of conferences, the classrooms will be open from 6:30 to 9:00 P.M. for evening interviews. Working parents will be given preference.

Please check one statement below on the tear-off sheet, indicating your preference for the time slot. The teacher will check your appointment and return the bottom sheet to you.

Sincerely,

_____
Principal

- -

(Please tear off and return to your child's teacher by _____.)

Dear _____,
      Teacher's name

_____ I expect to attend the parent/teacher conference on _____
      at

           1:00 - 1:30 _____
           1:30 - 2:00 _____
           2:00 - 2:30 _____
           2:30 - 3:00 _____

_____ I expect to attend the parent/teacher conference on _____
      at

           6:30 - 7:00 _____
           7:00 - 7:30 _____
           7:30 - 8:00 _____
           8:00 - 8:30 _____
           8:30 - 9:00 _____

_____ I do not expect to attend the parent/teacher conference.

_____
Parent's signature

Name of student _____ Class _____

Figure 13-1

The exact schedule for the conference day and the time of bus departure is also of great importance to parents. This is especially true of parents of primary youngsters. A special notice (see the sample) containing this information should be sent home about one week before the conference day as a reminder and to ensure that students will be promptly picked up on the day of conferences.

Your being available to parents on conference days is still another way to promote successful conference time. Parents who come to school to speak with the class teacher may want to also confer with you on various matters. Thus, your door should be open at conference times so that parents may freely communicate concerns and feelings. The open feeling of communication helps to reassure parents that you, as principal, are interested in each student and ready to assist every parent. This attitude helps to develop a feeling of trust in you and the school.

FACILITATE COMMUNICATION BETWEEN THE PARENTS ASSOCIATION AND THE PARENTS

The president and the executive board of the Parents Association should be integral parts of the school. Their needs and wants are important to the parents and general school body and contribute to good relationships and a healthy association between parents and the school.

During the school year, communications between the Parents Association and the parents should be sent. The Parents Association will need assistance in some, if not all, of the following ways:

- composing flyers to be sent home
- deciding about Parent Association events
- printing flyers, notices, and publications
- distributing the publications to students

You can be of great assistance to the Parents Association in helping them achieve their goals. The development of this trusting and helping relationship will also be of value to you; there is less chance of "surprises" coming from the Parents Association when you are involved in the development and implementation of all school-related events.

Today's Parents Association serves in a larger and more important role than ever before. Of great importance are its open lines to the parent body of the school. The passing of information of a general nature helps to establish its role and secure its importance with the parents.

A School Directory

One important communication is the preparation and distribution of a school directory. This publication can list:

- the names of the Parents Associations' officers and committeepeople, along with their telephone numbers
- time schedules of classes, bus arrivals, and departures

SAMPLE

Special Notice for Monday, March 23, from 1:00-3:00 P.M.
School Conferences Including Kindergarten and First Grade

Dear Parents:

You have received notice of conference time for Monday March 23 and Tuesday March 24. The schedule below is a reminder of the special school and bus schedule for afternoon conferences on March 23.

Sincerely,

_____

Principal

- -

Class	Arrival	Dismissal
Kindergarten—morning	8:40	10:25
Kindergarten—afternoon	10:30	12:00
First Grade	8:40	12:00

Bus Schedule for March 23

Class	Pick-Up from Home	Departure from School
Kindergarten—morning	as usual	10:25
Kindergarten—afternoon	10:15	11:40
First Grade	as usual	11:40

- -

(Please detach and return bottom portion to teacher.)

I have read the Special Notice for the children in Kindergarten and first grade and noted its contents.

Child's name _____ Class _____

_____

Parent's signature

- information about Class Mothers, visitors, early release, Parents Association membership, emergency telephone numbers, absences and latenesses, lunch and lunch money collection, report cards, and school newsletters/bulletins
- the school calendar
- dates and times of Parents Association meetings
- the school's administration and staff

Fund Raising

You can also help the Parents Association to successfully conduct fund raising efforts of all types. Assistance in these efforts range from involvement in the creation and development of ideas and strategies for implementation to notification of the parent and student bodies about the fund raiser.

To help raise funds for the continuation of a newsletter, for example, you might include "Tom the Birthday Clown" in each issue to wish participating children a happy birthday. If parents want their children's names to appear, they send 25 cents in an envelope with the child's name and birthdate written on the front. The envelopes are given to the class teacher. (Students born during the summer months can have their names listed in the June bulletin.)

COMMUNICATE WITH EXECUTIVE BOARD MEMBERS

The Parents Associations of the "cake sale fund raiser" status are long gone. Today, Parents Associations enjoy importance and indeed may have extensive influence. They often foster relationships with members of the school board and in that situation may be more successful in gaining services for the school than the principal.

A close and trusting relationship between you and the Parents Association board members or the president is important so that information concerning pending and current board issues can be shared. Objectives that have the mutual support of both the principal and the Parents Association have a much better chance of being accomplished.

Periodic meetings between you and the Executive Board should be scheduled. Each of the parties should have an agenda to be covered, with minutes of the meetings kept on file. These meetings serve several valuable purposes.

1. They provide an opportunity for the Parents Association to communicate areas of concern to the parent.
2. You can be made aware of certain school problems that require attention.
3. You and the Parents Association can share ways and means of helping each other to solve problems.
4. You and the Parents Association can discuss and plan joint actions to help provide the school with larger resources and greater services.
5. Both you and the Parents Association can act as resources for each other.

6. You can make the Parents Association aware of school problems and concerns that face school personnel.

WRITE ARTICLES FOR THE SCHOOL BULLETIN

Another way for you to communicate with the parents of the school population is through the school bulletin. An article from you should be featured in each issue and should convey a timely, informative, and important message. The bulletin can be the vehicle to state a position or communicate facts about a situation. Here are two samples.

Sample Letter 1

Dear Parents,

I look forward to the pleasure of greeting you during "Open School Week" November 13-16. Visiting the school to watch the educational process in action can only help to bring understanding about how we are working together towards an optimum educational opportunity for our children.

Parent/teacher conferences have already begun in kindergarten. They will shortly be held in grades one through six. Our mutual objectives for these conferences are:

1. To acquaint you with the progress of your child. Each individual strength and weakness will be discussed with you. You will see a diagnosis of skill needs in both reading and mathematics and the specific prescription prepared to assist your child to achieve the skills needed. An analysis of progress thus far this year will be shown to you through samples of work. The manner in which your child is performing in class and filling individual needs will be clear.

2. To plan together additional ways in which the school and the home can work towards mutually established goals. The teacher has many suggestions about how you can help your child at home.

3. To develop understanding about the role of the school in the life of the child. The student spends a large part of each day in school. Through your help and support of the school and its objectives for the student, we can work together to foster the development of children who will be life-long learners.

A second means of communicating with you is through the report card. Before the conference time, you will receive a report card from the teacher. All of the classes use a special type of report to parents. Students are not rated in comparison to other children in the class or on the grade. We are interested in telling you how *your child performs* in the class, in *each area, every day,* not just the test results.

In this way we tell you about only your child and what he or she does each day. The school and the parents are partners in the development and growth of the youngster.

Sincerely,_____

_____
Principal

Sample Letter 2

Dear Parents,

Our school, as a small representation of society as a whole, contains students with a large range of talents, abilities, needs, and disabilities. Over a period of years, we have worked to meet this wide range through the development of effective programs to provide services to every student. This article will briefly describe each program.

Our diagnostic/prescriptive approach to both reading in grades 3-6 and mathematics in grades K-6 is a sound approach to instruction in basic skills based upon the needs of the individual student. The teacher works with small skill groups in each skill area, thereby achieving a maximum instructional effect. In addition, each student has his or her individual prescription to fulfill on an ongoing schedule. This provides a second emphasis on instruction directed at the specific skill needs of the individual student.

The individual needs of the students are also serviced in both the Primary Media Center for grades K and 1 and the Media Center for grades 2-6. These needs range from advanced work to remedial work. Both the Primary Media Center and the Media Center house special programs.

ECPC (Early Childhood Prevention Curriculum) is a special program focused at diagnosing perceptual needs of young students and providing special instruction to strengthen skills. This program and the foreign language program for Kindergarten and grade 1 are housed in the Primary Media Center. The foreign language program is focused on both students who are bilingual Spanish and students for whom English is a second language.

In grades 2-6, our Spanish-speaking students, who are eligible, work with the bilingual teacher on a daily basis. Those students in grades 2-6 for whom English is a second language receive instruction in the Media Center as a part of the PSEN (Pupils with Special Educational Needs) program.

Beginning in grade 3 and continuing through grade 6, our gifted students are involved in the IDS (In-Depth Study) program. They meet in small groups to study a particular subject, with a special teacher, twice a week for four weeks. One week of independent study and research follows. The students then move on to study in a new area. The areas for IDS this year include: Science, Music, Art, and Spanish for all students, and Poetry and Careers for grades 3 and 4, Literature and Archaeology for grades 5 and 6.

Differentiated Curriculum is a sixth grade program. Twice a week for a four-week period, the students are involved in one of three areas with a particular teacher. Every four weeks the groups move on to a new area. The areas are: Environmental Education, Family Living (including Health and Sex Education), and Dialogue 28, a specially funded drug prevention program aimed at helping young students find ways to solve their problems.

It is with great pride that I write to you about the many fine programs here at the school. The programs are excellent because of the continuous and dedicated work of our outstanding staff.

Sincerely,

_____

Principal

MAKE YOURSELF AVAILABLE TO PARENTS

The principal serves as arbitrator, peacemaker, decision maker, problem solver, and counselor for students, teachers, and parents. In these varied roles, you must be available to the parents of the students as well as to members of the community at large. Requests to speak with you vary greatly and relate to problems about:

- the individual and personal needs of students
- interpersonal relations problems with teachers
- student-to-student relationship problems
- school policy problems
- personal family problems

An open and welcome attitude should be presented to the parent who wants to speak with you. There should never be a time when you are not available to parents. This does not mean, however, that parents may enter the school at any time and demand a conference. If possible, try to see parents who come without previous notification; most times, however, an appointment will have to be made for a more convenient time. This appointment should be made with an explanation of why you are unavailable at that moment, and should be made as soon as it is mutually convenient.

This open, honest, and available attitude with parents is the main ingredient in building good public relations and developing a feeling of trust in the school and its personnel.

ENSURE THE AMENITIES

The very first evaluation made by anyone having business within a school is the courtesy extended by the personnel in the office. To promote good public relations, àll personnel should be cordial, courteous, helpful, considerate, and—most of all—polite. Guidelines should be established for anyone working in the office who will answer the telephone or meet people who walk in.

How to Answer the Telephone

A school should appear as a well structured and organized institution. Part of a school's image is created by the manner in which the telephone is answered. Callers should immediately know that they have reached the correct number and that the person answering the telephone wants to be of assistance. The following manner of answering the telephone should be required of all school personnel who may be called upon to perform this task:

"Good morning (afternoon), this is the elementary school. May I help you?"

Certain procedures should also be established for dealing with requests that frequently occur.

1. The caller wants to speak with a classroom teacher.
   Response possibilities:
   a. "Mrs. Jones is in class with her students."

    b. "Mrs. Jones cannot come to the telephone at this time because she is working with students."

    c. "Mrs. Jones is not able to come to the telephone."

And add:

    a. "May she return your call?"

    b. "Would you like to make an appointment to see her?"

    c. "May I take a message for her?"

2. The caller wants to speak with the principal.

    Mandated response:

    "May I say who is calling?" THE PRINCIPAL IS THEN TOLD ABOUT THE CALL.

    Response possibilities:

    a. "The principal is in conference."

    b. "The principal is not available."

    c. "The principal is not in the office."

    d. "The principal is at a meeting."

    e. "The principal is on another line."

    And add:

    a. "May I take a message?"

    b. "May he (she) return your call?"

    c. "Will you be able to wait for a few moments?"

    d. "Would you prefer to call back later?"

3. The caller wants information.

    Mandated response:

    "Who is calling, please?"

    Response possibilities:

    a. "Please wait while I obtain that information."

    b. "I will return your call with the information."

    c. "I must secure permission to give that information."

An Office Courtesy Procedure

Each person who enters the office should not be required to wait more than a few moments for assistance. Office personnel should be aware of people entering the office during the day, and greet these people with: "Good morning (afternoon). May I help you?" Every effort should be made to be polite and courteous with all requests.

No person should be allowed to enter the building without going first to the office. This requirement is, of course, dependent upon school security personnel. As a general rule, people other than school staff should not be permitted to go to classrooms. Parents should never be allowed to go to the classrooms without a prearranged appointment with the teacher at a time when students are not in the room.

Parents' requests for homework or student pick up can be met by sending a message to the appropriate classroom while the parent waits in the office. Allowing parents to walk unannounced into classrooms while teachers are involved with students can cause disruption of classes and possible problems.

USE PARENTS AS RESOURCES

Parents represent a wealth of resources that can be used to enrich the school. They can be of valuable assistance with administrative details, supervision of students, and curriculum programs.

In the Library

Parent volunteers can be invaluable in the library. They are extremely helpful in assisting to sign out books as well as shelving books that have been returned. Parents also can be of assistance with adding new books and materials as well as updating inventory lists. All parents who assist should be involved in a training program first, to orient them to the particular process in use in the library.

In the Classroom

Involving parents in the classroom can either be an advantage or a disadvantage. Parents can assist a busy teacher with such administrative details as lunch money collection or attendance, as well as with such curriculum details as collecting homework. The decision to involve a parent in the classroom should be made individually with consideration for the particular parent involved. In all cases, two factors are of prime importance: (1) that the teacher wants to have a parent assistant in the classroom; and (2) that the parent works in a classroom in which his or her child is not in attendance. In all cases, confidential information about any student should not be made available to any parent except the particular child's.

In Security

One extremely effective involvement of parents is with school security. Parents can sit at a desk located at the front door of the school and ask each person who enters to sign the visitor's book and go to the office. In addition, parent patrols of exit doors will help keep those doors closed and securely locked.

During Lunch

Parents are very effective assistants during lunch hour. They can help younger children open containers and packages, and offer the reassurance and guidance that youngsters may require when separated from their parent for the whole day. Since lunchrooms are usually overcrowded and school aides or teachers are in short supply, the addition of parents may be of great benefit.

During Recess

Parents who want to become involved with school programs can be of tremendous assistance during the recess hour. First, they provide additional adult supervision in the yard or recess area, and second, they assist with emergency situations that may occur while students are at recess.

As Tutors

Support personnel for students with special educational needs, whether remedial or English as a second language, are never sufficient. Parents who are properly trained can give invaluable one-to-one assistance for these youngsters. Parents who are tutors can be housed in the library, media center, cafeteria, or the classroom with the teacher. These parents help to develop the students with whom they work in the particular area of concern as well as to provide emotional support.

As Speakers

Parents can serve as a community resource for career topics. Students will benefit greatly by listening to and questioning parents who address them on the subject of various career opportunities. Parents who have special interests or hobbies also make fascinating speakers for assembly programs or for groups of students who may be interested in that particular hobby. Parents who are involved in the speaker program can feel they have contributed to the students of the school by sharing their talents, training, interests, and hobbies.

ORIENT THE PARENTS

Orientation and training programs are essential for any parent or community member who is interested in contributing to the school. The rules and regulations involved with the particular program and process in which they want to become involved should be discussed, explained, and reinforced. The more carefully developed and implemented the orientation program is, the more effective the parent participation program will be.

A WORD OF CAUTION

Parents and community members are wonderful. They are filled with good intentions and a sincere interest in the school and the youngsters. However, never lose sight of the fact that they are volunteers. They begin with enthusiasm but personal problems, illness, other commitments, and family responsibilities may make their contribution inconsistent, sporadic, short lived, and disappointing. So never rely completely on parent volunteers; at most, they should be supplementary. If the parent program is the entire program, it may not be in effect more than a few weeks. Allow parents to enrich and contribute to the school, but always remember that their efforts are always *in addition to* rather than *in place of* other professional educational programs.

INDEX